"Religious life has always had a prophetic role. In this book Gittins points out how it can maintain its prophetic edge by modelling how we can live fully and interculturally in an age of unprecedented migration. In almost every country we are in the birth pangs of a new way of being human. But migration and intercultural living are full of pain and possibilities. Living happily and productively in the future will involve learning not only how to respect cultural difference but the ability to enjoy living with difference. Gittins outlines the missionary and prophetic role religion can play and gives practical insights into culture, marginalization, and mission and the skill and attitudes required to live in such communities.'

— Noel Connolly, SSC
Columban Mission Institute

"*Living Mission Interculturally: Faith, Culture, and the R*   y . .....s is a treasure and seminal work on intercultural living as an expression of mission, an actual participation in God's mission. This book is essential reading for international congregations committed to intercultural living and willing to 'do the work' necessary to make this a lived reality. The inclusion of questions for personal and communal reflection after each chapter and the appendices challenge the reader to move beyond the text and enter into a process that can lead to transformation. The freedom and openness to engage in a critique of culture is essential for the creation of a community of 'radical welcome.' The actual formation of intercultural community is crucial for the unfolding of religious life in a global context. Gittin's experience, wisdom, and profound insights are both gift and blessing for religious life and the Church. This is not reading for the fainthearted."

— Joan Marie Steadman, CSC
Executive Director
Leadership Conference of Women Religious

"In *Living Mission Interculturally*, Fr. Gittins provides the most comprehensive resource to date integrating the gifts from sociology, cultural anthropology (intercultural studies), and theology as they apply to religious communities. In his multidimensional approach to the topic, he guides his readers on a multifaceted journey with clarity of definitions, on the one hand, and landmarks for personal and community commitment and transformation, on the other. If the complexity of intercultural living is like a sphere, then each chapter of this book is like a slice of the sphere offering opportunities for deeper understanding and exploration of what it means and what it takes to be a faithful missional intercultural community."

— Eric H. F. Law
Executive Director of the Kaleidoscope Institute
Author of *The Wolf Shall Dwell with the Lamb*

"I am a leader in an international congregation that is currently discerning just what interculturality can mean for us and for others. I've participated in workshops by Gittins on this topic and I welcome this further study as an aid to deeper listening and more focused response to what the world needs today from international communities. In a clear and accessible way Gittins goes to great depth at each turn of this very timely topic. His mission-driven exploration of intercultural living is immensely practical, challenging, and solidly based on scholarship, lived commitment, wide dialogue, and prayerful reflection. Gittins has given us a great gift and incentive to live our unity in diversity from a stance of radical faith and heightened cultural awareness. I am eager to share this gift with my whole international community and all of our partners in mission."

> — Mary Ann Buckley, SHCJ
> American Providence Leader, Society of the Holy Child Jesus

"Many of us in religious communities, dioceses, and parishes are looking for advice and resources to address the growing challenges and opportunities of intercultural living today. *Living Mission Interculturally* is an excellent resource for practitioners. Drawing on his social-science background and in-depth knowledge of the actual situations of mission/ministry, Anthony Gittins provides a very fine tool with relevant information and practical exercises that can be used by groups and individuals. And he does this with an insightful, concise, and clear writing style that we know well and appreciate from his other writing. In his own words, Gittins 'attempts to offer ways of approaching the "otherness" of other people and to stimulate readers into remembering their own "otherness" in relation to those among whom they live and work' (xix). He has achieved this goal and left us with an excellent resource to respond to real-life situations."

> — Roger Schroeder, SVD
> Louis J. Luzbetak, SVD, Professor of Mission and Culture
> Professor of Intercultural Studies and Ministry
> Catholic Theological Union at Chicago

"*Living Mission Interculturally* is a must-read for anyone who wants to live more fully and deeply our call as church and global citizens. Anthony Gittins's book comes out of years of engaging theologically and living practically the invitation, challenges, and possibilities of intercultural community living. Gittins explains with great examples the dimensions required to move us toward living mission interculturally, whether as religious congregations or as parish communities. He both gives us an understanding of what we mean by intercultural community and shows us how to open ourselves to growth in very pragmatic ways. In the midst of all this, he reminds us that thinking and acting differently require a radical conversion, which God longs to live in us. This book is for everyone who wants to participate in building the reign of God here and now!"

> — Maria Cimperman, RSCJ, PhD
> Director, Center for the Study of Consecrated Life
> Associate Professor of Theological Ethics, Catholic Theological Union

Living Mission Interculturally

Faith, Culture, and the Renewal of Praxis

Anthony J. Gittins, CSSp

Foreword by
Gerald A. Arbuckle, SM

A Michael Glazier Book

LITURGICAL PRESS
Collegeville, Minnesota

www.litpress.org

A Michael Glazier Book published by Liturgical Press

1   2   3   4   5   6   7   8   9

Library of Congress Cataloging-in-Publication Data

Gittins, Anthony J., 1943–
    Living mission interculturally : faith, culture, and the renewal of praxis / Anthony Gittins, CSSp.
        pages   cm
    "A Michael Glazier book."
    Includes bibliographical references and index.
    ISBN 978-0-8146-8318-7 (print) — ISBN 978-0-8146-8343-9 (ebook)
        1. Catholic Church—Missions.   2. Intercultural communication—Religious aspects—Catholic Church.   3. Christianity and culture.   I. Title.

BV2180. G579   2015
282.09'051—dc23

2015002203

Contents

Chapter 8

Mission, Margins, and Intercultural Living   115

Chapter 9

Psychological Responses to Intercultural Living   131

Chapter 10

Cultural Responses to Intercultural Living   147

Foreword

The world is fractured by ideological conflicts, genocide, pathological forms of nationalism, and intercultural tensions—a world "groaning in travail" (Rom 8:22) in need of reconciliation across and within cultural frontiers. We need wise people to help us to understand what is happening and to offer us down-to-earth guidelines to live harmoniously together. Wisdom is information and understanding gained through contemplation on experience that will guide behavior. It is a form of understanding that combines a reflective attitude and a practical concern to act virtuously.

Author Anthony Gittins has the wisdom we need to live interculturally. This book is the consequence of his years of intelligently contemplating, and living in, many different cultures. The reader will discover, as I have done, that behind the book's text is his unquestioning belief that God calls us to build cultures purified of whatever obstructs the presence of the Spirit. His enthusiasm is infectious. Readers will also find it irresistible.

Though the book is written for members of international communities of religious (women or men, lay or clerical), much of the book's theoretical and practical insights can apply equally well to anyone committed to a ministry involving relationships between people of different cultures. To illustrate the wider and urgent relevance of the book, Anthony mentions, for example, the urgent need to foster intercultural living for clergy who have been recruited from overseas, and the need for religious congregations to cease their customary cultural assimilationist policies that are "increasingly ill-adapted to the realities of a global church and incapable of producing integrated communities composed of mutually respectful and supportive members" (p. xii).

He also claims that the book's themes are needed to assist pastoral lay ministers in multicultural dioceses. He is right. Once while I was researching in a village in the South Pacific, I overheard villagers speaking about the "Backhome Man." Each time they used the expression there were hoots of laughter. I then discovered the man who so delighted them was a pastoral worker from another country. He began his sentences with the expression "Back home . . ." so often that the people nicknamed him the "Backhome Man." The generous worker had the gift of internationalism—that is, he was prepared to live in someone else's culture—but he lacked the skills to learn anything from, and integrate with, the host cultures. In brief, Anthony's insights into the complexity of culture and its practical implications are valid for anyone living and working in cultures other than their own, not just for faith-oriented people committed to intercultural living.

The book's blending of theory and practice is so effective that the book could well have been called *A Handbook of Living Mission Interculturally*. Intercultural living is an intentional and unequivocally faith-based venture. But faith must be lived in a cultural context, for "we have this treasure in clay jars" (2 Cor 4:7). Hence the importance of perceptively grasping the complex dynamics of culture. If we are to be authentic members of international faith communities, we need to uncover, respect, and honor the genuine demands of our cultures and commit ourselves to meet persons of other cultures with both gratitude and a willingness to learn. This means we must grasp the nature and power of culture. We need to identify as we strive to live interculturally what may be stifling or freeing us in our cultures.

The author proceeds to explain these points in ways that are easily understandable by the nonacademic reader. Rightly, he insists that intercultural living demands skills that must be gained and worked at diligently and unceasingly *if* people are to live amicably. Goodwill alone is not enough. How true! He masterfully draws on the lessons offered by the social sciences with particular reference to psychology, sociology, and social/cultural anthropology in particular. The author not only clearly articulates the skills required but also describes practical ways to achieve and assess them.

The second word in the book's title is "Mission" because, referring to the exhortation of Pope Francis, *"everyone* is called to be a 'missionary disciple': there is no other kind of disciple of Jesus" (p. 164).

We cannot have intercultural living *if* we are not in mission; a community that turns inward dies. That is, the essential aim and validation for intercultural living is God's mission and our joyful and enthusiastic sharing in it. Intercultural living humanly will always be challenging; it means letting go of cherished cultural attachments and being open to new cultural experiences. It demands constant effort inspired by faith. In the words of the author: "Intercultural living is in fact revolutionary: it affects everyone involved, it favors no one, and it demands of each one a transformation" (p. xiv). Transformation is the ongoing fruit of conversion to the mission of Christ; it is our changed lives that will invite others to listen to us.

In J. R. R. Tolkien's *The Hobbit: Or There and Back Again*, Bilbo Baggins initially turns down an invitation to go on a journey. He is too comfortable in his way of life to be bothered with the trials of an adventure. He finally accepts the challenge and even begins to enjoy it. But he soon tires of the relentless need to adapt to, and learn from, new cultures, so he turns for home and retreats from the world of adventure, singing: "Feet that wandering have gone, turn at last to home afar. Eyes . . . Look at last on meadows green." Anthony explains that we can commit ourselves to intercultural living, but there is always the temptation to weaken our efforts, to seek refuge once more, as Bilbo Baggins, in our own familiar cultures and our prejudices. He writes: "Jesus calls us to transform our particular cultures by defying sin and seeking grace as he strove to transform his. And it costs no less than everything: this is the measure of our faith, lived culturally" (p. 78). St. Paul uses the analogy of a runner when he explains the process of conversion required of intercultural living. To stop running for the Lord is to fall back into purely human insights and comforts (1 Cor 9:24-27). Constant discipline of the whole person is required: "Athletes exercise self-control in all things. . . . So I do not run aimlessly . . . but I punish my body . . . so that after proclaiming to others I myself should not be disqualified" (1 Cor 9:25-27).

Gerald A. Arbuckle, SM, PhD
Refounding and Pastoral Development Unit
Sydney, Australia

Introduction

Challenge and Opportunity in Contemporary Mission and Ministry

Some topics prove to be of perennial interest to many people, while others become interesting because of particular circumstances; fires or floods in general may not capture people's interest or imagination—until a particular fire or flood involves themselves or their loved ones. With the phenomenon of globalization in recent decades, intercultural living has proved to be a topic increasingly relevant to more and more people and, quite frankly, very challenging to many whose circumstances bring them into frequent contact with people of different cultures. There was a time when most people spent their entire existence within striking distance of home or moved to places where people spoke the same language and lived very similar cultural lives as their own. But affordable jet travel, human migration (freely chosen or forced), the expansion of markets and trade, the availability of near-universal education, and increased pastoral missionary outreach have radically altered the nature of human relationships across the globe.

Internationality and multiculturality describe aspects of the changes affecting individuals and groups, but the words frequently conceal as much as they reveal—they are not always adequate to describe certain social processes. Rather, they describe situations or social facts: "international" usually applies to any situation involving people of different nationalities, from "an international crisis" to "international cooperation"; while "multicultural" is typically invoked where those involved are primarily distinguished or differentiated not by nationality but by culture. Neither word, however, identifies the actual quality of the relationships involved. International aid can be unilateral and token without creating a positive or meaningful relationship of mutuality between donors and recipients. Indeed, many donors never encounter any recipients, while recipients often have no idea where the aid originated. International aid can easily create resentment in the recipients and complacency in the donors.

The word multicultural can apply to a *de facto* social reality without disclosing anything about the quality of relationships involved. Millions of people live in multicultural cities or neighborhoods, side by side with people from very different cultures, but without ever trying to learn another language or encounter their neighbors in other than a perfunctory or conventionally civic fashion. Multiculturalism has been described as "living together separately." For ourselves as people of faith, that simply cannot be enough.

In today's world, something is occurring with increasing frequency, whether for commercial or humanitarian reasons or due to an intentional commitment to "the other" (any person, but particularly one of a different culture or language). The phenomenon is that certain people under certain circumstances deliberately choose to work through linguistic and cultural divisions in order to build a community that can be called "intercultural." That is the focus of this book. But, like the words "international" and "multicultural," the word "intercultural" can either describe a simple social fact, or it can apply to a particular quality of relationships between the people concerned; it is the latter meaning that we will define, identify, and promote.

Written primarily for members of international communities of religious (women or men, lay or clerical), much of this book's content can apply equally well to anyone committed to a ministry involving relationships between people of different cultures—the vast majority of ecclesial ministers in today's globalized world. The single most important denotation of the word "intercultural" in these pages is that it is a theological word and therefore applies to people who are explicitly and implicitly motivated by faith in God. But before exploring this, here are four possible scenarios or situations in which intercultural living might be called for and in which this book might prove relevant.

1. *International Clergy in Vast Dioceses*

There are many reasons why people of different languages and cultures might attempt to form an intercultural community, virtual or actual. Consider some far-flung diocese in Canada's Prairie Provinces or in many other parts of the world where clergy are few and aging, and the bishop is concerned to provide priests as pastors and sacramental ministers. He travels far and wide to countries with more clergy and manages to recruit a handful from the Philippines, Africa, Poland, and India to complement his current diocesan clergy, all of whom are Canadian. His hope is that this new influx of priests of various cultures will bond in such a way that they will demonstrate to the local people the possibility and power of intercultural living. After three or four years, however, his experience is that a considerable number of his carefully recruited expatriate clergy have returned home or somehow failed their bishop, their people, and perhaps themselves. Moreover, those who remain seek the company of fellow priests from their own culture and do not mix very well with those of other cultures. The local Canadian clergy also find them difficult to understand and consider them problematic in some ways, while the bishop believes not only has his experiment failed to bear fruit but also that an increased number of pastoral problems of staffing, effective pastoral service, and oversight have been created.

The details of such a scenario can be filled in by anyone with imagination and a little experience. The question then becomes: what, if anything, might be done? This book attempts to provide some answers.

2. *The Expansion of a German Congregation of Sisters*

Imagine a religious foundation dating from the middle of the nineteenth century that establishes a new community in the United States in the 1860s. It is composed of only a handful of German-speaking sisters. Initially, their ministry is confined to a single diocese where they work among mostly German-speaking immigrants. But as they find their feet and their apostolate, they increase their proficiency in English and begin to seek and welcome local vocations. By the time of Vatican II, they have become well-established, with communities and schools from the West to the East Coasts. Many of the younger sisters are from second- or third-generation German stock, so there is a strong German *ethos* and attachment to the German founders, although a substantial minority of the sisters are from English, Irish, Italian, and French stock. The religious habit, liturgical and praying style, and many customs and menu items derive, however, directly from the community's German origins. Characteristic of this community is that would-be postulants and novices are admitted by a process of assimilation: they are required to modify their behavior so as to accept the well-established conventions of the community with its heavily Germanic stamp, and anyone unable to do so will sooner or later leave the community. This assimilationist model was the default model in religious life for centuries: the order or congregation considered itself to possess a founding charism (an identity and specific purpose or "mission") embodied in its rule and constitutions, and this charism was to be lived from one generation to the next with very little variation and very much fidelity to the tradition. The approach was unremarkable in itself and ensured continuity and conformity by minimizing or suppressing individual differences of personal, temperamental, and cultural natures.

Spurred on by the reforms of Vatican II, such communities gradually diversified and expanded beyond their former territorial boundaries. With changing social conditions, new members now entered as mature adults rather than school-leavers, and the assimilationist model became increasingly ill-adapted to the realities of a global church and incapable of producing integrated communities composed of mutually respectful and supportive members. Today, while some communities remain largely monocultural and homogeneous, the majority of post–Vatican II religious have examined their original inspiration and attempted to focus it on today's world—incorporating people from cultures and local churches beyond Europe and America. Many have discovered, to their own surprise or chagrin and at great personal cost to aspirants, that it is impossible to continue with time-honored patterns of formation. Slowly but surely, they have become convinced that the assimilationist model is no longer fit for purpose if international and *de facto* multicultural communities are to be appropriately equipped for today's apostolate. But they are also aware that simply living under the same roof does not make people into a community or family. Unless they meet the challenge of *intercultural* living, communities risk fragmentation, loss of membership, and the inability to serve the mission. This book is an attempt to chart a course for the future.

3. *Individualism in Established Missionary Communities*

Not every international or multicultural group is intercultural. True intercultural living is both a faith-based undertaking and requires that each individual be truly committed to others of different ethnicities and cultures. A spirit of independence and individualism will undermine any intercultural project, and membership of international religious communities does not automatically produce intercultural living. Some people have lived for decades outside their original cultural environment without becoming truly accepted by, much less integrated into, the community in which they live. Some maintain far stronger links with home than with the people they claim to serve, seeking the company of other expatriates rather than local people and clinging to their own language rather than making any serious attempts to learn the language of their hosts. Not only are their lives far from intercultural, they are doubtfully even cross-cultural in any real sense. Ironically, some recently internationalized communities (international in both recruitment and outreach) seem more committed to intercultural living than long-established communities. We will identify some blind spots that limit people's vision and commitment and attempt to offer some relevant pointers for intercultural living.

4. *Pastoral (Lay) Ministers in Multicultural Dioceses*

In the past half century, the number of officially qualified and employed pastoral ministers has grown at an unprecedented rate. In the United States alone, there were none in 1967, 10,500 in 1986, and 22,791 in 2013.[1] Given the radical shift from monocultural or single ethnicity parishes to today's multicultural parishes, it is evident that pastoral ministers are now called on to work with and among a wide variety of cultural styles. The work of Eric H. F. Law has been a major contribution to multicultural ministry; his work will be examined in these pages. But this book is also structured in such a way as to offer to pastoral ministers some assistance in identifying challenges that are part of their ministry. Since all Christians are called by baptism to reach out not only to the sisters and brothers they already know but also those they have yet to meet, and given that we live in a globalized, multicultural world, there ought to be something in these pages for anyone who takes the cultural component of their faith seriously. Intercultural encounters and intercultural living does therefore not only apply to people *within* communities of consecrated women or men religious but also to relationships *between* communities and their constituent members. Hence, anyone undertaking pastoral work in *favelas*, hospitals, prisons, retirement homes, parishes, and so on, where oneself (*ego*) is the outsider committed to learning about and from the insiders, is undertaking a form of intercultural living.

Everyone committed to this enterprise will experience vulnerability, limitations, and "outsider-ness" to some degree. But by identifying the way Jesus himself embraced such a status and called us to do the same, intercultural living is not only possible (with commitment and the determined acquisition of appropriate skills and sensitivity) but it also can be redemptive for both insiders and outsiders.

Intercultural living is in fact revolutionary: it affects everyone involved, it favors no one, and it demands of each one a transformation. It affects all new recruits, including the recruiters; it affects the way people adapt to new appointments, including their mentors; it challenges members of the dominant culture in any community or group; and it affects the way people within minority groups are treated and respond. Leadership styles and the process for the selection of future leaders will need to be scrutinized and modified in response both to the reiterated call of Pope Francis and to the needs of the actual people we serve. And if there is to be a viable, long-term future for intercultural living, every aspirant—clerical, religious, or lay—will need to demonstrate not only willingness but also a real commitment and proven capacity for intercultural living.

The Limits and Limitations of This Book

The topic of interculturality and intercultural living has generated a virtual library of academic scholarship, initially and in great part within the social sciences and more recently from the field of theology.

The present work neither claims nor aims to be a narrowly academic addition to this literature. If we distinguish academic or outer knowledge ("knowing about") from apprentice or inner knowledge ("knowledge of"), the former being more theoretical and the latter more practical, the aims of this book are squarely directed to practical and apprentice knowledge. Theory is involved of course, and there are many bibliographical references for further reading; but my primary concern is to describe features of intercultural living and to invite readers on a path that can lead to the actual experience of such a mode of living. Throughout the book there are suggestions for experimentation and practical action for individuals and whole communities, and each chapter ends with suggestions for further integration. Some of the diagrams ought to provide food for meditation or faith sharing in community, while others, like the one on Social Profiles (chapter 6) or Psychological Responses (chapter 9) might be helpful for a workshop for community members. This book, then, is primarily for practitioners rather than theorists.

Living Mission Interculturally is not the result of primary research into daily practices in various communities, although some knowledge and experience of that has contributed to the presentation. Rather it offers a series of "approaches to" intercultural living, based as much on other people's research as on practical wisdom distilled by anthropologists working with people of different cultures. In that sense, the book is eclectic or synthesizing in nature, aiming to present intercultural living not only as a serious challenge but also as perfectly feasible and worth striving for. It attempts to offer ways of approaching the "otherness" of other people and to stimulate readers into remembering their own "otherness" in relation to those among whom they live and work.

There are plenty of resources that offer paths of spiritual discernment or psychological testing of readiness for cross- or intercultural living. This book, however, is more of a "discovery procedure" by which people can gauge their own temperamental suitability, readiness, or willingness to adapt and learn the elements of intercultural living through exposure to some social analysis, some theological reflection, and some personal *examen*. In the course of such introspection and conversation, individuals ought to be able better to understand whether they are ready for the demands of intercultural living, and, if not, whether they can offer moral and spiritual support to those who are. There is no shame in acknowledging that intercultural living is beyond one's current abilities, whether due to age, state of health, or other limitations. What is important is to know how one can best contribute to the good of the community and the missionary goal to which it is committed.

This, then, is something of a "how-to" book, but since intercultural living is at heart a theological or faith-based undertaking, some of its deeper theological and philosophical underpinnings are raised throughout. But in final analysis, no amount of theologizing or philosophizing can replace the necessity for individual commitment and for persistent efforts.

Here are two points to carry with us, each of which will recur throughout these pages. First, we must learn to appreciate our differences and not simply amalgamate or blend our similarities; the intercultural community we build must become a home (away from home) for everyone, not just for those of the dominant culture or for dominant individuals. The words of Jonathan Sacks give us fair warning if we fail in this: "Segregation is rapidly replacing integration as an ideal. Communities are turning inward."[2] And second, we must learn to identify the way we think and then rethink it for the sake of the mission. Later we will quote Rudy Wiebe's wise words: "You repent, not by feeling bad, but by thinking [and acting] differently."

And lastly, here is a parable or fable. As a child I loved to play cricket. I would have loved to be good at it. I had great enthusiasm. I had a modicum of talent. But I never had any coaching. I never received any encouragement. And I had no access to any decent equipment. Consequently, I never did develop whatever talent I may have had. But I might have if circumstances were different.

Many individuals and communities might like to live *in unum* interculturally. Many individuals and communities have a modicum of talent and a fund of goodwill. I would like in these pages to offer some equipment, a great amount of encouragement, some coaching, and some suggestions for continuous practice, alone or as a team. Not everyone will want to pursue this subject. Not everyone can become exceptionally good at it. But everyone is able to generate some enthusiasm and some encouragement for others. And everyone is able to commit to learning some skills and approaches and to endorse and affirm others rather than belittle or criticize them.

Are there any true intercultural communities? Yes, certainly in practice there are, wherever people are intentional about living as a community united in their differences and truly respectful of "the other." But there could be many more if people believed that intercultural living was not only desirable but also really possible, and if they felt that it was something that could be learned and practiced systematically and effectively. Although goodwill alone is not enough, it is an important prerequisite. Some of what else is needed is described, offered, and encouraged in the pages that follow.

Chapter One

Called to Conversion

The Changing Face of
International Religious Communities

The social organization of religious institutes of both women and men religious (including brothers and clerics) varies widely, consistent with their founding *charism* and pastoral purpose and is rather different from that of the parochial or secular clergy. In principle, at least, the latter used to be drawn from men living within the boundaries of a particular diocese, and they generally shared a common language, culture, and nationality. By contrast, many religious orders and congregations spread rather rapidly and far beyond their historical origins. Recruiting from many cultures over time, they became truly international in extent and membership. Others again, though also international in membership themselves, deliberately refrained from recruiting new personnel from the distant areas they evangelized ("the Missions" as they were then called) until first an indigenous clergy or a diocesan community of women religious had been established in and for the church of the region. Still other communities, more local in ambition and scope, flourished for many years relatively close to their original foundation but later (particularly since Vatican II) began to reach beyond their previous area of influence in order to share their *charism* and personnel among people seeking pastoral assistance and expertise in other and unfamiliar parts of the world.

Times change. Gone now are the days when the membership of different provinces of international religious communities was largely homogeneous, ethnically and linguistically. And if each of those various provinces once bore the unmistakable and heavy stamp of the original or "mother" province (in attire and daily *horarium*), their identity in the twenty-first century is often very different—in membership, theology, missiology, focus, and works—from what it was as late as the mid-twentieth century. Social and geographical mobility are far more evident today than before the advent of the globe-shrinking Jumbo Jet in the 1960s; and the impact of such mobility is currently affecting and reshaping the contours of international religious communities.

The classical model for recruitment was that of assimilation: after a suitable period of scrutiny or vetting, prospective members were admitted on the general and specific understanding that they were to learn to accommodate themselves to a preexisting and well-tried way of living. If and when aspirants were admitted to a particular community but brought with them a different culture or first language, the adaptation required would be largely one-way: the new member was simply expected to "fit in," while the community as a whole would continue as before—with a minimum of disturbance.

The thesis of this book is that, given the global demographic changes that have occurred in the lifetime of today's senior members, the future of international religious communities must increasingly and intentionally become intercultural. Indeed, without the tectonic shift from international to intercultural, there will be no viable future for international religious orders. Unless we can live together interculturally, we shall fall apart, retreat into our respective cultural groups, or continue half-heartedly, perhaps professing unconvincingly what we do not really live.

The challenge facing everyone now—not only new members but also the current membership—is to identify and respond to the specific demands of intercultural living. Aspiring members will more naturally acknowledge that their own cultural identity must not only be respected but also seriously engaged with by current members, while the latter will be challenged to acknowledge not only that the former assimilation model is no longer fit for purpose but also that it is now incumbent on every older member to identify and respond to the real challenge of intercultural living, whether by embracing it wholeheartedly, halfheartedly, or by resisting it and waiting for death.

Everyone must be willing to stand and be counted: the future, viable or not, demands and depends on it.

Definitions and Usage

In the course of these pages we will gradually build up a composite picture of the meaning and significance of the word "intercultural," used theologically. In that sense it is not in many dictionaries; and where it is employed it can be seen to have several referents. As used theologically, its focus is clearly different from that of the social sciences, where it most probably originated, and this book uses it explicitly in a theological sense: that is, intrinsically, it has something to do with God and faith. Where it does occur in a dictionary, its standard meaning is something like "of, relating to, or representing different cultures," and it usually appears in the phrase "intercultural communication," which, in turn, is described as communication-sharing across culturally different communities. Both of these are perfectly helpful and worthy as far as they go; but we will take them considerably further by placing them in a theological context. For several decades now, theologians and missiologists have been speaking of "intercultural theology" and "interculturality."[1]

When used in these pages with a theological focus, the word "intercultural" is most often associated with a way of living: "intercultural living" is our topic. It will be distinguished from "internationality" and "multiculturality." I take the following as a working description that I will attempt to expand by describing its workings and implications:

> [The intercultural approach] aims, in the final instance, to establish in reality the practical conditions that enable the subjects of any cultural universe to utilize the "reserves" of their tradition of origin as a point of support for their own personal identity, without discriminatory consequences, and to participate in using these cultural references in the process of exchange of ideas. All this is towards the common goal of searching for truth.[2]

This is clear and helpful, though the goal of these pages is not simply that of searching for the truth; it is primarily intended for people who sense that something more than internationality or multicultural community living is urgently needed. Some, indeed, are already committed—and may have been so for many years—to intercultural living as a way of life that serves the pastoral and missionary purposes of their international religious community; but today's circumstances demand that many more undertake this way of living.

Ten Theses about Intercultural Living

For more than a half century now, the need for cooperation across cultures[3] and for vastly improved cross-cultural communication skills has been identified by multinational companies and addressed by the social sciences.[4] The earlier and widely used term "multicultural" has now been largely replaced by "intercultural"[5] in order to focus not simply on the social fact that people of diverse cultures often live in close proximity but also on the specific challenges facing multinational corporations attempting to create a concerted workforce of culturally diverse personnel. Because these words are still sometimes used interchangeably—and social science and missiology address different social realities—I will clarify usage when necessary.

Just as the word *inculturation* has become a specifically theological word, unknown or insignificant to social scientists, so it is with the word *intercultural*; it may well be used to emphasize cross-cultural cooperation and mutuality, but in common or secular usage, that is all it means. So it is important for us at the outset to identify some features that are specific to *intercultural living* as it will be developed in the following pages *as a theologically weighted term.* Here are ten:

1. Intercultural living is an intentional and explicitly faith-based undertaking. It is therefore radically different from simply being a member of an international community and living under the same roof as others, including people of diverse cultures.

2. Since a particular culture (or constellation of cultural traits) marks every single person, it follows that a person's faith can only be lived *culturally*: there is no lived faith without a corresponding lived culture. Faith is expressed in practice. This requires that everyone be encouraged to express faith through one's culture and be made aware that failure to live deeply

within and through one's own culture can produce a kind of religious or spiritual schizophrenia.

3. Intercultural living itself should not be imagined primarily as a *problem*. It would be far preferable if people were to identify it as a *challenge* to be faced and dealt with appropriately. Nor should it be seen as someone else's challenge (or problem); it is a challenge that faces everyone alike. A community that is polarized into "us" and "them" will never achieve intercultural living; only in a community striving to become "we" can it possibly succeed.

4. For the vast majority of people, intercultural living is undesirable and unnecessary. In fact, it is unnatural or at least not "natural" (as we shall see). But it is possible, perhaps "supernatural," if undertaken from a supernatural motive. And since it is a form of faith-based living, it is not achieved by a simple mastery of new techniques;[6] it requires virtue and indeed the transformation or conversion of all involved.[7]

5. As anyone who has attempted intercultural living will attest, it is far from easy. But it is highly desirable and appears to be urgently desired by God, lest one single culture comes to dominate in a culturally diverse community and individuals become significantly distressed, alienated, or worse.

6. Goodwill is not enough to bring about intercultural living. Goodwill has been responsible for the perpetration of many human tragedies and scandals, both within the church and beyond it. Goodwill is surely very necessary, but alone it remains quite insufficient. Also required are commitment and the sustained hard work necessary for the acquisition of both skills and virtue.

7. Intercultural living demands graciousness, diplomacy, compromise, mutual respect, serious dialogue, and the development of a common and sustaining vision. A vision is something that inspires the common effort of a lifetime and also provides appropriate means to achieve a desired end.

8. For the majority of people—even in established international religious communities—intercultural living is something quite new. Most humans throughout history have been monocultural,

and this remains true in modern times even when people live in a multicultural or international environment.

9. Intercultural living is increasingly perceived as necessary for viable international religious life, but the cost is high. Where it succeeds it will bring about a revolution in religious life as we now know it, but such a revolution is obligatory if dry bones are to live.

10. Intercultural living—at least in a modified form—is not just required of members of international religious communities; more broadly, it presents a challenge to any person of faith who undertakes ministry to any "other," whether other by gender, age, ethnicity, religion, culture, or any criterion of difference.

As we proceed, these statements will be exemplified and clarified as necessary, but they are articulated here in order to provide an initial perspective on the journey that lies before us—the journey will require both careful preparation and strategic planning.

Three Guidelines

The following might serve as a guide, an orientation, or a framework within which we attempt to build intercultural communities and intercultural living.

1. *We are called to build a home together.*[8] Intercultural living only becomes possible if we have somewhere to call our own to which everyone can lay equal claim, for which each assumes equal responsibility, and where all can live in harmonious coexistence. But this is not to say that everyone, or indeed any one, will feel completely and entirely "at home" at all times, nor that coexistence will be like a perfect *Shangri La* or paradise. This is partly because the call to missionary religious life is also a call to leave home for the sake of the Gospel. So we will need to approach the paradox carefully.

It is important not to romanticize and to be realistic about what is feasible, but if people under a single roof become alienated from or unconcerned about each other, or cliquish or isolated, intercultural living is clearly impossible. Jonathan Sacks, former chief rabbi of

United Hebrew Congregations of the Commonwealth, contrasts a range of different places in which people might live, whether as permanent resident or transients. He considers the differences between a family home and other living spaces: a hotel, motel, country house, elite club, nursing home, hospital, prison, castle or fortress, and so on. Sacks distinguishes each of these according to rights, responsibilities, degrees of freedom or ownership, comfort level of each, as well as other criteria. The following paragraphs provide a few examples.

A *retirement home* is sometimes known tellingly as a place of "independent living." Here, many people may live under one roof, but each with his or her own freedom, budget, privacy, and self-determination. The larger community may come together for meals and some entertainment, but each person is free and nobody is held to any moral or legal requirements apart from observing normal social conventions governing such things as excessive noise and habitual rudeness. It is a form of independence or "alone-togetherness."

Prison, euphemistically known as a "correctional facility," is very different. Here, the rules are specific, all-embracing, and strictly enforced. The "inmates" have some human rights but are deprived of many others like free association and freedom of speech. Each inmate must keep to a regime for a specified time, after which he or she may be released into the wider society, often having received little or no help to adjust to the society from which they were forcibly and legally removed. This might be characterized as a form of "together-aloneness."[9]

A *motel* or *hotel* operates on a host/guest or principal/client basis. A "guest" has certain entitlements depending on what has been advertised by the establishment ("host"/"principal") and paid for by the "client." A special fee may be extracted if the property is damaged, and the usual civil conventions apply, with increasing force as the motel or hotel is more expensive and elitist. In principle this is neither aloneness nor togetherness.

A member of a *country club* may first be required to pass a vetting process requiring sponsorship and a declaration of certain personal and private details. Once admitted to membership, a person will be subject to the rules of the club and entitled to its privileges. The annual fee is designed to cover the provision of the club's amenities, and these should be freely available to the member. Normal "wear and tear" of the property will not be penalized, but strict rules will govern the member's responsibility in the case of damage or disruption. This is an example of loose affiliation.

As we reflect on communities we ourselves have known and perhaps lived in—whether specifically religious communities or residences of any other kind—it might be instructive for us to identify the images they evoke and consider whether or not they were appropriate for their stated purpose, especially if they purport to be religious communities as such.

The title of Rabbi Sacks's book is *The Home We Build Together*. But as the adage reminds us, "a house is not a home." A *family home* is much more than a group of relatives living under the same roof and very different from a prison, an intensive care unit, or an expensive hotel. Membership in a select club may allow certain privileges without requiring the member to perform essential duties such as preparing meals, making beds, or tending to the garden. Once the annual fees have been paid and the member behaves with discretion and decorum, he or she is "entitled" to a range of perquisites, including privacy and the attendant status involved.

A *family home*, however, is an *evolving, organic entity*. Its shape is forever changing, as husband and wife become parents, as a child gains a sibling, and as siblings grow through different stages and at different rates. And all this time, each person in the home has needs and rights that deserve to be respected and negotiated in an environment in which everyone has a different temperament and changing moods. Family harmony, indeed survival, depends on the quality of interaction between each member and requires constant compromise, change of plans, and adaptability to unforeseen circumstances. And when the children begin to leave home, every member of the family unit is affected to some degree. Even when the last child has left, the identity of the family continues in a modified form. Family reunions help maintain the "family spirit" while each family member adjusts to a new life. No family can survive without drama and trauma, fusion and fission, and great mutuality.

Reflecting on the different ways in which people live, permanently or temporarily, might help us visualize an intercultural community as one with much more in common with a family home than with any of the other examples of communal living. A major difference, of course, is that people do not choose their family home, but in many significant ways, they do choose their religious community. But specifically chosen or not, a community in an international religious order today bears the weight of great expectations from its members and great responsibility for becoming fit for purpose. That is, it must become a nurturer of faith, a place of mutual support, encouragement, and challenge. Furthermore, it needs to bear public witness to the real possibility of people of different cultures and languages but a common faith and vision being able to survive and thrive for a purpose beyond any individual whim or comfort and a sign of the Kingdom or Realm of God. Such is the daunting, difficult, but not impossible task before us! But Sacks warns that "if identity resembles a hotel, identity will be, not in integration but separation."[10]

2. *We are called to discover the dignity of difference.*[11] One of the most enduring and intractable human challenges is to see difference in a positive and constructive light. But there is a pervasive human propensity to define things and persons according to differences rather than similarities. The very word "define" means to set boundaries around, to mark off, to delimit and distinguish. I am *not* Chinese, young, female, a physiotherapist, artist, or activist; but to define myself negatively, by saying what I am not, gives little indication of my true identity. To identify myself positively as British, elderly, male, cleric, professor, academic, and so on is just as true but conveys a vastly different image and identity, as would my self-identification as brother, son, uncle, adoptive father, friend, and so on. But it is so easy to slip into negative or differentiating descriptions of people: from labeling someone as non-Catholic, not a priest, nonpracticing, "just a layperson," or similar terms, it is only a short step to treating that person as "not one of us" or "other" in a highly pejorative, xenophobic sense. The great human paradox is that we are all the same and yet all different; the great human folly is that humanity is often alienated from itself by using differences not only to distinguish but also to disagree, dissent, and discriminate, sometimes with appalling consequences. We are members of a single race, and its name is *human*.

In an old familiar rabbinic story with many forms, the teacher asks the disciples: "When do you know it is dawn?" One says, "When you can distinguish a white thread from a black one." "No," says the teacher. "When you can see the outline of a tree against the horizon," ventures another. "No," says the teacher—to this and to all other efforts to answer the question. Finally he says: "When you can look into the eyes of a stranger, an 'other,' and see a brother, or a sister, then it is dawn; until then, it is still night." This, in a sense, summarizes the process that should ultimately produce intercultural communities. We certainly have to identify and learn the skills to engage with our respective processes of cultural conditioning, during which, and subtly, the cataracts of ethnocentrism and other biases and prejudices will have clouded our vision somewhat. Such skills are not easy to come by, however, especially as we move through the middle and later periods of life. But as we proceed, we identify some of the skills and virtues we need to seek. The example of Jesus himself will, of course, be our guide.

Part of our task, then, is to rediscover the dignity of difference and celebrate it in our intercultural communities. Pope Francis is explicit: "We must walk united with our differences: there is no other way to become one. This is the way of Jesus."[12] The agenda of those seeking to live in intercultural communities is lengthy and taxing and will not be accomplished easily. But by God's grace and our commitment, we can put our hands to the plow and not look back. As Rabbi Sacks puts it, "Peace involves a profound crisis of identity. The boundaries of self and other, friend and foe, must be re-drawn."[13]

3. *We are called to rethink the way we think.* Many of us, often trained in and certainly influenced by Western cultures, operate out of a largely dialectical (oppositional or exclusive) mode of thought. Perhaps more simply expressed as "either/or" thinking, a dialectical mode of thought pursues an argument to a conclusion that judges one person or thesis right and another wrong. By contrast, an analogical (complementary or inclusive) mode of thought looks for compromise between two extremes, finding some truth or validity in each: this is "both/and" thinking.[14] As we strive to develop principles and practices of intercultural living, we need make a conscious shift between these two modes. Each approach or perspective can yield valuable insights, but the analogical way is probably better placed where common living and unity-with-difference are sought. Each person involved in developing intercultural modes of living needs to feel that there is no *us* and *them* but only a community seeking to identify itself inclusively as *we*. As Rudy Wiebe expressed it, "[In a Jesus

society] you repent, not by feeling bad but by thinking different[ly]."[15] On reflection, to think differently is considerably more difficult than to feel bad; it is relatively easy to do the latter without anything or anyone really changing; but after a lifetime of learning just how to think, and then to think that our thinking is right thinking (and even to think that the way we think is actually the way God thinks), we all become rather resistant to thinking differently.[16] To think and act differently often requires nothing less than a radical conversion.

As members of international religious communities of the twenty-first century, we need to face the urgent and pressing task of learning the skills and virtues required of each person, even though the challenge is formidable, especially perhaps (but not inevitably) for some of our older members.[17] New challenges have arisen (and will not disappear) in today's multicultural, globalized world. And today's religious—especially those who have been socialized in (or indeed live amid) strongly ego-focused and rights-based cultures and societies[18]—face an ongoing call to conversion. Xenophobia is not new and has taken on alarming religious (pseudo-religious, of course) forms in recent times. These are the poisoned fruits of bad religion, but we can all be tainted by that. As Jonathan Swift, of *Gulliver's Travels* fame and a clergyman himself, said: "We have just enough religion to hate each other, but not enough to make us love one another."[19] This must change—and members of international religious communities should surely be leaders and exemplars of the change.

The Call to Conversion:
What, Who, Where, When?

We are called to continuous conversion, and conversion always takes place in a particular—and changing—context. But for persons invested in intercultural living, that very investment entails not only the willingness but also the authentic desire to be converted yet again. Here, for personal and (even better) for communal reflection, are two authors' ways of distinguishing three components, aspects, or partners in our own conversion, followed by a number of definitions of conversion in general. Since conversion underpins everything in this book, they may help focus us individually and as a community.

Taking words from the prophet ("Act justly, love tenderly, walk humbly with God," Mic 6:8), Donal Dorr identifies three aspects or facets of conversion: *political conversion*: that is, conversion to public, systemic issues ("act justly"); *moral conversion*: that is, conversion to the neighbor ("love tenderly"); and *religious conversion*: that is, conversion to God ("walk humbly with God").[20] Orlando Costas (and see the definitions below) also speaks of a triple conversion: for him, it is conversion to *Christ*, to one's own *culture*, and to the *world* or other cultures and persons.[21] These perspectives can be very helpful in the context of the *raison d'être* and experience of intercultural living.

As for definitions: the first is very comprehensive, consistent with its being found in a dictionary. The author is Lewis Rambo:

> Conversion is a process that takes place in a dynamic force-field of people, events, experiences, ideas and groups. Cultural, social, personal and religious dimensions infuse and shape the process in numerous ways, in different settings. It is a process in which God makes us vulnerable to the transcendent; a lifelong process of breaking away from any obstacle or idol, and turning to the living God and to the needs of other human beings.[22]

The operative terminology here, as many students and retreatants have indicated over the years, includes: "process," "dynamic force-field of people," "cultural," "vulnerable to the transcendent," "lifelong," and "breaking away from, turning to, God, humanity." It is a rich definition, and some of its features will recur in other definitions.

Jim Wallis, an evangelical Christian and one of the founders of *Sojourners*, emphasizes our social responsibility and God's justice, entirely consistent with his own commitments: "A turning to God that is always deeply personal but never private; both a moment and a process of transformation that deepens and extends through the whole of our lives; the beginning of active solidarity with the purposes of the Kingdom of God in the world."[23]

Here, people are often struck by words or phrases like: "personal but never private," "moment and process," "transformation," "active solidarity," "kingdom," and "world." This is not focused on, nor does it seek justification from, the church alone but looks to the realm or kingdom of God, as Jesus did, for the ultimate realization of God's purposes.

The third definition, from Orlando Costas, a Pentecostal Christian, represents a profound change in his own spiritual journey. From a youthful naivety that assumed that as long as one accepted Jesus as one's personal savior, little work remained, to an appreciation for the real challenge of engaging with the process of one's personal and lifelong conversion, he offered this definition: "[Conversion is] a dynamic, complex, on-going experience, profoundly responsive to particular times and places, and shaped by the context of those who experience it. It constitutes both a break with and a new commitment to society, placing believers in a dialectal relationship with their environment. It is personal but also ecclesial."[24]

Again, some words and phrases jump off the page: "dynamic," "ongoing," "times and places," "shaped by context." We may note that a "complex" experience does not mean "complicated," but something much closer to "delicate."

Nikos Nissiotis, an Orthodox Christian, came from a tradition that deeply valued the community in which one was formed and subsequently worshiped. His succinct definition emphasizes the community's role very well: "[Conversion is] not simply an individual, once for all act, but a process of continuous personal change and growth, with and for the other members of the community."[25]

In the context of intercultural living, this is particularly pertinent: "with and for the other members of the community." Finally, Canadian theologian Bernard Lonergan seems to be inspired as he reflects on conversion in the words that follow. In the course of a reflection on a very different topic, he suddenly takes wing in a great lyrical passage that continues for a couple of pages. Here is a partial paraphrase but wonderful taste of what is well worth tracking down in its entirety:

> [Conversion] is entirely personal, utterly intimate, but not so private as to be solitary. It can happen to many, and they can form a community to sustain one another in their self-transformation and to help one another in working out the implications and fulfilling the promise of their new life. Finally, what can become communal can also become historical . . . pass from generation to generation . . . spread from one cultural milieu to another

> . . . adapt to changing circumstances, confront new situations, survive into a different age, and flourish in another period or epoch.[26]

If this had been commissioned by someone looking for some inspirational words for members of a fledgling intercultural community, it could hardly have been improved in any way; but it is not simply a pious inspiration or a utopian dream. People of fierce faith—united in a clear and common cause, committed to personal and mutual transformation, sincere about undertaking the hard work of learning other cultures, and willing to persevere throughout a lifelong process relying heavily on mutual goodwill and the grace of God—have indeed experienced what Lonergan describes. If what can be imagined can actually come to pass, intercultural living can be a reality—not simply by imagining it but by allowing the collective imagination of a community of faith to stimulate and sustain individuals in community through the vicissitudes and victories of their daily lives.

Suggested Follow-Up

1. Looking at Sacks's description of various living spaces and the different rights and duties associated with each, can you reflect on the nature of the community space you live in? Identify features it shares with a true family home (refer to the description) and in what ways it resembles one of the other residences Sacks mentions—or perhaps identify one that he does not include.

2. Reflect on the distinction between dialectical (either/or) and analogical (both/and) thinking, in your own case and in the way your community tends to operate. Are any adjustments called for?

3. Refer again to the various definitions of conversion and their focus on God, others, culture, and the world. Worth pondering personally, they might also be the basis of a community discussion.

Chapter Two

From Monocultural to Intercultural

Defining and Clarifying Terms

Without a shared understanding of major ideas, mutual comprehension is frustrated and sustained communication may even become impossible. Though this is widely true, it is of particular importance for culturally different people aspiring to form an intercultural community. Everyone needs to feel assured and comfortable with a common working vocabulary that will facilitate discussion of intercultural living in a mutually intelligible way. Yet even when people do have a common language, discussions sometimes produce only failed communication and deepening frustration. If one or more of the parties speaks English as a second or subsequent language, or when some of the terminology is technical, deeper misunderstanding, sometimes leading to mutual recrimination, can result. Understandably, any discussion of intercultural living for members of international religious communities will of necessity include language with explicit theological meanings, as we noted; intercultural living is a theologically charged undertaking. But a significant amount of language and terminology derives from the field of sociology or cultural anthropology, and when used in a nontechnical or imprecise fashion, it may simply add to the confusion. So we must be careful; precision of language is necessary. What follows is an overview of critically important terms. For any mutually enlightening and fruitful conversations about intercultural living to occur, these terms need to be understood and used appropriately.[1]

1. *Monocultural*

Historically, most people other than nomads have lived and died within a world of perhaps no more than ten miles radius. Statistically, therefore, very few people are truly bicultural. Exceptional circumstances regarding climate, warfare, or access to food can dictate a move from one cultural milieu to another, but usually this involves a significant number of people; adjusting to changed circumstances is usually somewhat easier in a group than it is for a lone individual. Where people live in a stable environment where virtually all social contacts are with "people like us," we have a monocultural group (figure 1). Beyond the arena of "people like us" are "people not like us" (those outside enclosure "A"). The majority of the members of culture A have little or no real contact with such people. External contact would be made largely by traders or explorers. Most of us live and die within our own social group or culture.

Figure 1

MONOCULTURAL

B A B

2. *Bicultural*

True biculturalism develops primarily in people who grow up from childhood within a stable domestic arena in which each parent speaks a different native language. These children will be socialized in a bilingual context and may also benefit from moving physically between the territories in which each of their parents was raised. They find it perfectly natural to shift between two languages ("code-switching") and geographical territories (figure 2). The term bicultural, however, is sometimes also applied to a person who grows up in one culture and later encounters another culture and language, learning each sufficiently to be able to pass more or less freely between two worlds. But if such a person is not living in the milieu in which he or she was raised, the more appropriate term would be cross-cultural. For clarity and consistency, I will use the word bicultural in the broader sense to apply to anyone living in two cultural and linguistic worlds simultaneously,[2] as do many bilingual Mexican Americans, Korean Americans, and so on.

Figure 2

BICULTURAL

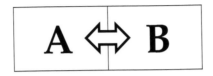

3. *Cross-Cultural*

A cross-cultural person is one who crosses over from one cultural milieu to another in a very particular way. Originally firmly rooted in a particular culture ("culture A"), the cross-cultural person chooses to move beyond its confines to reside for a significant number of years in another environment ("culture B").[3] In so doing, he or she is no longer "at home" but has "crossed" a boundary, visible or invisible, to culture B (figure 3). It is important for us to realize—and surprisingly easy to overlook this—that the people of "culture B" themselves are perfectly "at home" (it is after all, from their perspective, their own "culture A").

Figure 3

CROSS-CULTURAL

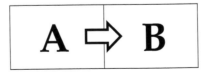

The intentionally cross-cultural person thus becomes an outsider or stranger in "culture B" and undertakes to learn a new culture (including new *mores*) and a new language, the former being as challenging as the latter.[4] Some people naively think that learning the culture will happen naturally, given time. This is a dangerous simplification: adults must learn a new culture with as much care, attention, and trial and error as they would learn a new language (but without a grammar or vocabulary in hand). And an essential component of the authentically cross-cultural person is the ability to communicate in the language of the members of "culture B." Millions of people who have lived in the same neighborhoods as people with different languages—or perhaps in the midst of the dominant language of the territory—never learn the rudiments of that other language, even after a near lifetime.

Even if successful in learning the host language and cracking the cultural code, the cross-cultural person nevertheless remains an outsider, since an adult cannot simply be assimilated into a new culture and become a true insider.[5] But there are significantly different kinds of outsiders, typically labeled "participating" or "nonparticipating."[6] The former can be of great value to the insiders,[7] while the latter are at best irrelevant (like tourists whose value is not in their intentional contribution to the community) and at worst destructive (like an invading and occupying army). Not surprisingly, the host population will take time and carefully scrutinize well-intentioned newcomers before giving them the kind of welcome they seek.[8]

Becoming a cross-cultural person evidently depends as much on the response of the indigenous population as it does on the *bona fides* of the incoming person. A transitional "testing time," often lasting months or years and not without pain and frustration, will precede wholehearted acceptance;[9] it is a necessary form of self-protection for local communities that often carry bad memories of previous ungracious and threatening strangers. During this time, the incomer is expected to be learning the cultural rules, responsibilities, and sanctions necessary for smooth day-to-day living.

4. *Multicultural*

Any neighborhood, country, parish, or religious community composed of people of many cultures is *de facto* a multicultural community; but this says nothing about *how* people of one culture actually relate to people of another (figure 4). The *how* is the great challenge to every person committed specifically to *intercultural* living. The evident social fact is that many neighborhoods and many countries are home—but not a single, common home—to people of several or many cultures, as noted above. Where different cultural groups co-exist in the same region, we have a a multicultural society and living conditions. But this is often as far as it goes. In general, people do not commit themselves—or seek—to build a new, integrated community. They may live in peaceful coexistence, with tolerance or mutual respect and even some degree of good-neighborliness. But each of their respective cultures is only minimally affected by the surrounding cultures, and they are certainly not committed to learning each other's languages. They are not cross-cultural because they do not leave their own cultural reference points and live among people to whom they themselves are the stranger. In fact, they remain "at home" while their neighbors of different cultures likewise remain "at home." So we describe this kind of multiculturality as many people who are all equally at home but separately rather than together.

Figure 4

MULTICULTURAL

A	B
C	D

Multiculturalism, then, can express itself in many ways, ranging from indifference to hostility, tolerance to friendship, civility to collaboration, and so on.[10] Cultural differences may be eliminated, blended or tolerated, or managed.[11] This is not the place to pursue this theme very far, but specifically for intercultural living, we can note several points. Eliminating differences can be accomplished in a number of ways: brutally (by genocide), forcefully (by relocation), painfully (by assimilation), and more subtly (by the promotion of uniformity). The outcome in all cases is that the "problem" of differences is, or appears to be, solved. How this may apply to intercultural living is a matter for reflection and, if necessary, action.

Likewise, there are many ways of blending or tolerating differences as the images of the melting pot, the salad bowl, or the mosaic can illustrate.[12] But none of these can provide an adequate human solution to the challenge posed by the social fact of human differences. A melting pot is a crucible in which one or several metals are superheated until they fuse, or a pot of soup in which the separate ingredients become blended. But human beings do not "fuse"; they may be herded like cattle or treated like slaves, but they remain individuals. Thus the melting pot construct is ultimately unhelpful in theory and in practice. A salad bowl conjures up the image of a wide variety of people thrown together and coexisting. But the limitations of this analogy are also quickly evident: no one makes a salad (except perhaps a green salad) in which all the ingredients are equally represented. Some (anchovies, onions) will give flavor even in small quantities; others (lettuce, spinach) provide bulk rather than taste. In a mixed society, various constituencies will be over- or underrepresented. The salad bowl is an equally unhelpful image for intercultural living. The mosaic is a more immediately attractive representation: many pieces together composing a single picture. But the limitations are just as obvious: no single piece in a mosaic has a discernible identity of its own: it is merely a fragment or piece of a much larger picture. Human society, homogeneous or heterogeneous, is not composed of anonymous individuals or clones: each human person has an autonomous identity. In some ways, this is the most dangerous image of the three, because below its immediate attractiveness lie dreadful implications for the actual individual community members.

So much for blending or tolerating (or overlooking) differences; but differences can also be managed in ways both negative and positive. Negative management might be accomplished by allowing for or expecting "separate development" (*chacun pour soi*: everyone on their own) or leaving apathetic or disinterested people to their own devices; this can produce a human group without a focus, center, or group identity, leaving everyone in a state of enduring confusion, identity crisis, or *liminality* (in a negative sense).[13] But there are also positive forms of management. One might use the analogy of a chorus (accommodating a wide range of voices and skills); an orchestra (harmonizing the sounds of many instruments; or a theater company

Figure 5

INTERCULTURAL

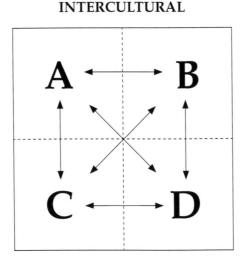

(creating an ensemble of many parts). But one thing that needs to be identified, specifically as we address the challenge of (long-term) intercultural living, is the need for appropriate leadership. Without competent leadership, a chorus can produce stridency or clamor, an orchestra can generate dissonance or din, and a theater company can become a disorganized crew.[14] But with mutual cooperation, encouragement of diversity, and appropriate leadership, greatness can be achieved. Issues like these deserve serious attention and provide a good segue to a consideration of intercultural community living, once we identify the meaning of intercultural itself.

5. *Intercultural*

From the 1950s, when study of the effects of cross-cultural contact was not a fully developed discipline and the vocabulary was unstable, the words multicultural and intercultural were often either used synonymously or employed by various writers for their own ends. The fledgling discipline first arose within the field of the social sciences, including cultural anthropology, sociology, and psychology. But gradually the practitioners of theological disciplines, specifically mission studies but more broadly pastoral studies, became aware of the enormous significance of cultural dynamics at work in situations of mission *ad extra* or parishes that were rapidly becoming multicultural. As theology borrowed and adapted terminology from the social sciences, standard usage generally now distinguishes *multicultural*, a sociological/anthropological term (figure 4), and *intercultural*, a specifically theological word (figure 5).

The sociological/anthropological term "multicultural" identifies a social reality within neighborhoods or voluntary associations, while the theological word "intercultural" carries specific overtones relating to God, faith, and practice. For our purposes, the anthropological and theological implications of intercultural living are equally salient, since elements of both culture (anthropology) and faith (theology) are combined in each person. An intercultural community shares intentional commitment to the common life, motivated not by pragmatic considerations alone, but by a shared religious conviction and common purpose.

There are evident similarities between figures 4 and 5. Both distinguish four cultures: A, B, C, and D. In figure 4, however, each letter or culture is isolated from the others by a boundary, indicating that members of each culture interact predominantly with their own: "people like us." Although they may be quite civil to people of other cultures, there is minimal social bonding. In figure 5, however, though the lines between cultures remain, they are porous, and internal arrows link each of the four letters or cultures to each of the others. This illustrates the nature of an intercultural community: a community-wide and explicit commitment to building a new social, cultural—and religious—reality out of the several cultures, which entails a cross-cultural commitment on the part of each to learning another culture and, if necessary or expected, another language.[15]

Nevertheless, members of intercultural communities do not surrender their individual cultural identity, though each is indeed "out of place" because of being away from home (living cross-culturally) and because no one culture will be allowed to dominate. Figure 5 indicates this by showing double-pointed arrows (rather than single-pointed) linking each person in the community with every other. But the challenge for all is even more dramatic: to create a *new culture* in which all can live fruitfully. This is what Sacks refers to as the home we build together, and it necessarily takes time. Nobody will be entirely in a familiar element, yet everyone must be able to find an appropriate degree of fitness in this new environment. Figure 5 would be completed, therefore, by the superimposition of the single letter E on the whole diagram, on all four quadrants (indicating a fifth culture, beyond A, B, C, and D, figure 6, below). This is a culture in the making and, paradoxically, *everyone* within the new community will be an outsider to culture E, but each is able to become a *participating outsider*[16] and to bring his or her particular culture to the emerging reality.

6. *Intercultural Community Culture*

In an intercultural community, *everyone* is directly affected by the presence of cultural others. This should be a stimulus to every member (not just those from minority cultures) to accept the challenge of cross-cultural living in the sense that they commit themselves to living *outside* their own comfort zone.[17] In that case, characteristics of cultures A, B, C, D, and so on remain part of the core identity of the respective members. But each is gradually *transformed* and *converted* to a way of living that is somewhat new and somewhat familiar to each community member. And as all cultures are always, everywhere, evolving or being "contested"[18] by the interplay of persons, contexts, and circumstances, we can identify *"culture E" as the existential identity of an intercultural community, formed of the raw materials of the component cultures (A, B, C, and D)*. Insofar as community members are committed to intercultural living, they are at once cultural, cross-cultural, multicultural, and intercultural: quite a challenge.

Figure 6

A NEW INTERCULTURAL COMMUNITY

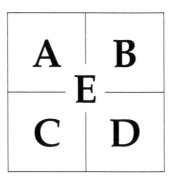

We have yet to discuss culture itself: its nature, functions, and pathologies. But before doing that, in the next chapter, it might be helpful at least to outline some of the features that mark a community striving for intercultural living. But we will need to revisit them later in order to show how each person's approach to them will be necessarily influenced by his or her own culture.

Characteristics of Intercultural Communities

"By their fruits you will know them" is not only a biblical principle. It is applicable in many situations. As we proceed to fashion a theoretical and practical understanding of interculturality and the demands of intercultural community living, we may note several indispensable features of any viable community. There is nothing inevitable about their occurrence and influence, and each needs careful attention and commitment from all the community members. Here are seven—biblically, the perfect number!

1. *Intentionality: A Common/Community Project*

Intentionality is considerably more than goodwill or good intentions. Whoever has the will must find the means, and a community must be able to identify common means and not simply individual goodwill. By religious profession, members of a religious institute embrace the common life, pledging not simply to plow a lone furrow but to work together with common dedication toward a common end. What is sometimes referred to as a "common project" or better, a "community project"—and sometimes misunderstood—is the focus that all must have for the common good and the good of the ministry or apostolate; it is not simply some practical task. A community may repair property after a storm or undertake a fund-raising drive; this may serve the community well but it is insufficient: it is not what a "community project" requires. For a faith-based religious community, that would be what really inspires, captures members' attention and imagination, and stimulates and challenges the faith of all. It may be expressed in the words of the community's "mission statement" or identified as its founding charism or *raison d'être*; but it needs to live, not simply in carefully crafted documents or nostalgic memories but in each person. As a plant or animal will die without water, so a community's zeal and focus will atrophy unless its common project is nurtured and tended. My own community, the Congregation of the Holy Spirit (Spiritans), articulates its "community project" or *projet communautaire* as follows: "Each (local) community plans what it wants to achieve and how it lives within the framework that the Rule provides. The planning sets down what community life asks of the members, in terms of time and occasions of prayer in common, of deeper sharing of our lives and of periodic evaluation of the community's life and of our apostolic work."[19]

A common project might be articulated as an answer to the questions: what are you really living for and what is worth dying for? But living such a common project requires several corollary features or qualities.

2. *Individual Commitment*

The common project is only common if everyone's contribution is sought and acknowledged; exclusion of any person, or disrespect for individual efforts, will undermine one's commitment, leave too much to specialists, or become an ideological preoccupation. The common project actually requires the commitment of all; leadership is vital, but a leader without followers or a teacher without learners is functionally impotent. However the common project may be conceived or articulated, it should require the commitment of each of the members, without whom it cannot be accomplished. This should be made clear to everyone. Thus each person knows what is asked for the good of the whole and the glory of God. For the good of the apostolate and the community itself, it is important to identify those who resist, actively or passively, because without a "critical mass" of commitment and energy, the prospects hover between dim and nil.[20]

3. *Mutual Tolerance*

The community atmosphere must allow or encourage people to take appropriate risks, even though they sometimes fail, such that mistakes and immaturity will not be so strongly sanctioned as to stifle future effort. Here is Pope Francis: "I invite everyone to be bold

and creative in . . . rethinking the goals, structures, styles and methods of evangelization in their respective communities . . . without
inhibition or fear. The Holy Spirit also grants the courage to proclaim
the newness of the Gospel with boldness in every time and place,
even when it meets with opposition."[21]

Speaking about the renewal and updating of religious life (and his
comments apply to the challenge to intercultural living), Pope Francis
acknowledged that "there is a danger of making mistakes, of committing errors. It is risky." But he immediately affirms: "This should
not stop us, because there is a chance of making worse mistakes. In
fact we should always ask for forgiveness and look shamefully upon
apostolic failures due to a lack of courage."[22] These bold and deeply
encouraging sentiments challenge everyone living in community.

4. *A Forum for Articulating Frustration*

Because of inevitable frustrations and misunderstandings, some
mechanism must be built into the community life—a forum or procedure that allows people to vent their frustrations publicly and
without feeling intimidated, inhibited, or accused of personal animosity. If one person identifies a particular personal difficulty, others
should not take offense or assume the air of "injured innocence." And
when someone is able and willing to name his or her frustration, it
can be of great help to others who can immediately identify with it
but were slower to articulate or even to notice it. Then the community
can take constructive rather than destructive measures or fail to act.
But each person must know that the gathering is in a "safe place"[23]
where they can feel respected and not attacked: a place for potential
bridge building rather than bridge burning. Moreover, the forum
must have some structure; it is not simply a "free for all," much less
a covert form of confrontation or complaining.

For example, each person might be invited to identify, on the one
hand, something specific that he or she finds difficult in community
life but then also something he or she would be willing to change.
Far from this degenerating into a personal attack, each speaker's
finger will point first at himself or herself rather than at someone
else. But then, if each one is also invited to identify some aspect of
community living that is of positive assistance in daily life and aspi-

rations, some consolation, as well as some success or achievement, a potentially confrontational or competitive situation will be defused before it can become toxic. People should be in no doubt about this: communities that do not avail themselves of some mechanism for constructive conversation about daily community living will ultimately fail to live out their call to unity and mission.

5. *Appropriate Correction*

A complementary feature is that correction is sometimes necessary, and the leadership is responsible for finding appropriate ways and means of correction, whether applied personally or through authorized personnel. Inaction or lack of leadership helps no one. A multicultural community whose members have professed their willingness to attempt intercultural living will be seriously hampered by unchecked and unsanctioned behavior that undermines the efforts of the community as a whole; leadership is vital.[24] Vindictiveness on the part of anyone is clearly unjustifiable—something much more positive is required: attentive listening and perhaps mediation and flexibility as well as sincere attempts at fence mending and an ongoing commitment to dialogue and development. Correction must never become humiliation, and the leader must seek not only to redress wrongdoing but also to become a bridge builder.

6. *Attention to Stress and Burnout*

A community of diverse membership in which each person carries responsibility can produce unhealthy competitiveness or its near opposite: inattention to others. Individuals' psychological well-being needs to be supported and misunderstandings (arising as much from overload as from language differences or bad will) resolved. This requires the sensitivity of everyone and the skills of leadership, especially at foreseeable stress times like the end of an academic semester, the preparation for liturgical feasts, or times of examinations or assessment. But given human nature and certain personality types, the community members need to be explicit here and pledge themselves to take seriously appropriate advice about signs of impending burnout.

7. Clarification of the Vision

Members of an intercultural community need to feel they are all on the same side, working for common goals and the implementation of a common vision; this requires compassion, concern, and sometimes explicit encouragement rather than a mere lack of criticism. A common vision is not simply generated from individuals and espoused by the wider community but is an attempt by everyone to identify *God's vision* for the community: what is God asking and how is the community responding?

We are striving to live, to embody, God's vision for a particular community and its constituent individuals. God is not fickle, and we believe that God's love—God's own self—is sure and enduring. But to remain faithful, we ourselves must change, adjust, and continue to seek God's will. The sun does not move relative to the earth and looking east in the morning we may feel its warmth and see its brightness; but unless we move by afternoon, the sun will appear to be behind us, and after dark it will have disappeared. Yet the sun remains! God's invitation and our life's work is to keep God's vision before us, lest we find ourselves taking the initiative away from God or simply going through the motions of religious life rather than remaining faithful to authentic "religious living."

Our attempts to keep the vision alive depend on our structures and strategies[25] and our willingness to review them continuously. This is a particular responsibility of Provincial and General Chapters and also of personal retreats. Structures are both our individual (bodily) structures and our institutional (architectural) structures. They not only facilitate but also limit what we can do. Minimal personnel, members declining in health as they increase in age, buildings in disrepair, and lack of property—these will limit our ability to sustain the vision as once we did. But we can still remain faithful to the vision that inspired us. In contrast, large numbers, fine structures, and splendid property are no guarantee: the Cistercians of the thirteenth century became too profitable and popular for their own good, and by the time of Henry VIII, religious houses offered rich pickings that a needy monarch could not resist. We must work within the constraints of our structures, neither wallowing in nostalgia nor being seduced by grandiose dreams. Structure is the springboard for any project, but it is not the only issue, since structures produce strategies.

If the structures are focused on keeping the vision alive, so must the strategies be. But structures can become self-serving and strategies prove to be hopelessly misaligned. Religious clinging to a "Mother House" (for sentimental reasons or until the centenary arrives) when it has long since become a white elephant are not using the structure appropriately: their strategies are failing to keep the vision alive, even if these people keep the buildings. A six-year plan adhered to because of the mandate of a General Chapter years before—after circumstances have changed beyond recognition—is not loyalty but lack of responsibility. Structures and strategies have a single purpose: to sustain the vision by and for which we live. If no longer "fit for service" in this respect, they need to be adjusted or discarded for the greater good of the mission. Here is David Steindl-Rast:

> Life always creates structures, and people are needed to support and refine the structures. However, while life creates structures, structures do not create life. So we have to keep the spirit going, the life strong, and then we will create the structures we need at a given time. The institutional structure serves life; it is not life that serves the structure. So look at the life. If that life happens to occur somewhere else—not inside the structure but outside [it] then be open to it. And if that life is so strong and so new that it bursts the existing structure, allow that to happen. The structure will renew itself. Life does that all the time. Every spring all the protective structures that are around the little leaves burst and fall off. So let it happen. Take seriously that for which you are created as a structure, and that is the life. That is very difficult advice to take, because institutions have a built-in tendency to perpetuate themselves. Structures are potentially dangerous enemies if you alienate them, and potentially helpful allies if you get them on your side.[26]

Changing Contours, Insights, and Needs

Multinational corporations hire people who travel extensively and internationally. They need skills for communicating with a wide variety of business partners. For decades, such skills have been identified, taught, and acquired across the business world. Meanwhile, many faith-based communities have encountered the challenges posed by their own increasingly multicultural membership and the awareness of the near bankruptcy of the standard assimilation model of recruitment. ("Come join us, and we will teach you to do things *our* way—as we have always done.") Over the years, the contours of intercultural living and ministry have become increasingly clear. But partly because they have been shaped by previously gained insights from the social sciences, the majority of people in today's international religious communities have either been unaware of, struggled with, or even resisted the challenge (which is fast becoming a real imperative) of intercultural living.

To summarize: intercultural living is a lifelong, faith-based process of conversion, emerging in recent decades as a requirement of members of intentional, international religious communities.[27] Healthy intercultural living depends on the level of commitment and support generated by *every* member of the community. Individuals vary in their adaptability and learning levels, but each generates positive or negative energy, and the quality of intercultural living depends significantly on the aggregate of positive energy generated by the whole group. A small, resistant group can generate enough negative energy to thwart the wider community. The future of international religious life depends significantly on the ability of each community (local and institutional) to live interculturally; those that fail to do so will fragment or die.

This is such a tall order, and to begin to measure up to it, we need to explore culture itself. Intercultural community life is the end: it is *what* we seek; culture itself is the means: *how* we actually live it. Culture is the totality of the processes that shape persons and by which they are related as a social group. By looking in some detail at culture, we should better understand how each of us is challenged to personal transformation or conversion and be better able to identify some of the skills and virtues we need to strive for, if intercultural living is ever to be more than a naïve and unrealistic hope. It is impossible to create a perfect community, but we do have a responsibility to cultivate assiduously the art of the possible.

Suggested Follow-Up

1. It might be good if a community gathering were to have a conversation in which the basic terminology—culture, monocultural, bicultural, multicultural, cross-cultural, and intercultural—were used frequently so that people would be able to understand and agree on the meanings of these words.

2. Four ways of handling cultural diversity are mentioned: eliminating, blending, tolerating, or managing. What is your experience in this respect (a particularly pertinent question for leadership)?

3. Four outcomes or ways of promoting a policy are mentioned: brutally, forcefully, painfully, or subtly. Reflect and discuss which of these might be present in your own community.

4. Differences in a community may be "managed" negatively (essentially when there is a vacuum where leadership is required) or positively (images of a chorus or orchestra—or both). Can this language and these images help facilitate discussion?

Chapter Three

Culture, "The (Hu)man-Made Part of the Environment"

Approaching "Culture"

Most people assume that they can identify and understand culture, but it is the very topic that needs the most clarification for our purposes. We do not, however, need a long disquisition on culture from a purely technical or theoretical perspective; more than a theory, we need to understand how to negotiate it in the specific context of intercultural living. Therefore our primary focus will be on the features of culture that we all engage with routinely but also find among the most challenging. First, we can locate the study of culture in the academic world, and then we can move on to a more descriptive and empirical perspective.

Gerald Arbuckle nicely locates the challenge we face by quoting from social historian Raymond Williams. His words should serve as a cautionary tale for anyone who assumes that "culture" is a univocal term, that they understand it adequately, or that they share a common understanding with others of their own community or culture. "Culture is one of the two or three most complicated words in the English language . . . mainly because it has now come to be used for important concepts in several . . . disciplines, and in several distinct and incompatible systems of thought."[1]

As do many authors, Arbuckle then reminds us that there are several hundred definitions of this shape-changing term, and that all of them can be classified under one of four broad categories: classicist, evolutionary, modern, and postmodern.[2] Briefly, *classicist* definitions identify "culture" in the singular: some (few, privileged) people or societies have it; others do not, or only in an attenuated form. An *evolutionary* perspective, by contrast, classifies cultures, contemporary and historical, as somewhere on an ascending scale that is topped by the European "culture" (or civilization) which, not surprisingly, happens to be that of the very people who created the definition in the first place.

By the late nineteenth century, however, people were beginning to identify a great plurality of cultures and using the word to describe the constellation of characteristics that defined or described particular social groups (usually a tribe, caste, or nation). Whereas classicist definitions tended to see culture as fixed and frozen, *modern* definitions tended to compare cultures to clocks or organisms: each part had a specific function contributing to the whole. Understanding cultures as in equilibrium, self-integrating and homogeneous, tended to overlooked cultural pathologies and rapid social change, not to mention the accumulating and sweeping forces of globalization. *Postmodern* definitions now tend to romanticize culture much less, to minimize the scientific nature of anthropology itself in favor of a more "interpretative" approach to cultural manifestations, and to view cultures not as discrete or static entities but as constantly "contested" (a helpful notion, this) by their members, who struggle to reinvent themselves, to make new choices, or simply to survive.

Theologian Robert Schreiter offers a very helpful profile of culture,[3] yet too much of the theological literature fails to take culture seriously enough, with the result being that some theological approaches to inculturation (the way faith is lived, and can only be lived, culturally, or in the context of a particular culture)[4] must be said to be naïve. Not so Schreiter, who creates a simple tripartite typology, seeing culture as *ideational* (concerned with meaning and interpretation), *performative* (expressed through ritual and bodily behavior), and *material* (identified in artifacts but also including apparel, language, and music).[5] While this can be a very helpful set of lenses, I would not include "symbolizations" (language, music) among the material aspects, and my approach here will be somewhat different, partly because it is explicitly addressed to people committed to intercultural living.

David Couturier, too, offers a helpful perspective on culture when he speaks of different "learning cultures" in seminaries or religious communities. These are "diverse patterns of understanding, emotions, rituals, and tools" [that help people] to mediate their world, interpret their experiences, and make decisions as to appropriate action."[6]

But however interesting, or frustrating, or inconclusive the study of culture (theoretically or empirically) may be, it is evident that ordinary people, nonspecialists, are intuitively able to recognize some of the gross features of culture and are perfectly able to make comparisons (not always appropriate or fair) between different cultures. We can begin, therefore, with these common intuitions: that culture is about people-in-society, about how they live, and about how individuals and groups are both similar to and different from others. This is sufficient for our present purposes as a foundation on which to build. Instead of adding one more to the plethora of (overtechnical) definitions, our approach will instead be much more descriptive. By identifying different facets of culture and offering some analogies that might be of practical help, we will first set them out in series and then consider how each offers us some specific challenges to, and means of, approaching intercultural community living.

But, first, to state a fundamentally important principle: culture is recognizable under many forms, and every human person, raised in a social environment, has culture. There is no such person as a cultureless person.[7] The significance of this as it relates to intercultural living will be explored later: faith is—and can only be—expressed *culturally*. And further, "culture" is a word that applies to a group of people rather than an individual. Culture as a social reality persists over time, certainly over generations and often centuries. Yet no one is *born* with culture; and, given different social circumstances, any individual might have become socialized or enculturated differently.[8] A baby boy born and raised in Shanghai by Chinese parents is ethnically Chinese and will become culturally Chinese, all things being equal. But that very same child, flown to Chicago soon after birth and adopted by Euro-American parents, will become enculturated as (that is, will become culturally) a Euro-American, though of course remaining ethnically Chinese. Ethnicity is *who we are*; culture is *how we live*, and environment and socialization are critically important for the development of cultural identity.

Descriptively, we identify culture in a number of ways. Each merits a much deeper treatment than we can offer here. For our present purposes, our treatment will be limited to practicalities. I will review five descriptive definitions from which we can derive some implications and applications. Culture, then, is (1) the (hu)man-made part of the environment; (2) the form of social life; (3) a meaning-making system; (4) social skin; and (5) an enduring social reality.[9] The rest of this chapter will occupy us with the first of these definitions, and the others will be the subject of the next chapter.

Culture as
"The (Hu)man-Made Part of the Environment"

Social or, in the United States, cultural anthropology, whose primary object of study is human society (cultural anthropology looks explicitly at culture: but in fact their focus and concerns overlap greatly) used to describe itself simply as the study of man. With the rise of feminist scholarship in the 1960s, it waggishly redefined itself as "the study of man—embracing woman." This very superficial description does point to the subject-object of study. Rather less superficial is the first of our descriptions of culture as "the human-made part of the environment." In other words, virtually every trace that humanity has left on the face of the earth—from the Great Wall of China to contemporary garbage landfills, from the Enlightenment to the *Shoah*, from nuclear medicine to nuclear war, and from poetry to pornography—reflects an aspect of culture. Culture identifies not only the greatest heights the human spirit can reach but also the lowest depths to which a society (not simply a lone individual) can sink. We may think of the depravity of ancient Rome or the corruption of the medieval papacy in these terms. But what constitutes the "human-made" can be more clearly identified under four headings: material, symbolic, institutional, and moral culture.

1. *Material Culture*

This is to be found in practical artifacts, including tools, implements, weapons, furnishings, decorations, pottery, clothing, objects of cult, and so on, as well as in buildings.

But it is important to remember that much material culture may be short-lived because it is perishable: mud-built houses collapse, wood gets eaten by termites, and the fabric of clothes rots or becomes unusable. Some things may be later found by archaeologists (or physical anthropologists, paleoanthropologists, or forensic anthropologists who unearth burial sites), but wherever societies do not use stone, concrete, or stressed steel, very little may remain after a few decades, let alone centuries. One consequence of this is that if we identify and evaluate "culture" *only* in terms of what the archaeological evidence reveals, we will erroneously conclude that whoever once inhabited a particular area was virtually without culture and thus "savage" or "primitive"—as indeed was the judgment of many Victorian explorers and anthropologists (and not a few missionaries). Hence the great importance of understanding culture as much more than material artifacts or skeletons.

2. Symbolic Culture

This can be found in things that stand for or represent something other than themselves. For example, a monolingual speaker of English can look at the written language of China, Korea, or Russia (with different writing systems), or France, Germany, or Spain (which use the same alphabet as English) without understanding a single character or word: Korean symbols and French words are signs or symbols that stand for something we fail to understand, and they point beyond themselves. Marks on a page may be random, but when brought together as part of a system, they become comprehensible *in a particular language*. This is an example of the symbolic component of culture: the characters or words carry a meaning beyond what is merely decorative or a random arrangement of runes or rebuses, glyphs, or graphemes. In a similar way, we can identify, as part of a symbol system, orality, ritual, dance, music, song, and story—and extend the list to include jokes, proverbs, parables, and other literary or oral styles.

Orality not only refers to the spoken word but also characterizes a primary medium of communication (there are others: touch, silence, proximity, mood, posture, and so on) in a culture where writing is nonexistent or not being used. *Primary orality* is found where people simply do not have writing (and manage perfectly adequately without it),[10] while *secondary orality* operates alongside literacy. Speakers are able to read and perhaps write but may have minimal use for such skills because their community is largely face-to-face and not dependent on literacy. The opposite of literacy is, strictly speaking, orality rather than illiteracy, since the latter signifies lack or absence, while people in primary oral cultures do not lack what they do not need any more than a human person "lacks" grass or wood for food.

The culture of Jesus was largely oral. Most of his contemporaries were certainly not literate and his message did not require them to become so. We need to understand that in a culture that does not depend on the written word, interpersonal relationships are face-to-face, frequent, and sociocentric, while in a highly literate culture, people's lives can be more independent, isolated, and egocentric.[11] Expectations, therefore, of different people in an intercultural setting may be very different and will need to be made explicit if communication and harmony are to be maintained. Another example of symbolic culture is communicative interaction. Edward T. Hall offers the helpful concept of "high context" and "low context" cultures,[12] to which we shall return.

Ritual, of course, is typically a wordless, established, and formalized procedure (though words may be used), often of a religious nature. Through a combination of words, objects ("condensed symbols" like a crucifix or chalice, compared to a simple cross or cup), and gestures, ritual contrives to "say the unsayable."[13] It may both regulate social behavior and have a more or less stated purpose; but it need not do so. If it does, it would be specifically *instrumental* (or manipulative) behavior, while if not, it would produce largely *expressive* behavior such as gratitude or sorrow. Much of human behavior, however, is a blend of the instrumental and the expressive.

Dance, too, may be ritualized or recreational, but it is always symbolic behavior, pointing to something else (from sacredness to self-expression to seduction). And so with music: it may be created and performed to create or evoke particular emotional responses (again, from the plaintive *Dies Irae* to the bacchanalian *Bolero*). But it may also be an effective conveyor of specific meaning, as when "talking drums" are used.

Finally, story or narrative in its many forms is symbolic behavior serving a variety of functions, from creating group solidarity to ridiculing a miscreant and from religious contemplation to orgiastic behavior. Attempting to refer beyond itself, and/or to say the unsayable, ritual is universal cultural behavior and is as varied as the American pledge of allegiance, the Nazi salute, or the prostration of an ordinand. In an intercultural community, therefore, its significance will need to be discussed.

3. *Moral Culture*

This is expressed and identified in the cherished virtues and values of a society, while its shadow side is revealed in vices and immorality. No culture is perfect, but every culture is not without virtue. Being a human-made creation, culture is always a carrier of vice: sin and grace operate within every person and social world. Values or virtues—and vices or immorality—may be conceptualized but need not be; but virtue and vice are always embodied, incarnated. Western thought likes to identify and play with abstractions and concepts: people, beauty, hunger, truth, hatred, and so on. But trying to identify vernacular words for abstractions may prove a thankless and frustrating task. Looking for a single word that "means" weather, hunger, or peace may be a waste of time. But as soon as we ask an interlocutor to identify a hungry *child*, a homeless *woman*, or a wicked *man*, or for words to describe *this* jealous person or *that* skinflint, the abstract becomes incarnated and contextualized, and people have absolutely no difficulty with virtue and vice when it is made concrete. Philosopher Immanuel Kant (1724–1804) liked to conceptualize, but Aristotle (384–332 BC) insisted that virtues and vices only exist in people, or in embodied form.

If no one in the world hated, there would be no "hatred"; and if no one in the world loved, there would be no "love" in the world. It is therefore profoundly important for anyone negotiating meaning and values across cultures to seek appropriate paths to discovery. How easy it is to generalize and condemn or affirm that "these people don't know the meaning of honesty" or "those people are poor but always happy." Moral—and immoral—culture is not to be found primarily in books but in people; not in philosophy but in behavior. And intercultural communities consist precisely of people behaving well or badly, not randomly but culturally. This means that people can be understood and can understand others with appropriate effort and information. Part of that information may be a simple reminder that for most people, thinking is concrete rather than abstract or conceptual, and that sometimes our community language can float off into a world of Platonic forms or idealizations when people are looking for something much more tangible. Much theological language is academic and abstract—alien and meaningless to large swaths of the wider community.

4. *Institutional Culture*

There are four essential building blocks or pillars on which every culture stands: the social institutions[14] of politics, kinship, economics, and belief and thought or religion. These can look very different from one society to another, so what exactly does each of them signify or denote? I will simply sketch the broadest lines of each of the social institutions, because the reason for looking at them lies beyond themselves and beyond theory; we need to know in broad terms both what they are and how significant they are in the context of our own efforts at intercultural living.

Politics concerns the organization and (smooth) running of daily life and is evaluated by the relationship between power and authority.[15] Authority can be described as the legitimate use of power, and power is simply the capacity to act on things or persons, whether such action be legitimate or illegitimate, moral or immoral. What constitutes "legitimate" power depends on the common understanding of individual cultures and is controlled (in theory) by the appropriate use of sanctions: rewards and punishments. A stable political system will have mechanisms for the peaceful transmission of authority from regime to regime or at timely intervals.

Social control or the use of positive and negative sanctions is invoked whenever effective law and order is compromised.[16] Disaffection and dissent, potentially leading to rebellion (the reaction against the prevalent social controls) or revolution (the intentional attempt to overthrow those in control and replace the system) usually follow. A reaction from those clinging to power, if not authority, may be to respond with an uncontrolled use of power (often called authoritarianism). The matter of social control is of great consequence in the context of intercultural living. Everyone must be apprised of how legitimate authority is mediated and under what circumstances it is exercised, and by whom. Moreover, members must understand procedures for "due process" or for referring grievances through established channels. Failure to reach a common understanding about, or the abuse of, authority by the exercise of unauthorized power, force, or threat will undermine the efforts to create and maintain a healthy community.

Every human society has political institutions and a political culture that can be identified and judged by various criteria of effectiveness, morality, or simple practicality. Codified and written laws are not always necessary; where the culture is largely oral, living tradition and oral transmission may suffice (as is often the case in religious communities). But any and every legal system is also susceptible to critique and modification.

Economics concerns the flow of goods and services within and between communities. Every society (culture)[17] must be organized in predictable ways, with rules and conventions. Otherwise, the day-to-day running of a community would become unmanageable. Societies differ according to who receives what and who is unable to acquire certain goods or services. They likewise differ in their conventional ways of relating economic considerations to the maintenance of good interpersonal relations; some transactions may be "purely business" and governed by rules of contract or law, but others have a clearer moral and interpersonal significance. The social institution of barter is a case in point, frequently misunderstood by outsiders but often important in cross-cultural situations.

Barter is a system of exchange, often independent of money or hard currency, underwritten by distinct but implicit moral values.

Behind the barter system is a community whose members are in a symbiotic relationship, so a *quid pro quo* principle will operate implicitly: "if you are kind to me, I shall be kind to you, but if I feel you are unfair to me, I may be unfair to you later." Nevertheless, the effectiveness of a barter system depends on the maintenance of a certain trust level between barter partners. One of the social functions of barter systems is to separate the mechanics of basic subsistence from those of wealth production, thus facilitating the equitable circulation of life's basic necessities.

Quite often however, outsiders or strangers, completely unaware of the principles of bartering, approach their transactions with a totally different mentality. They are looking not to build or maintain relationships but to apply rational economic principles (supply and demand, value for money, personal satisfaction) to get something cheaply and cannot understand why prices are not marked as they are in their own supermarkets. Trying to "beat down" the asking price, they may only succeed in being rude and giving a poor impression; but the wily trader will usually "win." He or she immediately identifies the outsider as having all-purpose "cash money" and acting either eager or phlegmatic, arrogant or respectful, combative or friendly, and will consequently strategize accordingly. After a purchase, the buyer may be very happy to have "beaten down" the original asking price, while the seller is happy to have earned more cash money than ordinary barter would have generated. But though the outcome may make both people happy, they have not become friends by the transaction. This is much more a rational contract (*do ut des*: I give so that you give) than a relational exchange.

Apart from bartering perishable goods, a local economy may or may not use hard currency (referred to as "all-purpose currency"). As the name indicates, all-purpose currency can be used to purchase anything from salt to cement, garden produce to gold ornaments. But, despite its usefulness—as with credit cards, one need not carry around quantities of goods for exchange—it also has serious limitations and has contributed to the undermining of many economies worldwide.[18]

The circulation of banknotes and currency in Africa and Asia, minted and underwritten by colonial powers, both "rationalized" and simplified a system. The new all-purpose money meant that the market was completely open to those who had sufficient wealth in goods and services; but it also undermined a system that operated with specific moral principles. When we consider kinship, we will see how traditional kinship and marriage institutions became compromised with the wide circulation of all-purpose money.

Applied to intercultural living, such information should remind us that not all relationships can be reduced to rational economics, and that value and worth are differently reckoned in different societies. This may challenge the more hard-headed members of a community to greater flexibility and to building relationships rather than operating only by the principles of cold logic and absolute equality. Some people need and deserve more or less than others. A world— even the world of a religious community governed by vowed poverty

—in which people seek absolute economic equality is an unsustainable world because individuals differ. Thus, in order for a multicultural community to become intercultural, people's immediate or long-term needs must be understood and approached with sympathy. Religious poverty is a topic that will come under increasing discussion and scrutiny in an intercultural setting. In a community where members share the vow of poverty and where the virtue of simplicity is prized, an understanding of common finances, distribution, stewardship, and some of the many unwritten conventions that govern daily living needs to be widely shared, lest patronage or partiality, inequity or injustice breed secrecy, jealousy, acquisitiveness, or dissension within the community.

No economic system can ensure the smooth flow of goods and services to everyone absolutely equally. Some people may be privileged or able to acquire more, while some are deprived. In other systems (sometimes dubbed "socialist") there may be a greater effort to ensure that the neediest people are not simply left to die. Therefore one must look at the principles on which a particular economic system is based: utilitarianism, capitalism, equality, privilege, or entitlement, and so on. A rule of thumb is that any enduring social group or culture—including intercultural communities—*must* be able to manage the flow of goods and services for its survival.

Kinship determines who is related to whom and how, who may or may not or should or should not marry whom, and how certain behavior is expected of various persons and what prohibitions apply. The study of kinship focuses on what humans do with these basic facts of life—mating, gestation, parenthood, socialization, siblingship, and so on. Kinship rules include the right and exercise of authority, marriage choices (or restrictions), residence, and entitlement to land. Every culture develops rules over time, and members of sociocentric societies with a strongly developed sense of duty are not at liberty to pursue private or personal aims, except at significant personal or social cost. Because there is an enormous variety of prescriptions and proscriptions and varying degrees of moral seriousness attached to them, it is particularly important for an interested outsider to learn the rules, conventions, and sanctions of a particular social group. Again, this becomes highly pertinent when we consider intercultural living itself, specifically in relation to celibacy as a cultural and religious value.

Descent rules stipulate how one is related to certain forebears or ancestors, and kinship systems can be broadly distinguished as patrilineal or matrilineal, double descent or cognatic,[19] each serving to locate every individual within a web of duties and rights. Universal rules of kinship nevertheless allow for a sometimes bewildering number of sophisticated systems, none of which can simply be understood by intuition or casual observation. The (virtually universal) rules are: women have the children; primary kin cannot mate; and authority is under male control.

An intercultural community may be composed of people with widely different understandings of what a family is, who is included, and what rules—especially rules of hospitality and filial piety (duty to parents)—operate. Formerly, religious cut the ties with their families in a rather dramatic way and in many cases were not permitted to be present for the death or burial of parents. Traditions like this are increasingly under scrutiny today when so many things have changed: travel and communication have become much easier, apostolic religious are much more engaged with the outside world rather than isolated from it, and people of many different cultures have a wide variety of customs, each with its own persuasive rationale. Dialogue is one of the life-support systems of intercultural communities, and evolving change is an imperative. The present and future must be negotiated both with fidelity to one's religious commitment and respect for those beyond the community, with whom the bonds of kinship and affinity need to be appropriately respected and affirmed.

Belief and Thought (religion) addresses (often informally as there may be no Scriptures or dogmatic propositions) life's fundamental questions: Why are we here? Where did we come from? Where are we going? Why are things the way they are? Is anyone responsible for the world? People may share a basic understanding or worldview, without speculating or philosophizing unduly about the smaller details. They may have a common understanding of causation and moral responsibility, without necessarily being able to itemize specific "beliefs." Thinking, as we noted, tends to be concrete, and the world (until science intrudes) is more or less accepted as a given; things simply *are*, and there is a relative lack of perceived alternatives— sometimes an objective lack, and sometimes a simple lack of awareness—to the way things operate.[20]

Christianity itself is rather unusual in having such a formalized system of codified beliefs and objective tests of orthodoxy. But many people who have become Christians in recent centuries would find questions like "Do you believe in God?" to be quite meaningless—like asking "Do you believe in Tuesday, or trees?" One does not "believe" in what simply is. Again, conversations between members of different cultures in intercultural communities risk foundering over questions of belief. Christianity has developed speculative and philosophical approaches to ultimately unanswerable questions, theologians have toiled to provide answers, and the church's *magisterium* has spoken about what is to believed and (sometimes) precisely how. But one needs to be careful when entering theological deep water in a community composed of people from very different cultures, levels of education, and philosophical perspectives.

Significant for intercultural living is the fact that the four social institutions—politics, economics, kinship, and religion—may be either *institutionalized* or *embedded*. In the first case, they would be freestanding (somewhat independent of each other—as in "the separation of church and state"). Thus, one might identify politics in the houses of Parliament or the Supreme Court in Washington, DC; economics could be understood in relation to Wall Street or the Stock Exchange; kinship in weddings or funerals; and religion in the mosque, the synagogue, or the church. The more institutionalized the social institutions are, the more they are organized in a formal or prescriptive way: "*this* is how things are done here." By contrast, institutions may be *embedded*—and globally this is much more common than institutionalization. Here, the four institutions would be interwoven, so that a marriage would be political *and* economic *and* kin-related *and* religious: not either/or but both/and. This makes for a more integrated system where roles are multiple and specialization may be less emphasized.

Unfortunately, many people (including Western missionaries) familiar only with a culture in which the social institutions are institutionalized tended to disparage cultures and people among which the institutions were embedded. One might hear the criticisms: "these people buy women for cattle; they don't have a (religious) marriage ceremony; they don't have any laws or (party) politics; and they don't have religion because there are no places of worship." Such critics failed to see that a particular political system may employ many ways to maintain law and order, that goods and services circulate quite effectively without a stock exchange or banks, that people know perfectly well who they are in relation to everyone else, and that religion and ritual do not need ordained clergy or cathedrals or even Scriptures but may be practiced in the home, within the village, or under the stars, by people who have no need for books, literacy, or dogma. In a wide variety of ways and innumerable contexts, the four social institutions support every culture on earth. But like different languages, their particular articulation or expression needs to be learned—intentionally and carefully: this kind of information cannot simply be picked up informally—by anyone who wants to communicate with the practitioners. In an intercultural community, a great deal of learning—some informal and gained by developing mutual relationships, but some done more systematically—is needed.

Suggested Follow-Up

1. Reflection and discussion on your community members' culture under the headings *material, symbolic, moral,* and *institutional* might be most enlightening.

2. To make abstract thinking more concrete and accessible to all, try to identify some of your own cultural virtues or moral qualities (and vices) as found in actual people: for you, what is "an honest man," "a beautiful woman," and so on, rather than "honesty" or "beauty" in the abstract?

3. If you reread the section on barter, can you apply it in any way to the interpersonal relationships in a community? Can you see how misunderstandings may arise between a person with a "barter for maintaining relationships" mentality compared to one with a "buy cheap and save money for later" attitude?

4. Social institutions may be institutionalized (more or less freestanding) or embedded (each interlaced with others). Can you discuss the significance of embedded institutions in some of the cultures represented in your community and help others to understand the power of integration rather than separation?

Chapter Four

Culture: Life, Meaning, Skin, Reality

Introduction

Our initial description of culture was "the human-made part of the environment"—or what people make of the world in which they live. For us, however, the implications are at least as important as the description. At any given time, every individual person is actually living in one of very many possible "worlds," ranging from the massively industrialized to that of basic subsistence level; from the aggressively secular to the devoutly religious; from the highly assertive and competitive to the more docile and collaborative; and from the tropical to the arctic or the ruggedly mountainous world to that of low-lying islands or plains.

We can well imagine what might happen if individuals coming from some of these many different "worlds" were to gather at a single location for any length of time. There would be many challenges and much demanded of everyone, particularly from those least familiar with the rhythms and annual cycles, the language and conventional daily life of the place they happened to be. Their responses would vary enormously and depend on many factors, including previous experience of different "worlds," temperament and age, and personal motivation. All this can be food for thought. But as we proceed, we will need to become more explicit as we explore how a hypothetical gathering might become an actual community with individual members committed to intercultural living for the long haul. In chapter 8, we will also consider how people might live "in-between" worlds or otherwise subsist in an uneasy and uncomfortable relationship with their environment and community.

At this point we turn to the other four descriptive definitions of culture as "the form of social life"; "a meaning-making system"; "social skin"; and "an enduring social reality." This will provide us with specific information useful for individuals-in-community as they strive to build a new home.

Culture as "The Form of Social Life"

As the shape or form of social life, culture comprises whatever occurs routinely in the daily life of a group, but it is also manifest in the responses generated in times of crisis or by unexpected events. Beyond a theoretical understanding of culture, we need a "cultural understanding" or sensitivity to actual cross-cultural experience. This requires us appropriately to contextualize certain behaviors that insiders judge as unusual or abnormal; not everything is normal, expected, or approved, and insiders know, far better than outsiders, how to judge events or behaviors along a scale from acceptable and approved to unacceptable and repudiated.

Before we can hope to create an intercultural community, individuals need at least to have had a significant cross-cultural experience where they have understood that they are the "outsider" in someone else's world.[1] Most, if not all, of those who attempt to build an intercultural community are outsiders initially (at least to the new community), and their corporate challenge is to build a new religious culture (identified in chapter 2 as "culture E") in which people of many ethnicities can dwell *in unum* as one community. As outsiders, therefore, everyone needs to develop at least three perspectives and abilities: first, to become involved in the daily social life for a significant period of *time*; second, to be able to discriminate between different *kinds* of behavior; and third, to understand the relationship, and the difference, between the *actual* and the *ideal*. Consequently, we consider the significance of the passage of time, different kinds of behavior, and the difference between the ideal and the actual.

1. *The Passage of Time*[2]

Everywhere on earth there are seasons and there is change. Seasons may range from two to a half dozen: dry/rainy, hot/cold, planting/harvesting, spring/summer/autumn (fall)/winter, or indeed named in an interesting variety of ways relating to climatic changes or occupational variations. Whatever is particularly significant in the course of the annual cycle will be identified and named in some fashion in different cultures. The annual cycle may determine not only planting and harvesting, fishing or voyaging, hunting or gathering, or working and relaxing but also marrying, house building, traveling, and other activities. But whoever understands and interprets culture as "the form of social life," whether they be an insider or an outsider, must have been present long enough to experience the annual cycle and identify its various moods and activities. Only then can the present be interpreted in terms of the past and the future.

For outsiders, patience is of paramount importance as they learn to wait, to withhold judgment, and to handle the daily frustrations with self and others. Thus they slowly, painstakingly, and sometimes painfully come to learn and interpret the form of daily life as it emerges and changes over time. But asking questions is also crucial. Some people try to work things out for themselves, believing that asking questions is a sign of weakness or only for the ignorant. But we are all outsiders and ignorant and weak to some degree: that is partly what defines us. Generally people are very willing to help us in our weakness and ignorance—if we ask in an appropriate way!

Beginning to write this in Chicago while the most severe winter on record refused to give way to spring, I found it easy to sense that the whole city was tired out by the interminable winter and keenly anticipating the signs that spring would indeed arrive. Yet one knew well that within a few months, people would either be complaining of the unbearable heat or noting the early signs that are the annual forebodings of yet another interminable winter. But someone experiencing a Chicago winter for the very first time has no real idea of its duration or severity, of whether this is a normal or extreme winter, or when it will ever end. Such a person, having no experience, can only endure and seek some comfort from other people's assurances. So "the form of social life" in Chicago, as everywhere else, depends to some degree on external (weather) conditions; and understanding it depends on the observer's acquaintance with the seasonal cycle and with what constitutes normal or abnormal conditions.

2. *Kinds of Behavior*

Everyone tends to interpret and judge things rather subjectively, by criteria familiar to themselves, and through the distorting lenses of personal bias and prejudice. Our second interpretive perspective, then, is people's actual behavior. But we need to refine this if we are to be able to distinguish normal from abnormal, legal from illegal, habitual from instinctive, and approved from disapproved. The challenge therefore is not only to *observe* behavior but also to *interpret it.* It is inadequate and often disrespectful to judge other people's behavior as meaningless or disgusting without having any idea of the criteria for either "meaning" or "disgust" (both of which are culturally coded); and if we simply impose our own categories and judgments, we will be acting either from ignorance or arrogance and certainly from ethnocentrism.[3]

There are a number of questions we would need to address in order to understand culture as a form of social life comprising people's actual behavior. Even to answer the question "What was happening?" we need to make some distinctions. First, "What do I think I saw happening?" To ask this is implicitly to acknowledge a potential discrepancy between the perception and understanding of the agent and the observer. An ignorant observer of a fly-fisher, a cricket match, a game of chess, or an air-traffic controller might be able to identify the gross behavior of these agents without either understanding its significance or knowing whether it was normal or abnormal, generally approved or disapproved, exceptional or routine. "What did I see?" is not amenable to a simple answer; and to it must be added several more. "What did I and the other person think *was* actually happening? What did each respectively think *about* what was happening? What did we think *should be* happening? We could also add "What did the community (whether my local religious community or the broader community of which we form a part) think/ think about/expect?" This will disclose just how subtle and complex is the matter of determining and explaining "the form of social life" on any given day and in any given community.

3. *The Ideal and the Actual*

There is a danger that the naïve outsider will judge by externals only. Actual behavior can only be adequately understood when linked to the underlying—invisible—system of belief and thought. There will always be a potential discrepancy between (visible) actions and (invisible) motivations. Beliefs may be implicit or explicit, but behavior does not always match even people's professed beliefs. "I am not a racist!" may be a firmly held conviction or belief which may be palpably belied by my actual behavior, whether or not I even admit it. Likewise, people may claim to respect others, to be concerned for the poor or hospitable to strangers, but "actions speak louder than words": it is easy to profess certain values or moral principles, but virtually nobody's actual practice lives up to the standards one claims to live by. Nor is social life always harmonious, virtuous, or lawful. People may have aspirations or good intentions, but pathologies occur, and insiders (and outsiders with appropriate knowledge) can identify ignoble or heroic behavior alongside what is normal or acceptable. Social pathology and virtue coexist within any social system, but reflexivity is required to determine who pins the designation "pathological" or "virtuous" on any actions.[4] Is it outsiders in general, the community of insiders, or simply individual insiders or outsiders? The student of any culture is challenged to identify people's own aspirations, yearnings for a more harmonious life, and the expectations they place on themselves and others. The outsider is rarely in a position to judge—from external actions alone—other people's actions and motivations.

Finally, it is important to remember that when we speak of culture, we do not simply identify the ways of individuals or their idiosyncrasies: cultural behavior constitutes both what is "customary"—the standard or normal and acceptable behavior of the group—and what behavior (sometimes habitual) deviates from expected norms. Social behavior is backed by positive or negative sanctions: reward or affirmation, or punishment or disapproval. Without such sanctions, people will not grow up to be affirmed or punished; and without sanctions there will be widespread confusion or anarchy, leading to the corrosion and even the collapse of a culture.

Culture as "A Meaning-Making System"

A system pervades an organism or field of thought. In a language, given certain standards and the appropriate application of rules, the system (grammatical, phonetic, phonological, and semantic) makes intelligible communication possible. All successful communication systems ensure appropriate information flow between sender(s) and receiver(s), but this can work at several levels, from the superfast and supereffective to the painfully slow and barely functioning. If a culture is seen as a meaning-making system, it need not be technically perfect, but it can only operate where there are minimal standards of mutual intelligibility. As it is with linguistic or nonverbal communication, so it is with culture in general.

An analogy from theoretical linguistics can enlighten us about languages as meaning-making systems but has a wider applicability as a way to understand how cultures work. We distinguish three criteria for judging effective communication as transmitter of meaning: *grammaticality, acceptability*, and *meaningfulness* itself.[5] As we identify these linguistic features, so we see their wider applicability to social relationships in general.

1. *Three Levels of Meaning*

(a) *Grammaticality.* Perfect *grammaticality* signifies that the language of the speaker or writer is strictly observing all the grammatical and syntactical rules (word order and relationship) of a particular language system. This produces formal correspondence between rules and their application. Yet it can sometimes produce pedantic or unnatural language (such as a slavish conformity to the rule that distinguishes "who/whom," or the rules about not splitting infinitives or ending a sentence with a preposition in English).[6] Noam Chomsky, the great innovator in theoretical linguistics in the 1950s, created a perfectly grammatical sentence to make a particular point: it conforms to every relevant rule of English grammar—and yet is perfectly meaningless! The sentence is, "Colorless green ideas sleep furiously." Grammaticality alone, then, is clearly insufficient for effective communication. But for our purposes here, it also reminds us that what is totally orthodox in theology or pedagogy (or to one person in a specific context) may appear to a hearer or recipient as gobbledegook: totally meaningless. Some theological statements or religious instructions are quite incomprehensible to most people. If the speaker fails to transmit a meaningful message or if the hearer fails to decode it appropriately, the communication system is patently inadequate. This principle applies very pertinently to communication in an intercultural context.

(b) *Acceptability* is another appropriate measure of successful information transmission. It is a way to determine whether the message is received and understood as the transmitter intended. It is not a matter of absolute norms but of relative correspondence: so long as information transmission is adequate or satisfactory, though it may not always meet the absolute standards of formal correctness, it passes the test of acceptability. In actual conversation, most people hesitate, repeat themselves, and deviate from formal rule keeping, but their conversation is nevertheless perfectly acceptable to both speakers. There are times and places, however, in which what is acceptable in one situation is not acceptable elsewhere: completing a written test in English usage requires answers that are more than what would be acceptable in casual conversation. Likewise, in order to meet the criterion of acceptability, addressing a person of particular rank or dignity appropriately demands a much higher standard of speech than what would be acceptable in casual or informal conversation. Someone who speaks English as a second language and does not observe all the grammatical rules with precision might be deemed a much more acceptable speaker than a native-language speaker who does the same: acceptability depends significantly on persons and circumstances. Sometimes acceptability is a mutually negotiated matter, particularly when communication of language or behavior is at issue, or when communication is between members of different cultural or linguistic communities.

(c) *Meaningfulness.* Again, this criterion is not absolute but relative to persons, places, and times. Semantics is the study of meaning in its myriad forms, and unless communication negotiates meaning successfully between two parties, it fails. Consider the stories and poems of Lewis Carroll, author of the classics *Alice in Wonderland*, *Through the Looking Glass*, and a great deal more. His poem *Jabberwocky* begins:

> T'was brillig, and the slithy toves
> did gyre and gimble in the wabe
> all mimsy were the borogroves,
> and the mome raaths outgrabe.

Of the many interesting things that could be said about these lines, two are pertinent for us. The verse is *perfectly grammatical*: it obeys the rules of English grammar, though the nouns and verbs cannot be found in any dictionary. And although it is not *acceptable* to pedantic native English speakers, it is, in a strange way, *meaningful*. To children who have not learned sufficient English vocabulary and therefore do not yet know which words are actually English and which are not, these nouns and verbs *could be* English words, in a way that many others are obviously not. (Children learning English are quite capable of identifying many words or combinations of lexemes that are definitely not English!) The poem appeals to the imagination and conjures up a possible world where imagination fills in what the words themselves only suggest. Intuitively, the bright child or native-language learner will be able to distinguish (though informally) a verb (outgrabe) from a noun (toves), an adjective (mome), or a possible adverb (mimsy).

So how can we characterize meaningfulness? *Jabberwocky* is meaningful because though many words in the poem are empty of actual meaning, they are open to many possible meanings. It is not "nonsense" but "non-sense": every combination of letters *could be* an English word, but they are empty of sense because they have never been used in a speech community to convey standard meanings. Parents whose children are in the process of learning to speak often hear their child produce sounds that do not actually occur in any dictionary; they are empty of actual meaning. But the parent may become very excited because they mean something *in the context*, and *to child and mother*. This linguistic creativity demonstrates the child's emerging capacity to use sound in a meaningful way. So we identify grades of meaning among language learners, adults, and by extension, members of an intercultural community struggling to make themselves understood.

A useful community exercise might be to ask what is and is not "grammatical," "acceptable," and "meaningful" in the daily community life.

(d) *"Rule-Governed Creativity."* "Rule-governed creativity" is the generative capacity found in every language that allows a virtually infinite number of utterances to be generated *and understood* from the application of a limited core of grammatical rules.[7] Natural to the native speaker, it is a difficult acquisition for those struggling to master a second language. As the rules of chess are few yet the moves are limitless, so it will be years before members of intercultural communities become as proficient as chess players. But members of intercultural communities should not need to learn intercultural living as if it were like mastering hundreds of different sentences for hundreds of different occasions. Slowly, as they become part of an organic and evolving community, they come to know the "grammar" of intercultural living. There comes a point—as there does in the process of acquiring a foreign language—when they actually become creative: they are no longer self-consciously applying community rules in a conventional or scripted way. The day comes when they become spontaneous and unself-conscious. This, coming as a great relief, signals a new phase in intercultural community life. To know that within the "rules" of daily life we can still be creative; to do and say things never actually done or said in that precise way before; and to be understood by others who share our intuitions—all this opens the door to a new level of intercultural living that will allow for a future not entirely dependent on the past, and a new, comprehensible, acceptable, and godly way of living religious life.

Culture as "Social Skin"

This image simply requires a little introspection and then anyone can play with it. The skin is the human body's largest organ; grafting is difficult and even impossible; if severely burned, death may be inevitable. And yet skin can tolerate numerous scars, blemishes, wrinkles, and many dermatological conditions. We cannot be "in someone else's skin"; and if ours were to be stripped or flayed, we would certainly die. By analogy, cultures, like skin, need not be perfect and can tolerate wear and tear and trauma; but the integrity of the skin is as necessary for life as is the integrity of a culture; if slashed, ruptured, and left unrepaired, a person may bleed out and die.

Just as no person's skin—when it has been lived in for enough years—is flawless, so no culture (which is fashioned and maintained by humans) is without faults, deficiencies, and sometimes pathological conditions. Human bodies may suffer amputation of limbs, life-threatening diseases, or trauma from external sources; likewise, cultures are vulnerable, from within and without, to debilitating or destructive forces. With appropriate treatment, human bodies may adjust and heal; and so may human cultures. But like human individuals or even whole societies, cultures have no guaranteed survival, and the sands of time are littered with the remains of now-vanished cultures that their people believed to be immortal.

For an intercultural community, this analogy offers lessons. Personal limitations are natural and inevitable, and some dysfunction may be overcome in time and with appropriate care. But some situations may be beyond redemption. Applying the "rule of one hundred" (familiar in hospital burn units): as the percentage of serious body burns plus the age of the patient exceeds one hundred, so the greater likelihood of survival approaches zero. If a community is severely damaged in its members and their resistance is diminished by virtue of their high mean age, so, the analogy suggests, the chances of continuing as a viable community diminish to the zero point. Where goodwill is both insufficient and wanting, and appropriate skills and virtues have not been developed,[8] there will be few resources for a community to fall back on in time of grave crisis. Attempts at intercultural living must be sustained over many years. Some have flourished for a while but withered and died of blight from external causes or from cancer growing undetected within. Though there are no guarantees of survival and no magical prescriptions to ensure healthy intercultural living, it is possible it can be lived, and—like good health and longevity—it is eminently worth striving for.

Culture as "An Enduring Social Reality"

Cultures rise and fall, flourish and fade, and die; here is food for intercultural living. Culture is transmitted over time, through the generations, in an ongoing process rather than a simple social fact. No religious community develops spontaneously; it takes generations to develop an identity and "mythology"—that is, the compendium of stories about itself, containing inspiration and heroism, though perhaps not literal truth. To develop a community *ethos*—the feel or shape that identifies and distinguishes a particular community— takes time. People then enter an established social entity and are incorporated into it in various ways. An intercultural community is not created overnight—it needs time to develop its own *ethos* or identity. Part of a preexisting social reality that may have endured for centuries, it is also in the process of further organic development or transformation. Members may appreciate how things have been done but are also fashioning something new: a new way of religious living; a new religious culture. To visualize culture as "an enduring social reality" may help in this process.

Although some cultures (termed "traditional") may appear to be in stasis or equilibrium, every culture is in a process of change, whether relatively slow or very fast. Some cultures adapt better to change than others. Reality (what people consider to be real) is socially constructed: people are born into a preexisting community that has already interpreted the world and determined the meaning of things, events, and relationships.[9] Certain things in every culture are accepted without question: they are "social facts." "This is the way we do things here" would be an example in every culture and every (religious) community. It speaks of tradition and permanence rather than chaos or randomness. Of course, cultures and communities do change, but the more "traditional" or established a culture, the more a certain built-in resistance to change will be evident. The process of socialization, by which an individual is aggregated to the preexisting world of meaning, extends far beyond the early years (see below). But once adequately socialized, it becomes increasingly difficult for anyone to think their thoughts or ways are wrong: this is the challenge of conversion for everyone, and this frame of mind is particularly tested when worlds of meaning collide or interact, as in the case of the formation of an intercultural community.

The Need to Clarify Terminology

It should be clear by now that culture is a complex topic and open to great misunderstanding, oversimplification, and essentialization or reification (the habit of saying things like "this culture believes that . . ." or "culture X treats people like . . ."). But because culture itself is not a personal agent, it therefore cannot "believe," "think," or "act"; it is people who do such things. So we distinguish between attributing things or actions to "a culture" and identifying the human agents; culture is an abstraction until animated by agents. To claim that "my culture does this" or that "cultures need to talk to each other" is inexact and unhelpful and quite often a fairly crude attempt to justify our own behavior.

Apart from not essentializing culture, neither should we be cavalier with other related terminology. Several words (some already noted: monocultural, bicultural, cross-cultural [in French, *transculturel*], and multicultural) are compounds of "culture," and others (enculturation, acculturation, inculturation, and intercultural) can cause confusion when used inappropriately. Here, as a point of reference, is a gloss on these four words, which belong in two groups.

Most terminology relating to culture belongs in the social sciences, notably sociology and anthropology: culture/enculturation/acculturation are sociological words. But theologians, having in recent years become increasingly aware of the importance of culture in relation to faith and religion, have co-opted sociological language, though not always deftly or precisely. But "inculturation" and "intercultural" are theological neologisms that borrow the sociological term "culture" as part of their meaning. As specifically theological words, they are largely unknown within the general discipline of sociology/anthropology. But a further complication is that "multicultural" has been used ambiguously or multivocally for decades, sometimes without a hint of theological connotation, and sometimes with decidedly theological overtones.

To understand the sociological words *enculturation* and *acculturation* and the theological words *inculturation* and *intercultural* requires a working understanding of the sociology of culture. But as we already noted, some theologians have a very untechnical view of culture, and some use the words inculturation and enculturation synonymously, mistaking what they identify as inculturation for what is really (sociologically speaking) acculturation. Massive confusion is compounded because many people are quite unaware of the linguistic labyrinth they have entered. Terms need clarification.

Enculturation[10] (or socialization) is the (cultural) process by which a newborn child gradually learns his or her culture and becomes an adult member of a social group.[11] It provides individuals with their cultural roots but invariably includes a degree of ethnocentrism; and it can be identified in three stages.

Primary socialization consists of all the processes that shape a child from birth to the age of reason (about seven years or so, universally). The ability to distinguish right from wrong is the major achievement of these years and is highly dependent on family stability *and* the particular culture. A moral sense is part of being human but can be distorted by poor socialization due to a broken or unstable home and is expressed variously across cultures. Every social group teaches virtue but also embodies vice, and children will be taught how they *should* behave; but a girl in traditional Borneo will have a rather different sense of morality than a boy raised in modern California, though both cases share common features and each child should be held accountable for his or her actions.

Secondary socialization refers to social processes that continue to shape a person as he or she approaches maturity. A maturing child makes personal choices, becomes less dependent on parents and home life, and comes under the influence of a peer group. Completed secondary socialization leaves the growing child with the capacity to rework his or her initial socialization based on learning, experience, and the (often contrary) attraction of the peer group and to be his or her own person, acting with freedom and responsibility. The key achievement during these years is a sense of autonomy, interrelatedness, and personal accountability. It does not always happen easily or consistently, and many people struggle for years into adulthood to become mature and balanced adults. Therefore, more time, energy, and focus are required, since secondary socialization is not the end of human development.

Tertiary socialization then, is a necessary and helpful adjunct, because people can and do change after reaching adulthood. Sometimes called "resocialization," for members of intercultural communities tertiary socialization can be glossed as "ongoing formation," "continuous conversion," or "transformation." Community members should acknowledge that the process of forming an intercultural community is itself part of each person's socialization. The whole subject matter of this book can be understood as an introduction to tertiary (religious) socialization—and in some cases, even remedial secondary socialization.

Successful enculturation, then, requires a stable community with enduring values and consistent modeling and example setting from the parents or "significant others" who hold moral as well as legal authority. Significant elements of daily life and expectations must be standardized and morally obligatory: otherwise chaos ensues. Precisely this happens in broken families where rules and expectations vary widely from one authority figure to another, or where one and the same person makes highly inconsistent demands. In the context of an intercultural community, therefore, since several people may be in the process of enculturation, it is most important that rules, expectations, and sanctions be clarified, lest massive confusion, frustration, and discontent ensue.

Acculturation is identified as the effects of the encounter between two cultures (or, more properly, the members of two different cultural groups), though the same word also does duty for what we call "culture change." Any culture-contact will affect each culture; but if we visualize each culture as having a slightly different consistency or composition from every other, we can imagine the results. If a fresh, newly laid egg and a piece of granite come into abrupt contact, the results for each are very different. The granite will appear virtually unscathed, but the egg might well be obliterated! Such are the effects of acculturation, which vary enormously from instance to instance. In an intercultural community, some members will find the process of acculturation relatively tolerable because of the resilience of their own culture and their previous exposure to other cultures. But others may find themselves rather like the newly laid egg after the encounter with the granite block: it can be quite traumatizing unless each person is consciously sensitive to the adjustment required of other members. Insensitivity and preoccupation with personal well-being can undermine the prospects for community building before some members have had a chance to adjust.[12]

Virtually no culture today exists in complete isolation, so culture-contact is a universal social fact, accelerated by the internet and associated technologies. At least one party is always changed in the process. Like a blood transfusion, it can be life enhancing—or death dealing. When we consider intercultural living, we would do well to remember both the potential and the danger.

A constituent of acculturation is the impact of the "speed of change" on each culture. One culture may be highly innovative while another is much more conservative. While members of the former will be used to and may expect frequent change, members of the other may find that they are expected to behave in a certain way, but no sooner have they adapted to that than the rules and expectations change, leaving them bewildered and emotionally unmoored. People of different cultures expect or tolerate continuity or change at very different rates, and attempting to shape an intercultural community of peace and cooperation, leadership especially must learn to deal with cultural habits and norms that are very different from person to person.

Inculturation. To understand this we must locate it firmly within the field of theology: it has to do with God and faith. Because, as we noted and will elaborate further in the next chapter, we can only live our faith though our culture, we identify inculturation as precisely the way each person's faith is lived out through the daily round of life. Given the distinction between acculturation (culture-contact) and inculturation (lived faith), we should note that the phrase "liturgical inculturation" is strictly incorrect: faith is the subject of inculturation, not liturgy, ritual, translation, or adaptation. Strictly, the term should be "liturgical acculturation" or "liturgical adaptation." If, however, liturgical modifications produce a harvest of renewal in the way the faith is actually lived, then that harvest—and not the liturgy itself—is inculturated faith.

But since inculturation as such is not the subject matter of this book—though it is of critical importance—we can only offer a few important definitions and descriptions.

> When we speak of inculturation, we are referring to a phenomenon that transcends mere acculturation. It is the stage when a human culture is enlivened by the Gospel from within.[13]

> The Christian faith cannot exist except in a cultural form.[14]

> [Inculturation is] the incarnation of Christian life and of the Christian message in a particular cultural context, in such a way that this experience not only finds expression through elements proper to the culture in question (this alone would be no more than a superficial adaptation) but becomes a principle that animates, directs and unifies the culture, transforming it and remaking it so as to bring about a "new creation."[15]

And finally:

> Inculturation is not limited to the initial stage [of introduction of the Christian message into a culture]. There must be a continuous dialogue between faith and culture.[16]

But, on this last point, since dialogue can only be between real people, the members of an intercultural community have the responsibility to develop their faith—through faith formation—in the context of the emerging culture of which they form a part.

Suggested Follow-Up

1. By reflecting on the distinction between what is "grammatical," "acceptable," and "meaningful," can you apply it to your experience of community life? Notice that there will be some disagreement about what is or is not acceptable.

2. Entering intercultural living requires that people undergo further enculturation or socialization into the new culture they encounter (and help to shape). Discuss some features of your own enculturation with other community members. Compare and contrast your experience prior to joining the community.

3. Everyone who joins a new community or culture is enculturated or affected by what and who is encountered. Sometimes this can be a mutually satisfying process, but at other times much less so. Identify some of the positive aspects of your own enculturation into an intercultural setting and also some of the things you find most challenging and difficult.

4. On the strength of material in this chapter, discuss in a community setting some things in your own life that you would be willing and able to change for the community's sake and other things you would consider nonnegotiable.

5. How the faith of each community member is inculturated becomes a matter of prime importance to the community as a whole. Discuss the difference between acculturation and inculturation and some of the challenges the community must face.

Chapter Five

Culture, Faith, and Intercultural Living

Lived Spirituality

The two previous chapters attempted to demonstrate that the only way to be human is to live in a culturally constructed world. Culture describes how people live, the shape of their daily lives, their worlds of meaning, communication, symbol, ritual, and more; it is "concerned with the spiritual, ethical, and intellectual significance of the material world. It is, therefore, of fundamental theological significance."[1] Since we cannot survive without culture, it is equally impossible to detach faith from culture: faith flourishes or atrophies in a cultural context, and culture provides the way of expressing faith.[2] There is no "naked Gospel." Like each human being, faith is specific, not generic; there is no faith in the abstract; therefore faith can only be incarnated and lived in actual people: people of culture.

Now we must explore more closely how faith and culture actually coexist. This chapter is largely about living *Christian* spirituality, which must be carefully distinguished from "spirituality" as the word is currently used by people who are neither Christians nor believers in God. Many of our contemporaries are honestly looking for "something more" or seeking to capture an experience beyond the mundane or an elevated state of consciousness. Such endeavors have been characterized as "feel-good spirituality," "New Age spirituality," and even "Me and Jesus" spirituality, but most (apart from the last) are explicitly separated from any religious tradition, and the last, despite its title, is not (yet) authentic *Christian* spirituality.

Christian spirituality is essentially the (new) life given at baptism by the Holy Spirit to guide our faith journey through life.[3] It might be described as *a way of being in the world with God*, when each of those variables—way, being, world, God—is shaped according to an individual's social and cultural experience. Through a single lifetime, a person may embrace a number of possible *ways* (single, married, celibate, divorced, widowed, professional, tradesperson, or service employee, and so on), experience different *states of being* (youth to age and health to sickness), live in a number of different *worlds* (rural to urban, tropical to temperate), and relate in different ways to *God* (Jesus, Spirit, Father, Lord, King, Warrior, Shepherd, Creator, Redeemer, Wisdom, and many more).

Christian spirituality is far more than simply a set of beliefs, formal or informal. It both shapes and is shaped by our attitude to the Creator and the whole of creation, how we pray or express our embodied selves, how we respond to suffering, disaster, and tragedy, and the life choices we make. It is critically important to acknowledge that there are many legitimate cultural and personal expressions of Christian spirituality and to realize that these will create challenges when, as an intercultural community, we gather to discuss liturgy, prayer, ritual, music, dance, language, silence, privacy, conformity, and so on. We must discover new ways to approach our cultural differences if we are ever to forge enduring community life. Some of the most contentious issues within a community can also, if approached sympathetically and creatively, be mutually enriching. Here we can only itemize the following four as among the most worthy of serious consideration. Each lends itself quite well to sharing in community as a way to appreciate the many paths we travel and the many ways we live.

Cultural Variables and the Shaping of Faith

1. *Social Location and Social Geography*

Everyone lives within a *microcosm* or enclosed world, whether that be one's own body, a room within a house, a neighborhood within a city, or a nation within the world. But beyond every *microcosm* is a *macrocosm*: a larger world, a community beyond the individual, a school beyond a classroom, a country beyond one's border, or a universe beyond one's world. All creation can be seen as consisting of worlds within worlds and worlds beyond worlds. In community building, the *relationship* between *microcosm* and *macrocosm* is critically important to identify and negotiate (figure 7).

A microcosm, then, is the "inner" world, whether it be the physical body or the "nest" we identify as home, while the macrocosm is the "outer" world, extending beyond our home to our country or even the universe. A particular microcosm may be closed (strong) or open (weak) in relation to the macrocosm beyond: the more closed it is, the more resistant it is to extraneous contact or interference; while the more open it is, the more accommodating or welcoming it will be to outside communication (see figure 7). The small, single-headed arrows within the large (macrocosm) circle on the left indicate external influences that are resisted by the strong/closed microcosm. The small double-headed arrows within the large (macrocosm) circle on the right indicate two-way movement between the microcosm and the (weak/open) macrocosm. The macrocosm boundary on the left is impermeable or closed, while that on the right it is permeable or porous.

Perhaps even more interesting than individuals' greater or less openness to external forces or relationships is the social fact that whole groups of people (different cultures) can exhibit the same dynamic: some individuals and groups welcome "otherness" in the form of other people, technology, or ways of living, while some appear almost programmed to be suspicious or wary of "otherness" in other people, technology, or ways. But when a whole culture exhibits such trends, social facts cannot be reduced to the whim or prejudice of individuals.

Intercultural community building requires that serious consideration be given to how members were shaped by their social location. Every community needs to learn how to accommodate legitimate cultural differences that cannot simply be dismissed as expressions of an individual's temperament, choice, or comfort. Openness cannot simply be crafted and managed by diktat. Openness to "otherness" (or the lack thereof) is a definite and formative cultural trait in its own right. Conversation about the social geography, the place where

Figure 7

MICROCOSM AND MACROCOSM

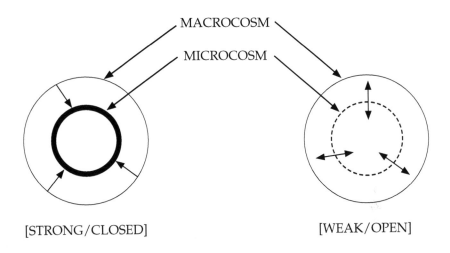

[STRONG/CLOSED]   [WEAK/OPEN]

individuals were born, the circumstances of their socialization, the climate, the amount of contact with outsiders, or the degree of social mobility will create an informed community and should lead to greater mutual understanding and empathy. The two points of departure then are, first, the individual, the self, the personal, and, second, the culture, the society, or the ethnic group.

As *individuals*, each person in a community can try to identify how one's own personal microcosm is more or less open (weak) or closed (strong). An open or weak personal microcosm shows itself in being at ease in one's own body and interpersonal relations, whereas a closed or strong microcosm is evident in persons who are more private, withdrawn, and somewhat uncomfortable with interpersonal relations (see the next section on "body tolerance"). Likewise, an open or weak *culturally marked* microcosm would be evident in the way people of a particular culture are generally open to strangers or people of significant cultural or religious difference. A culturally marked closed or strong microcosm would be evident where most of the people of a particular culture are naturally (or culturally) wary of outsiders, strangers, or different ways of living.

In order to perhaps facilitate the process of community building in an international and multicultural group, here is a series of questions both for personal reflection and group discussion. Even where a group perceives itself as homogeneous, individuals may be quite surprised at what they can reveal to others and what they can thereby learn about themselves to mutual benefit.

Questions about Social Location and Social Geography[4]

- Where were you born: village, town, city, countryside? Identify the major geographical features: hills, mountains, lakes, ocean, rivers, forest, etc.

- What significance was attached to geographical features?

- In what circumstances were you raised: economic, political, religious?

- How "big" was your world? Did you have extensive views and travel far from home, or live within a more or less enclosed local world? How free were you to explore and travel?

- What was your normal means of local travel: foot, bicycle, car, train, boat?

- How often did you travel beyond ten miles, and by what means, normally?

- Could you clearly see the sky and stars or the distant horizon?

- What was the climate: tropical, temperate, extreme?

- How many seasons in the year? What were they? How are they named?

- What kinds of boundaries were there to your world: linguistic, national, territorial?

- What were your images or ideas of God, and how were they related to your actual social geography?

- If the world were a theology book, how much of it have you read?

People do not simply inhabit the world—they live in a particular world, where certain features like *this* mountain, *this* lake, *this* ocean, or *this* forest have a particular importance in their lives. As God's creation, the world is indeed like a theology book that tells us much about God's creativity and humanity's relations with it. Members of an international community come from many different worlds, and what is familiar, unfamiliar, meaningful, or meaningless varies enormously among them. Intercultural community building entails attempting to live in a new reality. It requires that each member become able to *expose* existing meanings as understood by the current inhabitants and also to *impose* some order and coherence so as to be able to make a new home there.

2. Embodiment or "Body Tolerance"

Both individual temperament and culture shape human beings' attitudes to their own body, and people must become aware of the significance of cultural differences as they encounter them in others. "Body tolerance" is a way of identifying a person's comfort level regarding bodily display or reserve, something not itself directly correlated with immodesty or modesty: displaying one's body is not an absolute indicator of immodesty any more than covering one's body is an absolute indicator of modesty. Every society has norms of modesty, but there is a wide range of cultural difference: sensitivity and enquiry are required if people are to learn mutual respect.

We can visualize a continuum, at one end of which we would identify "low body tolerance" (Apollonian) and at the other, "high body tolerance" (Dionysian). "Apollonian" (after the god Apollo) designates a serene, ordered, disciplined, and predictable demeanor and bodily display that is poised and controlled (figure 8). "Dionysian" (after the god Dionysius)[5] refers to a more relaxed, spontaneous, demonstrative, or uninhibited person or style. Individual differences of temperament obviously exist, and there is also some correlation between colder or more temperate regions (Apollonian) where bodies are swathed in heavy, uniform clothing and the warmer, more tropical regions (Dionysian) where people are less constrained and more flamboyant in dress and demeanor.

Figure 8

"BODY TOLERANCE"

"APOLLONIAN"   *"DIONYSIAN"*

←――――――――――――――――――――――――――――――→

Controlled, Mannered,   Uninhibited, Loose,
Disciplined, Predictable,   Ostentatious, Relaxed,
Dignified   Spontaneous

But generally, as we encounter people whose body tolerance is very different one from the other, we can correlate that with cultural and climatic differences rather than simply with personal temperament or taste.

Official church documents refer to the "noble simplicity" of the Roman Rite,[6] a rather apt description of an Apollonian style. But this is adopted—indeed imposed—universally in our liturgies, despite the fact that people of many cultures find that style quite contrary to their own natural and cultural inclinations. Recently some things have changed, yet the Roman Rite remains—for individuals and communities in many parts of the world—overchoreographed and too predictable and controlled.[7] Generally speaking, African Americans and others are much more Dionysian than German or British people, while the Nunavut (Eskimos or Inuit) would be much more Apollonian than the people of the central Pacific. The style of many Asian cultures tends toward the Apollonian, which is quite well suited to the Roman liturgy. Many communities seeking liturgical renewal, however, often find that the rules and rubrics of the Roman Rite range from the awkward to the irksome and seem to inhibit rather than facilitate prayerfully integrated liturgies.

Within intercultural communities, cultural and individual behaviors relating to body tolerance can be very difficult to reconcile, and community members may well find that liturgy and prayer, designed to gather, unite, and lead to God, are major occasions for tension, disharmony, and frustration in the community. Open conversation and true dialogue are needed if community members are to appreciate that the significant differences between individuals are not simply a matter of whim or preference but coded in their cultural makeup.

Here again are some questions that might help facilitate personal reflection and group discussion among members of an intercultural community.

Questions about Personal Body Tolerance

- What was your usual mode of dress: formal or casual, loose or tight-fitting, uniform or varied?

- Did you dress "up" or "down" according to the occasion?

- How much did you wear? A lot or a little; seasonally varied or year-round?

- How did you present your body: (mostly) concealed or revealed?

- What was your attitude to personal and communal nakedness?

- How would you describe personal modesty?

- As a child, and in initial formation in religious life, were most people's attitudes to bodily display and concealment similar to or different from your own?

- How well does your normal style of prayer and liturgy suit you? What would you like to change, to make it more comfortable—or more natural—for you?

3. *Health, Well-Being, and Sickness*

People have very different culturally shaped attitudes to sickness and death. In a highly medicalized society, serious sickness is often presented as a temporary irritant to be cured with maximum speed and minimum pain, and death is thought to be something that can be postponed almost indefinitely. Even during the dying process, the prospect of recovery is routinely advertised by medical professionals, and so death often comes as a surprise. Before death, terminally ill people are routinely removed from home and institutionalized, thus minimizing their own and their family's encounters with death. To a significant degree, death occurs beyond the ordinary daily routine and away from the domestic sphere.

But by contrast, in societies where expensive and extreme medical expertise is not widely available, sickness is much more frequently encountered by almost everyone. A person who is evidently ailing is very often cared for and surrounded by family until death. One of the biggest challenges at the height of the Ebola crisis in West Africa was precisely that: family members often refused to admit a loved one was sick, fearing he or she would be taken away to the hospital. Even when someone is hospitalized, many family members remain to cook, tend for, and support the dying person; isolation is almost unthinkable.

Where people have minimal access to health care, few mothers have not experienced the death of one or more infant or small child, and few children have not seen a number of dead persons immediately prior to their burial. Death is part of life; so much so that in many traditions the deceased person will be buried at the threshold of the entrance to the house, or adjacent to the family home. Life expectancy ranges from below forty years in some places to over eighty years in others, a social fact that has a profound effect on individual and social life.

Cultural attitudes to health, sickness, death, and dying will inevitably show up on the occasion of the dying or death of a member of an intercultural community or of a parent or sibling. Talking about such attitudes so as to better prepare each member of an intercultural community is highly advisable, although it can be a delicate topic to raise dispassionately.[8] Here again are some questions that might stimulate personal reflection and community discussion and thereby help people understand the wide differences of experience and understanding among community members.

Questions about Health and Sickness

- Have you been seriously ill and hospitalized? Have you had serious surgery?

- What is the customary response to sickness in your culture? Isolation or integration, separation or inclusion, withholding or sharing of information?

- Do you know of sick people who are believed to be victims of witchcraft?

- Are you personally familiar with death? Are you at ease, or do you fear it? How many dead bodies have you seen, and in what circumstances?

- How many funerals have you attended?

- Do you often think about your own death? Are you preparing for it? How?

- If you or a loved one died far from home, what would be the expected procedure?

4. *Time and Space*

Cultural attitudes to time (chronemics)[9] are notoriously varied, as are attitudes to space and privacy. *Linear* or *chronological time* marks time's regular passage as measured by a clock—or the sun. But some people rarely see the sun, and others rarely tell time by a clock or watch. Not by chance do "clock watchers" speak of time using verbs associated with economics: they "save," "waste," "lose," "use," or "spend" time. Nor is it a coincidence that, in the past, where people worked long hours and years for a company or institution, if they survived long enough to reach retirement age they received—a gold watch! For years their time had not been their own but was largely governed by their employers. After retirement, their time is finally their own again, symbolized by the gold watch which puts time back into their own hands. Inmates in a prison, too, are spoken of as "doing time" and after release as having "done their time." Common phrases include "time is money" or "your time is not your own."

In a less-industrialized society, the sun rather than the clock is the primary measure of time. People rise and sleep with sunrise and sunset. If electricity is expensive, intermittent, or nonexistent, and "leisure time" is unknown, they may seem less driven and freer to do what they choose, depending on weather or season. Time is not a commodity to be saved or wasted but the backdrop to life. If "clock watchers" complain of having too little time, people elsewhere usually find that they can make their own priorities and accomplish what is needed: they have time. Their attitude is determined as much by culture as by personal whim.

Liturgical time is neither governed by clocks or watches nor is it linear or chronological, but it is more open-ended. It is sometimes spoken of as "time out of time": on Sunday or the Sabbath, people step off the daily treadmill and now have all the time they need to celebrate liturgically or playfully because holy days are not governed by the clock. When they celebrate liturgy or have a day off, they are free to take whatever time they choose, to worship or relax. Yet many people, particularly in Western industrialized nations, simply do not have time for liturgical time! Even during a solemn ritual or liturgy (or a homily), they constantly check their watch and become agitated if they think it is taking too much of their "precious" time.

Kairos time is another, special kind of time, as well as a way of perceiving time; it is "God's time," similar to liturgical time but not bound by any special ritual. It stands in contrast to chronological (clock) time, and, like liturgical time, is sometimes spoken of as "time out of time." But this is time for surprises and epiphanies, and anything may happen. It is also "quality" time rather than quantitative (the Greek word *kairos* refers to the right, apt, or supreme moment). For Christians, it is "God's time": a time for action, either by or for God. *Chronos* occurs fifty-four times in the New Testament, but *kairos* occurs more than eighty. An intercultural community will want to seek, and use, *kairos* time as an opportunity for heroism, daring, and submission to the movements of God's Spirit.

Mythological (or mythic) time is again different, but it has something in common with *kairos* time: it is the time of spectacular—larger than life or out of this world—happenings, or the time of the gods. "Once upon a time" signals that the story that follows takes place in mythological time where animals speak, children fly, and people live for hundreds of years without growing old. There are strong elements of myth and mythological time in the Genesis accounts of creation: the story begins before "chronological" time does; a serpent talks; all animals eat grass; God talks directly to humans; one human being is created from the rib of another.

Attitudes to space in general (proxemics)[10] are also significantly determined by culture. As far as personal space is concerned, individual temperament and particular contexts also come into play;

some people like to get physically close to their interlocutors, while others maintain a greater distance (partly related to the Apollonian/Dionysian disposition). But beyond personal preference, culture determines appropriate distance and closeness between specific people. The normal "standing distance" between two women is closer than that between two men; spouses may stand closer together than friends or strangers; and a man and woman will subconsciously negotiate a comfortable distance between them, based on many factors, including the level of their friendship, intimacy, or professional considerations. But when two persons of different cultures find themselves in conversation, the proximity or distance each finds culturally appropriate when "at home" will be challenged. People of different cultures must mutually adjust their expectations or assumptions, which can be delicate and even embarrassing.

Many people remember a time when, conventionally, clergy and women religious were not demonstrably affectionate and kept a strict distance. More recently they have become less inhibited as religious habits gave way to secular dress and standards for public demonstrations of appropriate affection changed. But one still meets situations where the conventional expectations of, for example, a cleric and a nun create moments of strain, embarrassment, or perhaps laughter. If one is too hasty and overcommitted, the other may pull back; while if one waits a fraction too long, the other may have already made a move. Whether a handshake or embrace is more appropriate is something each party tries to decide in a split second by reading the body language of the other, but not always well. And if it is sometimes a challenge to people of the same culture, it can be quite confusing to people of different cultures.

As an adjective, *"privato"* [private] in Italian has strong connotations of "deprivation," whereas for many people, privacy is considered a basic necessity and even a right. But one person's privacy is another's antisocial behavior, and one person's sense of deprivation is another's feeling of comfortable relaxation. Public and private spaces in community need to be mutually understood and respected, but people should not be expected to guess which is which or to know what exactly constitutes appropriate behavior. Questions arise and might be discussed profitably in a community setting, first pertaining to space and then to time.

Questions about Time and Space

- Do you treat time as a scarce commodity? (Do you "save," "waste," "spend," "keep" or "lose" time)?

- What common phrases relating to time can you remember?

- What irritates you about other people's attitudes toward time?

- Do you have—and make—time for *kairos time* and *liturgical time?*

- Do you ever wish you were somewhere else and doing something else?

- Are you conscious of trying to "turn the clock back"?

- Would you rather be younger?

- What is "privacy" for you? How highly do you value it? How do you protect it?

- Do you prefer prayer and liturgy to be controlled, quiet, interiorized, and private—or creative, lively, social, and public?

- Can you live alone, as a contented and contemplative person?

- Are you claustrophobic (afraid of enclosed spaces) or agoraphobic (afraid of wide-open spaces)?

- Are you comfortable with your living spaces and the spaces between people?

We identified only four cultural variables, but there are many more. Particularly significant for intercultural living would be a reflection and discussion about food and the etiquette of eating. Another would relate to comfort levels in community: not everyone is familiar with, or enjoys, air-conditioning in the summer or high heat in winter. Such variables should be sought out by mutually sensitive community members.

Cultural Understandings of Past, Present, and Future

Important but not immediately related to "ordinary time" is the cultural significance of time itself as the relationship between past, present, and future. We often refer to societies as "traditional," "modern," and "postmodern," and one way to distinguish them is precisely by looking at their understanding of the meaning or significance of time.

A *traditional society* identifies *past time* as the repository of tradition, when the community's values were determined and developed. It was also the "golden age." The *present time* is the time for learning from the past and assimilating the tradition of the forebears or ancestors (those who "have gone before us, marked with the sign of faith") for transmission to the next generation. Then the *future time* should be spent trying to recapitulate and re-create the past "golden age." This kind of ("traditional") society does not value, and resists, change or novelty.

A *modern* society tends to see the past as old-fashioned, outmoded, and as something to be liberated from. The present is not a recapitulation but a reinvention of the past: a correction of mistakes and an upgrading of quality and efficiency. If there is such a thing as a "golden age," it is in the future and something to strive for. Meanwhile, it embraces change, lives for change, and loves innovation and in-built obsolescence.

A *postmodern* society tends to express disillusionment with the failure to realize the *modern* society's dreams and hopes. It has largely abandoned the notion that there ever was—or indeed ever will be—a "golden age." Experience seems to show that things in general do not get better, and there is no evolutionary inevitability about progress. War, famine, floods, and epidemics are not under human control. The breakdown of the "metanarrative"—an overarching explanatory scheme or myth—leaves people struggling to find or make meaning, and many are persuaded that the only way forward is to look out for oneself. After the Second World War and for the rest of his life, Viktor Frankl identified the great malaise of the age as "meaninglessness."[11]

Members of international and intercultural communities need to identify the common faith and metanarrative (Scripture and the incarnation) by which they live, be convinced that life does have a meaning, learn from the experience of others, and, while living firmly in the present, have a focus on *eschatological time* and the future as fulfillment of God's promise.

Living Our Faith and Spirituality Interculturally

Far from being confined to the inner life of prayer and contemplation, Christian spirituality should manifest itself in daily interactions and, particularly for religious, in ministry. But within our homes and communities, our "way of being in the world with God"[12] will be challenged by the interactions with other community members. Moreover, intercultural living makes some stringent demands on our availability and willingness to strive to be authentic disciples whether or not engaging in formal religious acts of prayer or worship. And far from simply meeting our own personal needs, Christian spirituality has a centrifugal dimension, an outgoing missional dimension which everyone must embody.[13]

Some major features of Christian spirituality, then, are the following. First, it is intentional participation in God's eternal creative work brought down to earth in Jesus, taught to his disciples, and continued by them to the ends of the earth. Second, it is always a committed search for God, which can only take place in the life of each individual. Third, every individual is a person of a particular culture; it has an intrinsic cultural component. Each of us seeks God in the existential circumstances of our lives. Culture is not the only factor, but it is a necessary one (and historically, it has not been sufficiently acknowledged, respected, and worked with and through). Fourth, the purpose of Christian spirituality, to quote Inagrace Dietterich, is "empowerment for mission: for witness to God's mighty acts."[14] But if this is true, it must perforce bring each person into contact with the "other"; and such an encounter will be not simply a meeting of persons but a meeting of *persons of culture*, cultural persons, with all the implications of that fact. Fifth, and following up on the previous thought, people striving for authentic Christian spirituality should not become inverted, turned in on, or preoccupied with themselves but "everted," turned outward, open to, and concerned about the well-being of the "other."

Encounters with other people are encounters with other, and previously unrecognized, faces of God, the purpose of which is to glorify God precisely by continuing the mission of Jesus. Authentic Christian spirituality—spirituality of the Holy Spirit—becomes good news to the people of the margins by channeling God's compassionate concern for them through our instrumentality or agency. Dietterich phrases it very well: "A spirituality of the Holy Spirit moves beyond the inner self of private individuals, to speak of the all-encompassing power and love of the creating, redeeming and sanctifying God at work in the midst of personal life and history. Without the faithful worship and witness of missional communities, the concept of God becomes empty and irrelevant."[15]

In a highly pertinent book, Michael Paul Gallagher identifies several components, concerns, and implications of genuine Christian spirituality.[16] Its components include being rooted in one's lived faith experiences (orthopraxy) rather than codified doctrinal principles (orthodoxy). It is developmental in character: spirituality matures throughout a whole lifetime. And it has the capacity, through contemplation, to foster an ongoing, personal relationship with God. Each component is rooted in a person's daily cultural and intercultural living.

The basic concerns of genuine Christian spirituality are, first, to make and strengthen connections between the gift of faith that sustains us and life's everyday encounters that challenge and deepen that faith; second, to help us become increasingly conscious of the essential link between faith and culture in every life and to encourage people to live their faith through their culture (this is true inculturation of the faith); and, third, both to identify in oneself and to encourage others to attend to the Spirit's inspiration precisely in the humdrum daily cultural round so that our lives can be shaped by unfolding cultural events as the Spirit breathes life through each of us.

Finally, some implications of true spirituality are that we are being converted from egoism, ethnocentrism, and other forms of cultural blindness to openness to others, to the world, and to God, here and now; that we discover how to *receive* with grace, as a necessary counterbalance to the tendency to *give*, which places us in a position of superiority and power; and that we learn to discern, through the limitations of every culture, that we are offered freedom in Christ: wherever our personal freedom is compromised by the sin that touches every culture, cultivating a true spirituality can be a way to survive and thrive through God's grace.

Two Examples: Oscar Romero and Jesus

Writing of Romero's vision, Jon Sobrino[17] expresses how it synthesized his faith and culture. It is rare to find the convergence so well articulated, and I quote it at some length, though the full text is longer.

> Romero's hope was to evangelize the structure of society. He wanted to change the economic and political infrastructure, as well as the legal institutions, health care institutions, and media. He also wanted to evangelize the ecclesial infrastructure, with its curia, parishes [and] religious congregations. . . . He wanted to evangelize the country in its totality—everyone: individuals, social groups, and infrastructures—and to evangelize a country in which there was terrible oppression and state-sponsored violence, kidnappings, disappearances, and killings; where there was poverty and injustice, but also hope, solidarity, strength, faithfulness, and martyrdom. "Evangelize" meant "to bring salvation to a people."

Here is a splendid expression of Romero's faith-in-action, in the very concrete circumstances of his life. But to have been able to visualize, much less undertake, such actions, his conversion from the ecclesial centers to the margins where real people live had to happen first. So with us: the essential purpose and justification for intercultural living is God's mission and our joyful and wholehearted participation in it. To respond appropriately, we need a missional faith grounded in our context and lived culturally.

Finally, Francis Moloney writes:

> God's saving intervention in the person of Jesus became part of a religious practice, a culture and a history, but that culture, history, and religion were assumed and transformed by his life, teaching, death, and resurrection. Such a "life-story" broke through the expectations and limitations their religion, culture and history would have preferred to impose on him. Who Jesus Christ is . . . cannot be "controlled" or "contained" by *any* religion, *any* culture, or *any* history. The life, teaching, death and resurrection of Jesus stand as a challenge to the absolutization of any particular culture, religion or history.[18]

Jesus calls us to *transform* our particular cultures by defying sin and seeking grace as he strove to transform his. And it costs no less than everything: this is the measure of our faith, lived culturally.

Suggested Follow-Up

1. "A way of being in the world with God" might serve as a working definition of Christian spirituality. Ponder, or discuss, each of these variables in your life.

2. Strong/closed microcosm and weak/open microcosm represent two ends of a spectrum. Can you apply this notion to yourself as an individual and identify cultural factors that shape it in your life?

3. Discuss the questions relating to social geography, body tolerance, health and sickness, and time and space.

4. How does your culture evaluate the past, the present, and the future?

5. Since faith can only be expressed culturally, reflect on what frees you and what stifles you in the community context.

Chapter Six

Social Profiles and Social Interaction

A Caution and a Word of Encouragement

Even with the best of intentions, people—not just those of different cultures or faiths—sometimes find that mutual understanding is very difficult to establish. Hurts, or perceived hurts, can fester and undermine our best efforts, and frustration can paralyze our will to persevere. Indeed, frustration is particularly potent, since with its onset we can become persuaded not only that our best efforts are in vain but also that we simply do not know how to proceed without adding to the frustration. Frustration is self-perpetuating; it creates a vicious cycle: the more frustrated we are, the more frustrated we can become. The fact that we share a common faith with those we struggle to live with harmoniously can actually increase the frustration in a community. So if we are to move beyond monocultural communities and manage our cultural differences wholesomely in an intercultural context, we need first to believe that this is actually possible and not just a pious dream.

A thread running through these pages is that culture cannot simply be "picked up" or absorbed with the passage of time; it must be learned painstakingly, and the frustrations that are an inevitable part of all social interaction must not be allowed to overtake and demoralize us. The antidote to frustration lies in discovering the available ways and means to learn appropriate skills and advance in wisdom and knowledge, that is, virtue. As our reflection on cultural attitudes to time, space, and body tolerance might have demonstrated, so we might discover another key both to self-understanding and mutual understanding, without which we will never build a new intercultural home together.

Wherever people of different cultures attempt to do more than simply coexist or manage their lives according to a "live and let live" philosophy—that is, first to acknowledge, then to appreciate, and perhaps, in time, to respect each other's differences and accommodate them as an intrinsic component of their daily lives—they must generate and employ a variety of specific ways to negotiate inevitable frustrations and misunderstandings. It is not enough to bite one's tongue and say nothing, and neither passive-aggression nor a "martyr complex" will be adequate to sustain healthy community living for very long. Without some safety valves designed to address the unavoidable tensions that the common life produces, members will find themselves perpetually on edge—if emotional confrontations do not first produce mutual recrimination and festering enmity.

The purpose of this chapter is twofold. First, we compare and contrast "social profiles" as a way to identify some salient cultural features that both distinguish human beings and also disclose some shared social characteristics.[1] Having done that, we will look at suggested "safety valves" for communities so that such confrontations and their negative results might be minimized.

Characterizing Social Types

The diagram below (figure 9) can be read in two ways. First, it offers a set of horizontal axes or lines, each of which represents a continuum, with the ends marking an extreme contrast between two types. Anyone who takes time to ponder the implications of this diagram should be able to find a place *somewhere along the line* (rather than at one extreme) to represent his or her own current social location.

The designations at each end of the lines represent ideal types: no actual persons could live in society if they were totally egocentric or completely sociocentric. On each line we distinguish, characterize, and contrast two opposite (cultural) profiles of people. Of course, culture is not the only factor determining a person's attitude; temperament

Figure 9

SOCIAL PROFILES

1. *Egocentric* . . . . *Sociocentric*

2. *Rights-Based* . . . . *Duty-Based*

3. *Personal* . . . . *Positional*

4. *Elaborated Code* . . . . *Restricted Code*

5. *Achieved Status* . . . . *Ascribed Status*

6. *Novelty* . . . . *Tradition*

7. *Competition* . . . . *Collaboration*

8. *"Limited Good"* . . . . *"Common Good"*

or personality differences ("nature") also play a part in everyone's makeup. Sometimes, as when a person maintains "it's my culture!" cultural factors may actually be insignificant: personal temperament may be the real issue. But neither temperamental nor cultural habits are unchangeable or above criticism. Here, we focus on trends or typifications: generalizations about culturally marked features. Although no two persons are identical, they may share cultural tendencies that would place them rather closer to each other on each of the horizontal lines and rather farther away from the typical cluster that marks the responses of people from a different culture but within the same religious community.

As components are described, each person can mark a place on each horizontal line, locating themselves from one of two specific perspectives. First, as a result of our own enculturation or socialization: the cultural influences that have shaped us (see figure 10 and the "X" marks); second, according to our current understanding of the imperatives of Jesus and religious life (see figure 10 and the "Y" marks).

Figure 10

SOCIAL PROFILES

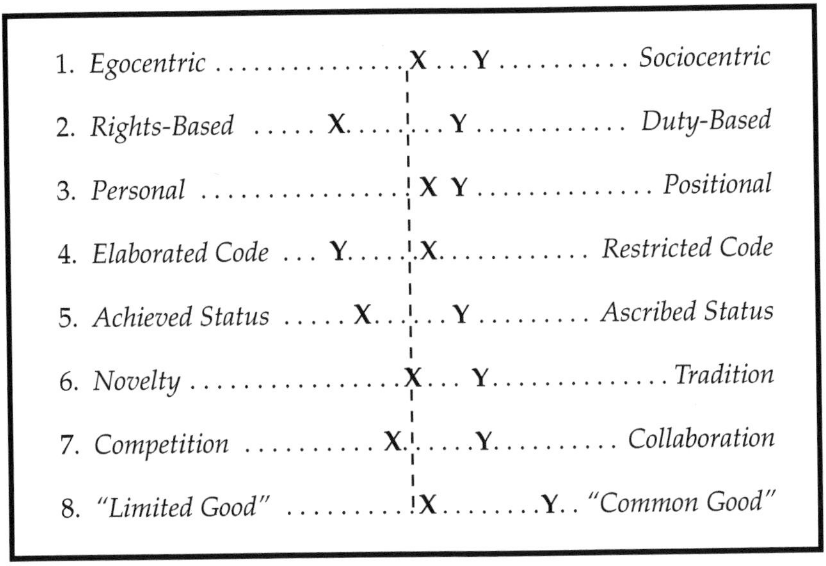

1. *Egocentric* . . . . .X . . .Y . . . . *Sociocentric*

2. *Rights-Based* . . . . . **X**. . . . . . . **Y** . . . . *Duty-Based*

3. *Personal* . . . .**X Y** . . . . *Positional*

4. *Elaborated Code* . . . **Y**. . . . . .**X**. . . . . *Restricted Code*

5. *Achieved Status* . . . . . **X**. . . . . . **Y** . . . . *Ascribed Status*

6. *Novelty* . . . .**X**. . . **Y**. . . . . *Tradition*

7. *Competition* . . . . **X**. . . . . .**Y**. . . . . *Collaboration*

8. *"Limited Good"* . . . .**X**. . . . .**Y**. . *"Common Good"*

The exercise could also be done by allowing each person to try to place *another* person on each horizontal axis. But that demands trust and mutual respect because the way we see ourselves and the way others see us may be rather different. (But at least the exercise would provide a talking point.) As everyone works through the diagram, where they mark each horizontal line may vary, so that the completed diagram might look like the "X" marks on figure 10. Then it is easy to compare and contrast one's profile with that of other community members and discuss the implications for intercultural community living.

Also note whether every point marked on the diagram falls on the same side of the vertical line. The likelihood is that most of them do; if not, can you identify why there is one or more exception? Then you might reexamine your own commitment as a person of faith, asking whether your current understanding of the call of Jesus—specifically in relation to intercultural living—is inviting you to move closer to the central vertical line. Again, this might make for a helpful community conversation.

The diagram, however, can equally be read as a set of two contrasting vertical columns, each one identifying a cluster or set of characteristics. The left-hand column shows a set of eight features that tend to co-occur in an *egocentric* individual or society. Likewise, the right-hand column shows features that tend to co-occur in a *sociocentric* individual or community. We begin with an explanation of the terms used in the diagram.

1. *Egocentric and Sociocentric*: These terms refer to the basic orientation of an individual, group, or society. Egocentric simply means that the *individual* (ego) is the primary agent, the focal point for choice making and decision making, while sociocentric identifies the *group* itself (society) as the primary determinant of choices and decisions. The subsequent distinctions on each line will make this point increasingly clear. It is important to remember that even in a highly egocentric society, individuals still have the freedom to exercise choice and thus to respond to the "duty calls" summons rather than the "I have the right" chorus; even in egocentric societies, altruism finds its place. Likewise, in a strongly sociocentric society, individuals are still capable of making personal and indeed selfish choices; a sociocentric society may nevertheless harbor much egoistical behavior. Nevertheless, the egocentric person is typically encouraged and endorsed by the wider society to make personal choices, while in a more sociocentric society, individuals are aware that their social responsibility is primary. And sanctions, positive and negative (rewards and punishments), underpin social behavior in both egocentric and sociocentric societies.

2. *Rights-Based and Duty-Based*: Beneath *egocentric* are the words *rights-based*, while the corresponding words on the right are *duty-based*. Not surprisingly, persons operating in an egocentric world will lay considerable emphasis on the claim to personal rights in various circumstances: "I have the *right* to vote, to smoke, to choose as I please" (always within limits stipulated by some law or rule, religious or civil). Such a person has a strongly developed sense of personal entitlement, mirrored or endorsed by the wider society. At the other extreme we locate a person situated in a duty-based world where personal and social responsibility are strongly emphasized and enforced more than, or even without, much regard for personal preference. That person's rights may be relatively few and not necessarily

codified or explicit—since social duty is understood to be of primary importance—and personal choices are not only limited but also frankly unimaginable. People growing up in a duty-based society will be left in no doubt about their primary obligations. But again, we always need to bear in mind that talking about ideal circumstances is very different from encountering actual behavior. Anyone and everyone can, in principle, be more or less selfish, more or less altruistic. Culture (or nurture), though a major contributing factor, is by no means the only one to be considered. Nature (or individual differences), temperament, and training all play a part in generating behavior.

3. *Personal and Positional*: These terms refer to one's existential social location and its effect on decision making or the exercise of choice. Since every human person exists in relation to others—we are *social animals*—the way we operate affects and is affected by those among whom we live: the other members of our society. And this way of interacting is often—and mostly unconsciously—invoked when we are in unfamiliar social situations. They will thus manifest themselves in intercultural contexts, where people with very different cultural norms and assumptions interact. In a strongly egocentric society where people prize their autonomy, it follows that people want to exercise *personal* autonomy and not be unduly constrained or motivated by other people's opinions or expectations alone. Contrast a sociocentric society or community in which the moral authority of the group exercises a strong influence over individual choices, and it is easy to see that one's position in relation to the group may be a more significant determiner of choice making than is individual whim or preference. Hence we speak of a *positional* constraint on behavior, or an individual as "positioned" relative to a larger group rather than independent of it. The stronger the sociocentric nature of a group, the more strongly *positional* its members will be.

4. *Elaborated and Restricted*: This terminology is used to refer specifically to a speech code:[2] the way communication is enabled, usually verbal (linguistic) but also nonverbal (gestural, attitudinal, or symbolic). People socialized in egocentric communities will be actively encouraged to have, and to express or articulate verbally, their opinions, feelings, and convictions. By contrast, the more sociocentric the focus of one's community, the more people will be identified *positionally*,

their social position in the community dictating the norms for social communication. An elaborated code identifies a person with a high degree of verbal articulation: redundancy, excessive detail, and verbiage or wordiness are sought, tolerated, and socially accepted both as one's personal entitlement and as indicators of fluency and sophistication. At the other pole on the scale, we find people who are raised to "speak when spoken to, and not before," to be "seen and not heard," and not invited to express personal opinions or even to speak freely. Their actual speech then becomes *restricted* to minimal responses and few verbal initiatives: "yes," "no," "please," and "thank you." Contrast then a typical middle-class American (elaborated) communication between mother and child over what to eat for dinner with that in a typical soup kitchen where homeless people are given a prepared meal and expected to "be fed, be grateful, and be gone." Their gratitude, such as it may be, is expressed in a restricted code (brief verbal "thanks," or restricted bodily gestures), and they would never be invited to create a menu of their own choice or to enter into a discussion about the quality, preparation, or presentation of the food.

Likewise, in any multicultural community, and *a fortiori* in a religious or faith community, where some members have been raised to express themselves in an elaborated fashion while others use a highly restricted speech code governed by convention, great problems will arise if the assumption of the dominant group is that anyone can speak and say whatever he or she wants as part of a "democratic" conversation among equals. While this favors "elaborated code" speakers, these will tend to perceive the "restricted code" speakers as surly, inarticulate, noncommunicative—or simply as having nothing to say. Meanwhile, the "restricted" speakers perceive the others as dominating and self-centered due to their unrestricted language flow and endless personal (unsolicited) opinions.[3] The situation is ripe for confusion, misunderstanding, and ultimately resentment by those using a restricted code—or the perception that those using an elaborated code are both dominating and insensitive.

5. *Achieved and Ascribed*: This contrast applies to social statuses and their acquisition in different cultures and communities. Status itself is the legitimate title to a social role, or the moral authority to exercise it. For example, a prince may choose to play the *role* of a servant even though his legitimate *status* is the far superior one: prince. Indeed

someone with the status of a servant or slave may "role-play" as a prince but clearly does not have the status of a prince. There are numerous examples across cultures or within the armed services, where "role reversal" is institutionalized. On an appointed day, those with the legitimate status of officers will serve those with the status of enlisted men; the officers simply take on the role, but not the status, of enlisted men—for a day, after which everyone assumes one's true status as before. But if an enlisted man were to role-play as a person with the status of an officer, his actual status nevertheless remains that of an enlisted man. Similarly, a chief or even a king may act as a servant and wait on some of his people as a demonstration that allows the lowly people to act as if they were "king for a day." So, while a person with the status of brain surgeon or bishop may choose to take on the role of servant, an actual servant who assumes the role of professor or company director will either be "role-playing" or duplicitous, unless he or she also has the appropriate credentials (status) of the person in question.

In strongly egocentric societies most statuses are achievable by virtually anyone; in strongly sociocentric societies, most people are excluded from significant statuses. The USA proudly proclaims that anyone can become president—if he or she *achieves* that end and is an American citizen. Barak Obama proved that this is factually correct (as would a woman president); the status of president is achievable in principle by virtually anyone, irrespective of gender, creed, or ethnicity. But in many parts of the world, inclusive competition for office or other status positions is simply impossible. Currently in the Catholic Church, women cannot achieve the status of deacon or presbyter (and where they have been ordained *womanpriests*, the orthodox position is that they have thereby excluded themselves from the church and that their ordinations are invalid and certainly illicit). Meanwhile, in other Christian churches, women are routinely ordained priests or bishops, thus serving a vital role in the survival of many congregations.

What then, characterizes strongly sociocentric societies in this respect? They allocate—or ascribe—many statuses according to birth order, gender, descent, and so on; such statuses are not open to anyone, in principle or in practice. For example, a younger sister may not be allowed to marry (receive the ascribed status of wife) before her older sister has done so. A girl, whether older or younger than her brothers, may not be allowed to go to school; the status of "scholar" may only be ascribed to boys. And a line of descent, usually recognizing descent only through the father and continuing only through sons, may determine who the next Chief will be, irrespective of the fact that there may be other competent persons and even family members, including daughters. If the status of Chief is ascribed rather than achieved, there will be no room for competition and no considerations of meritocracy among the offspring; the choice and identity of the next Chief is fixed and nonnegotiable.

6. *Novelty and Tradition*: In modern and postmodern societies, novelty and change are prized. But so-called traditional societies set great store by custom and—as the designation implies—tradition; they tend to resist novelty and rapid change for perfectly defensible reasons. But in a globalized world, such resistance is proving increasingly ineffective, though the consequences of rapid change and innovation are often destructive, divisive, and traumatic. Strongly egocentric societies tend not only to value but also actively to seek and stimulate novelty and change, in contrast to more sociocentric and traditional societies.

In order to grasp the motivations behind such contrasting approaches to the values that can be found in both novelty and tradition, it may be helpful to identify some characteristic features of a "traditional" society, but bearing in mind that these do not only refer to so-called tribal, simple, or primitive societies (terms which tend to be used pejoratively at best). They should be used with great caution because they often connote a superior or judgmental attitude on the part of their users and a quite inadequate understanding of the people they designate by those terms. But "traditional" as used here may very well apply to many contemporary religious communities, rural or farming communities all over the world, and numerous other groups of people whose values are not always those of the dominant culture in which they are found.

"Traditional" applies to those who set a high value on "tradition" as "the way things were handed on to us." It can also be understood in terms of people's attitudes to time and history and to the way innovation is viewed, as we saw previously.[4] More pertinent here though would be some observations about novelty itself. The contemporary, postmodern, high-tech world—wherever found, from Silicon Valley to some of the most isolated places on earth—is driven by innovation. As everyone with a computer or a cell/mobile phone knows, what amazed one only a year or two previously, is now deemed obsolete, old-fashioned, or much too slow for current needs—and not by chance. "In-built obsolescence"—electronic devices intentionally designed to be replaced by new technology within months or years—ensures both that the user will have many more models to choose from within a short span of time and that the model itself will remain serviceable but replacement parts will no longer be available when needed. A consumerist culture thrives on insatiable demand for newer, better, and faster labor-saving devices, and it is not only the young who are seduced by the media and by their peers to seek innovation for its own sake as an index of fashion at least as much as for utility or durability. Thus is addiction created and fed.

By contrast, a more sociocentric community will (theoretically at least) raise its members to share, redistribute, and minimize wastage: this is the antithesis of a novelty-driven culture. Here, great social value will be accorded to the careful and prudent person who looks after things, repairs them when necessary, and thus ensures that they continue to function for the longest possible time. Wastage and carelessness will be strongly sanctioned, and people will be raised with a sense of respect for property and for extracting use from whatever continues to work adequately, irrespective of its vintage.

In an intercultural community, at least some of whose members may have been raised in a strongly sociocentric or "traditional" society, there might be a significant clash of values and of persons. Where one person sees value in conservatism, recycling, and simplicity, another is motivated by greater speed and efficiency and judges that the latest models are quite justified because of those qualities and their time- and labor-saving properties. For one person, the fact that perfectly usable machines or devices lie unused in cupboards is amply justified on the grounds of efficiency; to the consumerist mentality, this is enough. But an ethic of community sharing and a spirit of "waste not, want not" sits uneasily in this environment, and people may even be subject to joking or ridicule for their "old-fashioned" attitude. The vow, the virtue, and the spirit of religious poverty will come then under great scrutiny and even threat.

7. *Competition and Collaboration*: Our social profile offers us a contrast between the respective values of competition and collaboration. In a society where hard work can bring success, where virtually everyone has the potential to achieve, where personal goals are encouraged,

and where people are brought up to speak for themselves and be assertive and articulate—in other words, where many of the features of an egocentric society are to be found—competition is a standard feature of social life, from kindergarten to company boardrooms. This kind of society promotes the notion that people thrive on competition and that it is an essential characteristic of a modern society to value progress and improvement. But while competition can indeed stimulate individuals, bring out the best in them, and contribute to social and national achievements, a darker side must be acknowledged. In a competitive world, not everyone succeeds, or even survives. That is the nature of such a society or world; some people thrive on competition while others are threatened and may even be destroyed by it. "The survival of the fittest" can be a cold reality.

In today's multicultural and globalized world, and even within a predominantly competitive society, there may still be people whose values are based squarely on collaboration. But the interaction between "competitors" and "collaborators" can lead to great confusion and dystopia. One therefore needs to be careful. In a multicultural religious community, the clash of persons from the opposite ends of the spectrum (competition-collaboration) can quickly produce a dysfunctional community unless addressed with speed and understanding.

The more sociocentric a society or community (religious or other) is, and the more it emphasizes duty over personal rights and social position rather than personal ambition, the more highly valued collaboration will be. Teamwork rather than individualism will be encouraged, with the corollary that the individualist will be seen as anomalous, perhaps dangerous, and certainly a destabilizing influence on the group. In smaller-scale, face-to-face societies in which people not only know their immediate and more distant neighbors but also are related to many of them by blood and marriage, or as members of cohorts or peers who have been schooled or initiated together (through specific cultural rites of passage or in a common novitiate, theologate, or tertianship program), collaboration is a virtue honed over many years and a sign of solidarity and moral support. But when people with such experience are separated from their community of peers and find themselves in a multicultural community of high achievers and naturally competitive individuals, the task of intercultural community building becomes acute and requires both a great deal of clarification of a variety of social norms and conventions and a concerted and focused effort to compromise and collaborate.

8. *Limited Good and Common Good*: There remains one more social driving force or motivation. Quite consistent with an egocentric society in which people compete for achievements and statuses is the notion that such competition does not leave everyone equally rewarded; that is the nature of competition itself: "To the victor, the prize." People know perfectly well that this is a world of "limited good." There can be only one (individual or team) winner, and therefore there must also be one loser. If the winner is said to gain one point and the loser loses one point, then the quotient is always zero (hence we speak of a "zero-sum" game). A competitive society thrives on winners and losers.

But there are other ways of working. In sharp contrast to the notion of limited good is the notion of common good. Where this is espoused, the "good" is achieved without polarizing winners against losers. Some societies operate quite efficiently (according to clear criteria) on the principle of limited good, while others find that emphasizing the common good and the collaboration of all makes for a more harmonious, if not always the most highly efficient, society.

Sport offers a good illustration of the contrast between these two approaches. All sport is, to a degree, agonistic: a struggle or competition between individuals or groups. But not all human labor is agonistic; laborers building a bridge or roadway must learn cooperation. Competitiveness is not appropriate. Likewise, a village overcome by fire may mobilize all able-bodied people to fight the fire as a community. But where homes are widely separated and communities very loosely constituted, neighbors may simply look on while homeowners watch their homes burn. And interestingly, not all sports are agonistic. Not every sporting occasion need be a zero-sum game, producing a winner and a loser. Soccer has a long pedigree, and many soccer games end in a draw or a tie: neither team "wins." Cricket too is legendary as a game that can last five days and *still* not produce "winners" and "losers." Participation itself or the sheer "fun of the game" or "the spirit of the thing" counts for more, and if members of different teams are not to generate mutual animosity, a game that is enjoyed by all is more important than one in which one team is, and is made to feel, defeated or even humiliated.

By contrast, in the United States, a highly agonistic and competitive society, all sport is designed to produce a winner and a loser: so much so, that soccer—the most widely played game on earth—was very slow to catch on. And when it finally did, it was partly due to the fact that the United States succeeded in changing the rules at international level—so that there would be no ties or draws, but every game would produce a winner and a loser. Hence the penalty shoot-out that so often concludes games, much to the chagrin of the conservatives, purists, and traditionalists, who claim that it is destroying the "noble game" as it is called, by making it always and forever a zero-sum game!

"High-Context" (Sociocentric) and "Low-Context" (Egocentric) Communication Styles

In chapter 3 we mentioned high- and low-context (HC/LC) communication styles, identified by Edward T. Hall.[5] That topic needs to be more clearly described in the present context. The issue here is how information is held and transmitted between any two people. Imagine another continuum then with "high context" (HC) and "low context" (LC) at opposite poles. In an HC communication, most of the information being shared is located in the persons themselves and the specific context. The actual message may be brief and contains relatively little of the total communication. It is the person, posture, emotion, and shared context (not only physical but also "topical," or relating to the topic of the communication) that bears the weight of the message. In LC communication, however, precision and explicitness are needed in order to transmit the message adequately, since the interlocutors have very little in common with respect to implicit knowledge or context.

Family members who share implicit knowledge (they can interpret or "fill in the blanks" of the actual conversation) are HC communicators. They understand not only what is actually said but also what it really means, as in "Are you angry with me?" "No!"—when "no" clearly means "yes" here. But in a courtroom trial, where every detail needs to be spelled out and nothing is left to the imagination, communication is LC: here, facts are all. There is a strong correlation between HC (informal) communication and sociocentric relationships, and also between LC communication (more formal) and ego-centric relationships that is worth reflecting on in the context of intercultural living. Close friends are HC; a superior interviewing a candidate is much more LC (see figure 11).

Figure 11

HIGH CONTEXT AND
LOW CONTEXT COMMUNICATION

LOW CONTEXT	HIGH CONTEXT
The parties share very little common information and need to be explicit and precise, sometimes tiresomely so.	The parties have much information in common and there is no need to be long-winded or treat the other as a child.
A novice director would be very explicit and wordy when speaking to a new member unfamiliar with the community.	Long-separated confreres could easily pick up from years before and build on shared experiences without undue wordiness.
Some people speak as if they are giving instructions to a slow-witted person rather than having a conversation. This can be inappropriate and offensive.	Some people wrongly assume they are talking to someone familiar with the community, but the other person does not know what is going on.
Strongly "egocentric" people tend to operate with an LC communication style: professional rather than warm.	Strongly "sociocentric" people have an HC communication style: sensitive to the other's feelings and mood.
Assertiveness and confrontation may result in open conflict.	Deference and subtlety minimize conflict, but passive-aggression may result.
LC persons are direct, unsubtle, and sometimes insensitive and hurtful.	HC persons avoid open disagreement but are sometimes indecisive or ambiguous.
Emphasis is on rational problem solving.	Emphasis is on maintaining relationship.

Interpreting, Applying, and Living with Communication Styles

In an intercultural community, one would expect that, as in a family, people share a great deal of common information—about their common aspirations, common faith, and common membership—without needing to make it explicit every time they talk. This implies that a community represents a high-context (HC) situation. Characteristics include sharing "insider" information not shared with outsiders; familiarity with each other's personalities and temperaments and ability to adjust to different personalities and shape conversation accordingly; a degree of intimacy consistent with a long-term relationship within the community; and an assumption that others understand and are sensitive to one's feelings without being oversentimental. Genuine mutual concern and enquiry about each other's well-being would be expected, and community members would avoid a confrontational style with each other. Nevertheless, miscommunication can all too easily occur between two people, one of whom is operating with an LC understanding, while the other approaches with an HC attitude. One person can then sound patronizing to the other. Evidently, sensitivity to each person in a community is required of everyone if the community is to be united in faith, friendship, and common purpose. A low context situation is much more appropriate between a traveler and a gas station attendant or two members of a parish who are only nodding acquaintances. In LC communication, each person needs to be explicit and not assume that the other knows what one is thinking.

An intercultural community, then, is not made without effort, and if its composition changes relatively frequently, careful attention must be paid to facilitating a spirit of inclusion and welcome. Unless this is done, incomers can feel very isolated and uninformed, and cliques or pockets of two or three members can become exclusive. If, after an initial period of familiarization, a community member feels that he or she is living in a low-context community, it would be extremely difficult to thrive. This can occur when individuals are too strongly ego focused, or where there is latent racism or simply a failure to attend appropriately to other community members. Where it does, the spirit of an intercultural community will evaporate, and people will find that although they live under the same roof they are far from sharing a common fraternal spirit. Many religious acknowledge that even after decades they have few close friends and fewer confidants within the community; people treat each other amicably and respectfully, but something intangible is missing. A true intercultural community must be built slowly; it cannot happen automatically. As we have noted on several occasions, goodwill is simply not enough; there must be mechanisms in place to facilitate community building, from faith sharing to strategic planning, and from sharing of leisure pursuits to socializing.

The threads of this chapter can now be pulled together with a summary and a suggestion for each individual and community committed to trying to move from simple membership of an international community to real community living in an intercultural context. Culture, as we have seen, is an intrinsic component of one's social persona and indeed (for religious) a major factor in the shaping of our faith. Therefore, as members of international faith communities, we must discover, respect, and honor the legitimate demands of our respective cultures and undertake to approach persons of other cultures with both appreciation and openness to learning. Bearing in mind that in every single culture, as in every person, there are elements of both grace and sin, we must beware of noticing only the grace in ourselves and our own culture yet seeing in others and their cultures little more than the sin we judge to infect them. That is sinful ethnocentrism and bespeaks a narrow and bigoted perspective; it is absolutely no basis on which to build intercultural communities.

Playing the "culture card" may just be an example of perverseness, inflexibility, or prejudice that prevents someone from trying to change and adapt. If a person thinks that nobody else in the community is in a position to make a judgment about its culture, one may be tempted to overplay that "culture card." Everyone should self-monitor and understand that disruptive behavior in community needs to be challenged. Looking then at the diagram with its contrasting social profiles (figure 9), we should be clear that there is value and virtue in each side of the vertical median line. Two things, however, will need careful attention. First, the conventions of any and every culture are not above reproach and appropriate criticism, and no culture models the Gospel imperatives and the call to discipleship in a totally adequate, much less in a perfect, way. Therefore, every culture and its constitutive members must first bend the knee before the revelation of Jesus Christ, and every Christian disciple must become countercultural at some points, in order to conform to the Gospel and to the particular call of religious life. Second, in order for people of different cultures to live harmoniously together, everyone must make a concerted effort to better understand what makes other people "tick," both culturally and spiritually. Ultimately this can only be done through the development of mutual trust, and the willingness to explore together, in faith, the contours of different cultural approaches to the common challenges of life.

People are very different and shaped by many factors. Intercultural communities thus comprise people of many different styles—outspoken, reserved, dominant, submissive, extroverted, introverted, opinionated, receptive, competitive, collaborative, thick-skinned, or thin-skinned. Careful consideration of how these can be managed appropriately will remain an imperative for each community and each person. St. Paul knew this well: "Be of the same mind, having the same love, being in full accord and of one mind. . . . Let each of you look, not to your own interests, but to the interests of others" (Phil 2:2-4).

Suggested Follow-Up

1. Try to spend time with the diagram (figure 9), placing an X on each horizontal line, according to the primary social/cultural factors that shaped you.

2. Identify—by placing another set of X's—where Jesus is challenging you to move, as a religious committed to the Realm of God. Then consider the implications of any differences between the two X marks.

3. Let the broader community (local or regional) find time—and not just once—for real dialogue in which individual members are encouraged to identify their own cultural profile, explain its values, and articulate what they find (a) the most challenging and difficult aspects on intercultural living, (b) what they find the most rewarding, and (c) what they would like to modify in their own expectations of others for the greater good of the community.

4. See if you can make sense of the High Context/Low Context comparisons. Discuss this as reflective of community relations, especially if some individuals feel they are not being treated like adults and family members.

Chapter Seven

Developing Intercultural Competence

"Models of" and "Models for"[1]

We can identify two types of model. A scale model of a ship or skyscraper is a physical or material model showing many details and an overall perspective of the larger reality it reduces to scale: it is a "model of" whatever it represents. As such, it can be very helpful in providing a wider context than a person confined to a ship's cabin or a skyscraper's elevator would ever have, even though they would actually be inside the ship or the building. A "model of" provides a simplification and systematization of a complex reality while at the same time offering satisfying attention to detail. But not every "model of" is simply a scale model of a physical reality; such models can also be constructed to help us retrace our steps in order to see where we have been or what brought us to the present situation (figure 12). So we can legitimately speak of models of mission or pastoral ministry, or models of community life, that attempt to schematize what is already, or was formerly, taking place. These would be "normative" models.

But we can also identify a "model for" or "descriptive" model as a projection or stimulus for future endeavors. Here we will consider a "model for" intercultural living, based on one already in use, but for circumstances different from our own, so it needs to be modified accordingly. But it has been found very helpful for several years now.

Figure 12

A "MODEL OF" AND A "MODEL FOR"

MODEL OF	MODEL FOR
Helps show how we got to where we are.	Helps indicate how we can move forward.
It "domesticates" or summarizes reality.	It generates or creatively imagines reality.
It demonstrates the workings of a system.	It indicates how a system might work.
It is deductive: starts from given premises.	It is inductive: starts from actual circumstances.
Its origin is in concrete circumstances.	Its aim or outcome is something new.
It provides information and clarity.	It provides inspiration and ideals.
It describes what does already exist.	It describes what might exist.
It is based on reality.	It is based on needs or imperatives.
It is neat and complete.	It is provisional and unfinished.
It is built on previous or past achievements.	It will arise from present aspirations.

It is obviously not a model of what is in process, nor is it a physical model, since intercultural living is an existential experience. But it can be seen as a kind of guidebook or practical "how to" presentation, offering specific advice and instructions for negotiating various circumstances and avoiding some avoidable issues or causes of embarrassment. Like any other "model for," it can also provide a gauge or self-administered test for an individual or a whole community—particularly if assisted by a suitably competent person—to assess progress in becoming a more mature, dedicated, and truly intercultural person. It can also help individuals to understand their own and others' reactions and motivations, strengths and weaknesses. Understanding other people does not come automatically, any more than does understanding a foreign language.

Someone who has contributed both to the theoretical under-standing of the challenges of intercultural living and provided much practical wisdom and guidance for people who are striving to meet the challenges it presents is Milton J. Bennett. Having taken his initial steps in the cross-cultural journey through his years in the Peace Corps, he learned—as indeed we all should—from his mistakes, gradually refining a model for "intercultural competence" which has been widely used and applied. It is a "model for" intercultural living and, used by a whole community, it can be of considerable practical help. It may also help to persuade the as-yet unconvinced of the real possibility of achieving a way of healthy intercultural living.

Beginning in the 1980s and with subsequent refinements, Bennett produced what is now called the *Developmental Model of Intercultural Living.*[2] There have been further refinements and developments by one of his former colleagues, which we will refer to later.[3] But first I will identify each of Bennett's six stages, adding some words of cri-tique and potential application specifically for those committed to intercultural living that is explicitly shaped by faith and religious commitment.

From Ethnocentrism to Ethnorelativism

Some people seem to manage in cross-cultural situations much better than others. Some appear to learn quickly or cumulatively, while others struggle, give up, or are blissfully ignorant of their own cavalier or frankly disrespectful attitude toward those with and among whom they live. If the former are strongly motivated and want to improve their skills and relationships, others are intimidated, self-conscious, or oblivious to the challenges posed not only to them-selves but also to those around them. Bennett's model tracks a six-stage movement or progression from *ethnocentrism* to what he calls *ethnorelativism.*[4] The first three stages exemplify various degrees of ethnocentrism,[5] while stages four through six describe a person who has moved beyond ethnocentrism and increasingly toward the target of ethnorelativism. Not everyone begins from the first stage; however, not everyone progresses to the sixth, and there is not necessarily a steady progress through each stage; there may be some regression before forward momentum is achieved again. It might be good to keep this in mind, for our own benefit and because it may help us better understand other people.

The Ethnocentric Stages of Development

In its most basic meaning, ethnocentrism is the propensity to see and interpret the world from a subjective, context-bound perspective: I see, judge, interpret, and act on the world as seen through my own eyes and thus from a narrow and personal perspective. This tendency is of itself perfectly natural and should not be cause for immediate consternation, since the purpose of our whole socialization or enculturation processes is precisely to help us become rooted in a specific cultural context and to provide us with a context-based perspective and a capacity for moral judgment. But ethnocentrism becomes problematic and even sinful when I act as if my perspective were the only possible or acceptable one; when I expect other people to adopt my perspective as absolutely normative; and when I even imagine that my perspective is actually God's. Bennett's working definition of ethnocentrism is "the experience of one's own culture *as central to reality*" (I would even say *as reality itself*). What this amounts to is that one's beliefs and behaviors, accumulated during primary socialization (up to the age of reason) and beyond remain unquestioned thereafter and are accepted as "just the way things are." Bennett says that "ethnorelativism" is his own coinage and is intended to be the opposite of ethnocentrism: it is "the experience of one's own beliefs and behaviors as just one organization of reality among many viable possibilities." For the moment, we simply note these two polar opposites, ethnocentrism and ethnorelativism, and then identify Bennett's series of six named stages moving between them. We begin with ethnocentrism and its effects.

Evidently nobody else can see through my eyes or see exactly what I see, any more than I can see through anyone else's eyes or see exactly what the other sees. But the merest human dignity and respect requires that we be aware of individual differences and perspectives existing alongside our own, whether they are purely personal in nature, or linguistic, religious, or broadly cultural. We should never attempt to coerce others or impose our perspective; rational argument and genuine dialogue are acceptable, but beyond that, we enter murky and dangerous waters. Bennett identifies three stages or grades of ethnocentrism, from the very crude to the more subtle: denial, defense, and minimalization. These labels identify different kinds of subjective experience.

1. *Denial*

This is the most biased or gross form of ethnocentrism. Denial refers to a crude attempt to disregard cultural differences entirely. Sometimes it shows itself as a kind of cultural blindness or tuning out, a blatant failure even to notice cultural differences. At other times, initial awareness of such differences is followed either by rather obvious avoidance tactics or more intolerant or confrontational efforts to remove them so that life can continue as before. Bennett makes the important point that denial is not only experienced by people of the dominant culture in any given place; minority groups may also operate with what he calls a "denial worldview" or propensity to avoid bringing to full consciousness, to acknowledge or negotiate, cultural differences. It also shows itself in people who, for example, think or speak of "Africa" as a vague entity somewhere "down there" or as if it were a single nation or ethnicity and all its denizens were the same (usually pejoratively identified). Crude characterizations of ethnicities—the "n" word, or derogatory terms like "polacks," "spics," "fuzzy-wuzzies," and the like—serve to distance the speaker from whole portions of humanity and to paste generic labels on them, thus dehumanizing them.

Denial is a way of evading the cultural realities that distinguish "them" from "us."[6] Those who deny are not completely unaware of the differences themselves, whether cultural, ethnic, and so on; they simply fail to reflect on their significance. Such denial therefore precludes any possibility of establishing any *rapport* with anyone categorized as "other." It betrays an incapacity or unwillingness to negotiate facts and to discuss cultural and personal differences. "Aggressive ignorance" is one of Bennett's telling phrases; it describes the person in denial very well.

Pastoral Reflection: Adamantly monocultural people may try to deny cultural differences by avoiding cross-cultural situations where such differences arise or are evident. If they are in leadership positions, they may become authoritarian in an effort to remove certain practices or behaviors by dictate, as in "No cooking of [foreign foods] in the kitchen because it leaves a very bad odor for days." Or, even more heavy-handedly, they may leave instructions or create arbitrary rules such as: "X is forbidden and will not be tolerated." This betrays an obtuse monocultural perspective. It is hard to say whether such blatantly insensitive behavior is worse than avoidance or passive-aggression, as when a person makes a loud and deliberate sigh before leaving a room in evident disapproval. Denial is found wherever people avoid noticing or negotiating cultural differences or when they interpret them simply as other people's bad habits. It is an expression of cultural ignorance.

2. *Defense*

Not quite as objectionable as the gross ethnocentrism labeled denial, defense is "the state in which one's own culture (or adopted culture) is experienced as the only viable one—the most "evolved" form of civilization, or at least the only good way to live."[7] A person operating in the defense mode is certainly *aware* of many cultural differences that someone in denial may simply fail to notice, but the defense mentality sees *only* differences from what one considers to be the norm, immediately judging them negatively and without adequate reflection or introspection. Here, the line of separation between "us" and "them" is even more sharply drawn, and an attitude of uncritical approval of whatever obtains in one's own culture dominates. Such jingoism or excessive patriotism is highly sensitive to any form of criticism from "them." The person in a defense mode will stereotype the other and may tell demeaning jokes—ostensibly light-hearted but actually deeply felt—about other nationalities, modes of speech or dress, or customs. Taken to excess, defense shows itself in affiliation with exclusive groups (racist, sexist, homophobic, and so on) whose policies are explicitly directed against "the other."

But defense may also characterize the attitude of persons from minority groups or cultures. This is an understandable form of self-protection against unfamiliar and dominant behavior, and virtually everyone who feels outnumbered or taken for granted in a larger group will create some defense mechanisms. These, however, should gradually diminish as a person feels more integrated and accepted into a larger or more heterogeneous group. But this is far from an automatic development; the attitude of some people may actually harden so that they become increasingly strident in their criticism of the dominant culture and in defense of their own. But Bennett also draws attention to what he calls "reversal" as a quite different response by some people from minority groups. This means that one becomes infatuated with the dominant culture, to the point of quite uncritical absorption or approval of everything it stands for. Sometimes called "going native" or "going bush," it may be extremely naïve or a not-so-subtle effort to ingratiate oneself with the host group. We will look more closely at this later.[8] But as Bennett says insightfully, this is really going from one extreme (total rejection) to the other (total acceptance), and "by changing the poles of the polarized worldview, this person has not changed [an] essentially unsophisticated experience of cultural difference."[9]

Pastoral Reflection: Take Bennett's definition—"the state in which one's own culture (or adopted culture) is experienced as the only viable one"—and simply substitute "religion" for "culture," and the dangers of defense become immediately apparent. Anyone intolerant of any religion or denomination espoused by "the other," instinctively hostile to or defensive before whoever wears a different religious label, and without any desire for dialogue or a sympathetic relationship is in the defense mode. Some crude attempts at proselytizing (using force or fear as instruments) and anything approaching a "crusading" zeal exemplify the extreme defense position. So, within an intercultural community, leadership that is didactic and nondialogical, or preemptive and inflexible in decision making, may be operating in a defense mode. Likewise, certain people in authority (even some clergy or formation directors) who proclaim rather bombastically, "You can't tell me anything about these people; I've been around/ doing this for twenty-five years," are clearly manifesting aspects of the defense response to cultural or religious differences. Carried to an extreme, this would produce an attitude of "do as I say, or leave," popularly referred to as "my way, or the highway."

Once again it is always useful to remember the sin and grace in every culture; no culture survives indefinitely without distinctive elements of virtue, and none is without weaknesses or deficiencies. So a tendency to compare the grace in one's own culture with the sin perceived in another must be resisted: we see the splinter in others but fail to identify the beam in ourselves. If we claim some cultural or personal virtue, we should at least look for some equivalent in another culture or person. And if we immediately identify some blemish or sin in another, we should be honest enough to look within before we lash out in response. Another way to approach cultural or religious differences positively is to remember the great paradox: human beings are simultaneously all the same (human) *and* all different (individual); we need to look at both aspects if we are ever to live harmoniously with others. The attitude named defense is an expression of assumed cultural superiority and crude judgmentalism.

3. *Minimization*

Still tainted with an unacceptable amount of ethnocentrism but showing signs of a more mature and tolerant approach to cultural or religious differences is what Bennett identifies as a third possible response. "Minimization of cultural difference is the state in which elements of one's own cultural worldview are experienced as universal."[10] The tinge of ethnocentrism that still marks a minimization approach is that one interprets the other by using the categories that are immediately familiar to oneself. Rather than identifying cultural differences as threatening and then condemning them (defense), one "subsumes the differences into familiar categories."[11] But this is to risk being closed to the possibility of valid or rational meanings intrinsic to other cultures or religions. "That's not the way to hold your knife/tie your shoes/say your prayers" betrays a person employing the minimization approach: the assumption being that there is a single universal way and that it is my own. It also risks jumping to an unwarranted conclusion about what the other person is actually doing; what I interpret as "praying" may actually be something else. Tellingly, Bennett observes that "people at Minimization are unable to appreciate other cultures [or religious actions] because they cannot see their own culture clearly."[12] This is due to our habituation or socialization, because of which we simply take many things for granted. We assume that the way we act is correct and even normative.

People in the minority may initially adjust to the expectations or demands of a dominant group, which may insist on conformity in order to minimize what it considers unimportant variations or on the grounds of necessary discipline or rational standardization. In both cases, minimization is operative if people on both sides of a cultural divide assume that variations are simply unnecessary and prevent the smooth running of an operation. But if conformity proves to be more than simply irksome to the minority person, resistance to it could provoke serious problems.

Pastoral Reflection: In religious communities, new members are aggregated into a preexisting community with many established or standardized ways of proceeding. The incomer is expected to learn, to adapt, and to conform. In a monocultural community, individual differences may be appropriately minimized in order to achieve a team spirit and common responses. But in a multicultural community, the person in charge (or of the dominant culture) and the incomer (from a minority group) may be unaware that standard procedure in the community has itself been significantly shaped by the cultural assumptions of the dominant culture or "the community." Unless leadership becomes sensitized to the purely cultural (and thus potentially adaptable) expression of various behaviors—posture for prayer, dress, privacy, and so on—serious tension can develop as new or minority community members feel suffocated and unfairly constrained. Those who may initially feel constrained, however, also need to learn how to tolerate unfamiliar ways and expectations. This, after all, is one of the necessary challenges of intercultural living. But if an "us"/"them" polarization occurs in a community, the dominant group will hold most of the cards and adapt the least, while the minority will feel powerless and manipulated. Just as the leadership (or dominant group) is challenged to learn how to be culturally sensitive, so minority persons must learn not to cry "foul!" as soon as they are asked to do something unfamiliar or challenging. Instinctively to invoke the "culture" card as a reason not to change one's ways is unworthy of anyone committed to intercultural living. But equally, never to have the opportunity to express one's core cultural identity in important matters is a failure of those in authority and will soon prove disastrous.

Minimization is typical of any first attempts to make sense of and adapt to another culture, since it is perfectly natural to try to interpret events and behaviors with the "grammar" familiar to us: our own cultural inventory. It takes a while to realize that this is not much help, any more than trying to understand Russian with the grammar of English would be. And there is a further danger in minimization: to assume that what works in one culture—the Myers-Briggs test, the Enneagram, and even IQ tests—is universally applicable. Many tests are culture-bound or culture- (or gender-, age-, or otherwise) sensitive, and to try to force an individual into a culturally inappropriate straitjacket can be devastating. Formation personnel must be careful not to minimize cultural differences; but at the same time, they need to remember that not only are people culturally different (in greater or lesser ways) but also that every one of us is a member of the human race and therefore able to communicate and cooperate, to empathize—or to tyrannize.

Here then, we are at three stages of ethnocentrism, from the more egregious (denial), via the intermediary stage (defense), to the more moderate (minimization). A person moves beyond simple *denial* by becoming consciously aware that there *are* indeed significant cultural differences; beyond *defense* by realizing that cultural differences are not always intolerable or incompatible and that there are significant similarities; and beyond *minimization* by perceiving that intercultural differences are intrinsically valid and effectively meaningful. We are now moving steadily toward what Bennett calls ethnorelativism, an acceptable and creative way of encountering cultural "others." It too can be seen in three manifestations or stages, as illustrated in Bennett's own simple diagram[13] (figure 13):

Figure 13

STAGES OF INTERCULTURAL DEVELOPMENT

Denial → Defense → Minimization	Acceptance → Adaptation → Integration
ETHNOCENTRISM ➡	*ETHNORELATIVISM*

The Ethnorelative Stages of Development

"Ethnorelativism," says Bennett, simply means "that one's culture is experienced in the context of other cultures."[14] Ethnorelativists are conscious of cultures other than their own and consequently adapt their approach and monitor their instinctive reactions to "the other." The term "ethnorelativist" is ungainly and could perhaps be replaced in ordinary conversation with a term such as "respectful" or "culturally sensitive," but it is now enshrined in the literature. There is, however, no inevitability about a smooth transition from crude ethnocentrism to sympathetic ethnorelativism: people who present themselves as crudely ethnocentric in the first place have already formed habits that may prove intractable. The stages identifying ethnorelativism are acceptance, adaptation and integration.

1. *Acceptance*

Simply to accept another person seems to be the minimal requirement of anyone hoping to negotiate the challenge of a multicultural situation, and yet for some people this already seems too much to expect. Anyone still rooted in an ethnocentric worldview will simply continue to react in an ethnocentric way unless encouraged, motivated, and assisted to become more open. And people with deep prejudice, a strong *idée fixe* or obsession, and a spirit of self-righteousness will be threatened by and intolerant of behaviors or ideas different from their own. So acceptance is not something we can take for granted, unless one is in principle open to alternative ways of acting or thinking as being at least tolerable and neither irrational nor ungodly. Acceptance becomes possible only if I can freely acknowledge that my ways are not the only possible ways. But personal religious prejudice and dogmatism first need to be identified because some people are simply unable to get beyond the notion that their own ideas and convictions are nonnegotiable absolutes.

Acceptance of cultural differences requires that we can distinguish our own cultural ways from those of others and at the same time accept others as just as human as ourselves. We can then countenance the idea that there can be many ways to solve a single problem and many ways to interpret external reality. But acceptance is not measured by one's knowledge alone; it requires sympathy for, and understanding of, other people's efforts to negotiate the circumstances of their lives. It is precisely here that some integrated anthropological knowledge becomes necessary (which is what some of the terminology, reflections, and exercises throughout this book attempt to introduce). It would be almost as bad for a person to be faced with cultural differences armed with some measure of theoretical or factual anthropological knowledge but without a "feel"—an attitude of real respect and openness—for the people involved as it would for that person to stumble blindly into a multicultural context with absolutely no preparation. So, while goodwill alone is insufficient, equally so is knowledge without empathy and flexibility.

Acceptance does not mean ceasing to think and judge; nor does it mean either agreement or capitulation. In fact, *uncritical* judgment, as Bennett reminds us, smacks of ethnocentrism. The real challenge is to be open-minded and tolerant of differences, without thereby losing all sense of principle or core values. "Relativism" is positive when it acknowledges acceptable areas of free choice (in dress, food, ways of praying, posture, and so on); this would be "relative relativism." But it becomes dangerous (and even worse) if people decide that *anything* and *everything* is acceptable (like cannibalism, torture, infanticide, human trafficking, and so on); this would be "absolute relativism." Absolute relativism would soon produce anarchy and the destruction of culture itself. Evidently, there are degrees of relativism, and one's tolerance of specific cultural differences will be built on one's socialization as well as on the theological and philosophical principles that shape one's moral character. So acceptance is always subject to careful reflection, real ongoing dialogue and mutual regard, so that people can reach a consensus or *modus vivendi* in relation to what is and is not acceptable under particular circumstances—such as intercultural living.

Pastoral Reflection: Acceptance is always related to other issues, such as what is and is not negotiable, changeable, or provisional. In an intercultural community, this calls for great patience and mutual respect, since all of us behave in certain (cultural) ways that we tend to consider normative—until we encounter other people who behave differently. This is not a problem when the lives of those others hardly impinge on our own; we can more readily "live and let live." But when actually living with and among people with different ways, habits, and even convictions, but with whom we must create a community of faith and common life, many delicate or neuralgic issues will quickly surface. Simply to try to accept, without working out the implications of such acceptance, can quickly produce irritation and then resentment, a breakdown in communication or a sudden eruption of real anger. One of the outcomes of successful acceptance is the ability to acknowledge other people's full humanity and goodwill without trying to make them conform precisely to one's own understanding of those things and of being able to make provisional judgments about other people's actions without thereby condemning their supposed motives. Consequently, each person is challenged to distinguish what would be personally unacceptable from what one might disapprove of in others but has no business to judge and condemn.

Pope Francis's disarming "Who am I to judge?" shocked many people who thought they had a right to judge—and condemn. The responsibility of leadership is onerous but also delicate. Leaders must lead, and that requires them to find a line between what is totally unacceptable and what is tolerable, but at the same time to struggle with the fact that the future shape of religious life, particularly in its cultural diversity, will be very different from what has hitherto been regarded as unquestionable, exportable, and of universal applicability.

Goodwill alone is evidently insufficient and can produce great frustration and a sense of impotence. Knowledge is also important, and people striving for wholesome intercultural living must learn directly about and from each other in much more than a casual way. We could watch people playing chess for a hundred years, but unless we know actual rules, we will never understand it well enough to play. Similarly, living under the same roof as others (whether spouse, children, or religious) is not an adequate measure of intercultural living. Hard work, constant questioning of oneself and others, but, above all, real compassion, concern, love for the other are a *sine qua non* for mutual—and especially cross-cultural—understanding.

2. Adaptation

The issue of relativity—the ability to acknowledge and respect a variety of approaches to common tasks (good) or the complete lack of any absolute standards and principles leading to uncritical acceptance of whatever anyone chooses to do (bad)—must be resolved before a person can move from acceptance to adaptation. Mature individuals must have a strong intuitive sense of right and wrong and the ability to follow their conscience without, however, imposing their views or convictions on others. After due consideration and with appropriate information, a person may learn to behave in new ways in the context of another culture. To see another's point of view and to respect and even adopt it is the essence of adaptation. But this requires a constructively critical approach. "When in Rome, do as the Romans" is a useful rule of thumb; but "when not in Rome there is no need to act as if you were" might be a useful corollary. Adaptation is built on mutual respect and flexibility, but it neither means that people jettison their principles nor that they become absorbed or assimilated, thereby losing their own identity. Successful adaptation would actually increase a person's range of possible responses; and since we are thinking of a multicultural context, it would also result in the transformation of everyone in the community and the gradual erosion of a dominant-culture mentality or deliberate manipulation.

Pastoral Reflection: Adaptation takes time and shows itself in different forms of uneven value. To copy another person's behavior because it seems "exotic" or "different" smacks of playacting or superficial behavior modification. True adaptation should be respectful both of other persons and their cultures; it should not simply be a change of behavior that fails to touch one's deeper convictions or belief. An example from Africa might help here.

I lived for a number of years in a society in which the threat, fear, and reality of witchcraft dominated people's lives. When I first arrived, I had brought with me a purely academic understanding of witchcraft but no actual experience of its social reality. Gradually coming to understand it as a real, existential, cultural attempt to explain and address various kinds of evil *common to people of every culture* (unwarranted ill fortune or sudden death, tragic "accident," crop failure, and the like), I was able to see it as a specific cultural response to the universal questions: "why evil?" and "why me?" In this, witchcraft is asking the same question as all religions do; but witchcraft is a *personalized explanation of evil* (the "what?" as in "what is the cause of this?" becomes a personal "who caused this?"). As such, the logic of witchcraft demands that an actual person in the community be charged and found guilty, whether consciously so or not. So long as I was surrounded by the "witchcraft mentality," I needed to bracket my own Western understanding of *impersonal* or *"accidental" causality* and to accept witchcraft as the lived reality, the (only) available explanation in the circumstances.[15] Few of my "Western" confreres could appreciate this, and some suspected I had lost my reason. But by accepting the palpable social reality rather than ridiculing the people, I became more empathetic and pastorally relevant. When I returned to my own cultural context, I returned to my own worldview, of which witchcraft was simply no longer a part. To be mutually intelligible while retaining one's core identity—one's authenticity—is the challenge for everyone.

This is a simple example of a situation that requires a person to rethink, reexamine assumptions, and be prepared for a modification or transformation of established and sometimes entrenched ideas about the world and social reality. Unless we establish a common base, a common language to address what is really real, we will find it impossible to live together as members of a single community.

3. *Integration*

This is not really a separate stage but rather, as the word suggests, the integration of both one's external or interpersonal experiences and one's internal or personal identity. The basic characteristic of integration is the ability to generalize from one set of experiences and apply one's learnings and adaptation to subsequent situations. Living in a community where the witchcraft mentality is pervasive would be an example of both adaptation and integration if it facilitated increased sensitivity to future cross-cultural experiences. One of the words Bennett uses in relation to integration is "cultural marginality," which I will address next.[16]

It is important to recognize that adaptation and integration are not achieved at the cost of one's core identity: I cannot become you but I can continue to improve ways in which I can be myself with greater integrity. I am neither absorbed into another community nor fully incorporated if that means I become lost within a greater organization or entity. In the case of efforts to create an intentional intercultural community, however, there are both losses and gains for each person, such that the new community is not identical with a former or, indeed, any other community. Insofar as it is indeed a new creation, one could argue that there is incorporation without identity loss, because each person is changed by the experience of intercultural living, and because that experience itself creates a new organism. This is where a return to a consideration of various forms of marginality would be valuable.

To summarize the three stages of ethnorelativism: A person has moved beyond acceptance and toward adaptation when there is a real commitment to, and palpable signs of, undertaking the task of learning a culture through study, research, and encounter. And the move from there to integration has effectively happened when a person develops respect for the culture of another that shows itself in authentic interpersonal relationships as well as appreciation of the cultural genius itself.

Pastoral Reflection: This rather summary description of a potential movement from the crass ethnocentrism of an individual to the successful integration of several persons into an intercultural community is intended to identify some pitfalls and perhaps some necessary skills and changes of attitude required of everyone. But the actual experience itself, of living with others and shaping such a community, remains the great challenge. Before that challenge can be met it must first be recognized; and if it is to be successfully met, it requires great and consistent commitment on the part of all. Other chapters in this book deal with other aspects of the call and challenge, but this one is primarily intended to sketch an approach and to affirm that it is possible to move from ethnocentrism to a more inclusive and respectful way of living. But of course many variables can affect the hoped-for outcome, and in a subsequent chapter we will consider the tension between our already well-shaped cultural identity and our attitudes to the prospect and challenge of personal transformation or conversion.[17]

Coda

In recent years, and largely as a result of Bennett's pioneering work, a number of models and inventories have been designed to assess the suitability of personnel in the corporate world of multicultural enterprises. Similarly, within the world of religious and missionary communities, there is a great deal of expertise and assistance available. At the corporate level, Mitchell Hammer's *Intercultural Development Inventory* can be found at www.idiinventory.com. But for international and multicultural religious communities, the best resource is Intercultural Consultation Services (currently under the direction of Sr. Katie Pierce, IHM, at ktpierce@interculturalconsultation.com). Their internet address is www.interculturalconsultation .com.

Suggested Follow-Up

1. A useful community exercise might be to attempt to construct a "profile" of some of the behaviors and attitudes encountered in each of the stages from ethnocentrism to ethnorelativism.

2. It is important at some stage for a community to identify specific requirements or undertakings that each community member might be expected to measure up to if an international, multicultural community is to move intentionally toward true intercultural living (i.e., courses, readings, "immersion experiences," and so on).

3. M. Scott Peck identifies six characteristics of authentic community: inclusivity, commitment, consensus, contemplation, vulnerability, and "graceful fighting."[18] How does your community measure up?

Chapter Eight

Mission, Margins, and Intercultural Living

Review and Preview

So far we have looked *within* an intercultural community, but mission is also a call that takes us *beyond* our little world. Before exploring this, it might be well to revisit several key themes already identified in order to emphasize their intrinsic relationships. Then we can focus on margins, marginality, and the missionary challenge to members of intercultural communities. After all, the very purpose of intercultural living is to enable us to move from the relative security of our community or comfort zone in order to reach out and encounter people. Our ultimate desire is not survival but greater commitment to God's mission—the *missio Dei*.

Nevertheless, intercultural living makes certain demands on everyone, even before we venture out. First, and fundamentally, we have to acknowledge and learn to respect cultural differences. To that end, we spoke of culture as "the [hu]man-made part of the environment," and then described it in a number of other ways, as "the form of social life," a "meaning-making system," an "enduring social reality," and even as "social skin." Each of these descriptive images (several others might easily have been added) can facilitate an understanding of culture that is something most people take for granted or believe they already understand. But culture, as we saw, is more complex, delicate, and subtle than many people realize. Unless we have a reasonably firm grasp on its component parts, it will be impossible to create an authentic intercultural community. Chapters 3 and 4 were intended to deepen our understanding of culture and to appreciate that such an understanding is crucially important for our commitment to God's mission within and beyond any local community.

In chapter 5, we brought together culture, faith, and Christian spirituality, attempting to show that faith *always* requires a cultural context, and that it can *only* be expressed in a cultural form. To attempt to destroy people's culture is to mount a head-on attack on their faith and spirituality itself. Nevertheless, every culture is called to "bow the knee" before God, which will entail the identification and transformation of its sinful elements. But since spirituality is "a way of being in the world with God," the world in which people actually live provides the immediate context for their encounter with God's creation and creation's God. In order to invite a personal and communal reflection on the relationship between faith, culture, and spirituality, we considered a number of anthropologically and theologically significant factors: social location and geography; embodiment and body tolerance; health and sickness; time and space; and finally some further theological reflection.

Moving to chapter 6, we considered two ways of living, contrasting (strong to moderately) ego-focused and (strong to moderately) sociofocused persons and societies. Various characteristics of each were contrasted, and readers were invited to locate themselves along a continuum. The intention here was to offer each person two possible aids. First, it should be possible to identify our own *cultural* emphases and contrast them with the influence that our *theology* or *spirituality* has exerted on the shaping of our cultural identity. It should be quite easy to see how both culture and faith have combined to shape our own identity (and therefore, on reflection, how they do the same in everyone else's life). The second way the "social profiles" diagram might help in an intercultural context is as a conversation opener to be used between people of different cultural and faith backgrounds, or as an instrument a faith community might use in order better to understand its individual members' moods and motivations. Then chapter 7, on intercultural competence, offered another way for people to identify and assess their current situation. Milton Bennett's six stages, from extreme ethnocentrism to real mutuality can help to clarify impediments to intercultural living and indicate a way forward from a less enlightened to a more enlightened way of living in community.

Each of the first six chapters can stand alone or be read in sequence. They provide some necessary (but only partial) background, vocabulary, and approaches to intercultural living. Chapter 7 forms a bridge between those somewhat theoretical chapters and the rest of the book, offering a kind of checklist or gauge for determining where we are on the journey toward authentic intercultural living. It includes theory but also offers some practical hints. Now, without completely neglecting the theoretical, the rest of this book will place increasing emphasis on the practical implications and applications of intercultural living, which, we always need to remember, is not an end itself but a means whose purpose lies beyond itself: the mission of God, of the church, and of each of the baptized. So now we can tackle the matter of margins and mission.

Margins and Marginality

The author of the Letter to the Hebrews reminds readers that "here we have no lasting city" (Heb 13:14). With that in mind, the present chapter looks for signs that we have assimilated this theological dictum; we also explore some of its deep implications for members of intercultural communities committed to outreach in missionary discipleship.

The related words "margins" and "marginality" are both ambiguous and polysemic: sometimes their meaning can seem vague, and sometimes they have quite diverse meanings and connotations: they can be elusive and subtly shape shifting. Nor are the words user-friendly to large numbers of people. Yet what is problematic or offensive to some can be life-giving and wholesome, even attractive, to others. Jesus himself, our teacher and model, adopted a marginal lifestyle and lived for those who subsisted at the margins, accepting the discomfort that entails. Consequently, the phrase "comfortably marginal" would be a near oxymoron; so we begin with clarifications of terminology, usage, and our own expectations.

Although our theme is theological rather than etymological or semantic, a little of the latter may help to sharpen our focus. If we think missiologically or about mission, we recall first that a *boundary* is a marker or dividing line serving primarily not only to separate but also, and significantly, to connect spaces or people. As we observed when speaking of *microcosms* and *macrocosms* in chapter 5, some boundaries are porous and undefended while others are closed and stoutly defended, some hardly noticeable yet others patrolled and virtually impenetrable. Second, a *definition* is itself a form of boundary creation. It identifies limits, limitations, and edges that clearly exclude what, or who, is not clearly included. And, third, a *margin* is an edge, but it also draws immediate attention to a center, against which it is polarized and by reference to which it is defined.[1] The word *marginal*—implicitly "hegemonic" because it rests on the perspective of the person at the center—refers to something or someone judged unimportant, of minimal significance, and not included in the main part of something else: thus—and critically important for the mission minded—marginal people are, by definition, incompletely assimilated into the mainstream, at the lower limits of someone else's standards of acceptability, and *liminal*. But how they become or remain marginal is also highly significant to our theme. And since the word *marginalize* in its verbal or adjectival form can carry very different connotations and denotations, we must distinguish imposed and chosen marginality, then active and passive marginality, and then make a brief reference to *liminality* itself.

All this might serve as an invitation for us to consider the very nature and purpose of our intercultural communities. Do they exclude, include, or both? Do we actually seek to move from the center (our intercultural community) to the edge, the margin, and beyond? Does our intercultural community facilitate our movement to and beyond its margins, explicitly in order to encounter those who live there, marginal and marginalized people? Since there are various kinds of marginality with different effects, we need to identify them.

Imposed and Chosen Marginality

Socially speaking, marginality, as a condition of being far from the center—of power, influence, orthodoxy, or lifestyle—is most often a label attached to, or a condition imposed on, people. Such people are forced into a situation by whatever social or religious agencies in which they are perceived—by those at the centers and sometimes even by themselves—as irrelevant, inferior, and often culpable. Most people do not seek the appellation "marginal." But there are some who do: people who for various reasons actually choose to leave the centers of power and seek an "eccentric" or marginal status. Such are those dedicated individuals who leave their home or center in order to seek the margins where other people—who are themselves "at home," such as it may be—live.

Insofar as those who choose marginality dedicate themselves to "the other," they are initially outsiders in the new social world they enter, and yet they can, with the gradual development of appropriate mutuality and the assistance of the insiders, become outsider-participants[2] rather than outsider-nonparticipants, as is the case of tourists or sojourners: people with minimal rights (*nokri* in Hebrew). The outsider-participant, by contrast, would be the sociological stranger: a person with certain specified rights in the community (*gēr* in Hebrew). This describes Jesus himself and his chosen ministry as a "marginal Jew" (in the striking phrase of biblical scholar John Meier). Later I will explain what being a "marginal Jew" entailed.[3] But anyone who attempts to follow the example of Jesus as a disciple and intentionally takes up the daily cross in order to follow the Teacher is thereby committed to choosing marginality. Yet relatively few seem to take this sociological identity seriously to heart as the major driving force of their ministerial and missionary lives. Nevertheless, it is critically important that we mark and appreciate the distinction between imposed and chosen marginality.

We can therefore identify chosen marginality as of two kinds. First, an individual who joins an established intercultural community is initially marginal to that community and its current members but seeks to become an active participant. But more is involved than the new member's choice of initial marginality; since the community preexists the new arrival, he or she is *de facto* marginal to it (quite apart from any professed willingness to be so) and must therefore negotiate whatever resistance or testing may be entailed. This will place the new member in a transitional or *liminal* state, which can be acutely painful. The second kind of chosen marginality is found in the commitment of a community member to those living outside or beyond it, on or across margins or boundaries of gender, ethnicity, economic power, religion, and so on. Each of these two forms of marginality must be negotiated separately. In the former case, one seeks to join a community; but because the members have already embraced a shared vision and purpose and established their own corporate identity and solidarity, adjustments will need to be made, and mostly by the incomer. In the latter case, the people beyond the margins (marginalized not by choice but by circumstance) may be disparate, alien, and naturally suspicious of one's motives. Again, the person who chooses marginality will need to make serious adjustments, since the other parties, within or beyond the community, will in fact impose an extra degree of marginality on the person who initially chose it. The consequences of our good-faith choices are not always under our control.

Active and Passive Marginality

We also need to distinguish active and passive marginality. Active marginality may take the form of an initiative or a response. As an initiative, it is essentially the same as chosen marginality. But there are some people, initially marginalized against their will, who manage to turn this imposition into a mark or symbol of new significance. One thinks of people who are gay or lesbian, bisexual or transgendered. By asserting their legitimate identity, they gained wide currency in social service circles and beyond for the designation "LGBT," thus removing some social stigma. More widely, active marginality describes what any countercultural Christian is committed to as a path to discipleship. There is, however, no absolute correlation between chosen and active marginality or between imposed and passive marginality; those who choose it may indeed be very active, just as those on whom marginality is imposed may respond by passivity. But it is possible to experience imposed marginality and to respond to it either actively (as did many people in Auschwitz) or passively (as did many others in identical circumstances). As for chosen marginality, one may initially undertake a very active role in working at the margins and with marginalized people but, due to burnout or disillusionment, become passive and unresponsive to previously sought challenges.

Economist and social justice theorist Amartya Sen speaks of active and passive "social exclusion."[4] The former happens when immigrants or refugees are "not given a usable political status," while passive exclusion happens "when there is no deliberate attempt to exclude,"[5] but poverty and unemployment create conditions that produce such exclusion. This can be just as harmful, as when the government or church has a responsibility to examine the effects—direct and indirect—of its policies or procedures but fails to do so. But whether we create or perpetuate the marginalization of people actively or passively is less important than the fact that to contribute to either form of marginalization is immoral, reprehensible, and completely contrary to the spirit of the mission of Jesus. In short, social exclusion describes any process that causes people to be relegated to the social margins by depriving them—individually or collectively—of their basic human rights through discrimination on whatever grounds. Therefore the boundaries or margins of our intercultural communities must remain porous if we are not to betray the mission. Whether we made an initial choice in favor of marginality or found ourselves marginalized due to the circumstances of a particular appointment or assignment is less important than the way we responded to the situation: actively or passively, fullheartedly or halfheartedly. And each community member must be sensitized to notice when another person is suffering marginalization within the community itself: alienation and loneliness can occur within any community.

Marginality as Burden or Opportunity

Classically, through Georg Simmel a century ago[6] and Everett Stonequist thirty years later, the social sciences described the marginal person as one who lives in two societies but is a member of neither, "poised in psychological uncertainty," in Stonequist's words.[7] But there is much, much more to marginality than this. In his influential 1995 book on marginality, Korean-American Jung Young Lee discusses its positive and negative aspects and offers a helpful scheme or scale. He distinguishes passive or even pathological marginality from other and more productive forms. Because, as he says, "to be in-between two worlds means to be fully in neither."[8] Therefore one must strive for more than becoming a nonbeing living in "existential nothingness"[9] or being defined negatively by others. Marginality is not only being forced to live "in-between" but also actively choosing to live "in-both"; then its positive elements become visible. But this can only happen when people affirm both their roots and their branches: their original home and their current domicile or sojourn. Identifying Jesus as the "new marginal person *par excellence*," he notes that "if God was in Jesus Christ, the people of God must also be marginal. . . . The fellowship of God's marginal people is known as the church, [which] becomes authentic when it is situated at the margins of the world. The way to overcome [negative] marginality is through the creative transformation by which marginal and dominant people create a new marginality. . . . Change and transformation take place at the margin because creativity flourishes there."[10]

But Lee is not finished. He then proceeds to make some specifically theological observations, saying that it is also possible to live "in-beyond," which describes the perspective of the Letter to the Hebrews already quoted: "Here we have no lasting city, but we are looking for the city that is to come" (13:14), by keeping our focus on our ultimate destination and aspiration. Lee says that being "in-between" and "in-both" "embodies a state of being in both [of these] without either being blended." This produces a new *marginal person* with "the ability to be continuously creative."[11] So, to live "in-beyond" does not mean to be free of the two different worlds in which persons exist, but it does mean that we are not bound by either of them because we are liberated by the example and promise of Jesus. Here is an insight that people in intercultural communities and working as marginal people in marginal situations might profitably ponder.

Positive and Negative Marginality (Liminality)

One form of marginality familiar to us all is *liminality*. From the Latin word for threshold or boundary, it describes a state of in-between-ness in a rite of passage as one is moved from a former social status to a new one. The middle or *liminal* stage places initiates in transition, identified with both danger and great promise. The intended outcome of the *liminal* stage is the reincorporation of individuals as a group into society but with a new, enhanced, social identity. As a transitional stage in a ritual, *liminality* is positive if it leads initiands to the intended outcome; but it becomes negative if it fails to do so, leaving an individual in an ongoing state of status confusion, anguish, and often real and enduring fear. The theories of Arnold van Gennep and Victor Turner,[12] which built on the ethnography of *liminality*, are not beyond lively critique, but they have afforded us very useful language and concepts, particularly in identifying a series of stages which, if successfully negotiated, will serve to confer on a person a new identity but, if not, can lead to disaster.

Liminality as a "Rite of Passage"

As a sociological term, liminality has a specific purpose: to hold a person in an "in-between" state for as long as it takes the insiders or host to scrutinize and test that person in order to determine whether they will accept or reject him or her. Classically, three stages have been identified in a "rite of passage," whether an initiation rite as such, or a transition into a community, which is our concern here.[13] If a person is to become accepted and welcomed, it will be necessary to negotiate the first two successfully. If this is not done, the second stage (true liminality) will serve to abort the process and reject the incomer. The stages are identified (figure 14) as preliminal (or preliminary), liminal (sometimes marginal, transitional, or betwixt and between), and postliminal (or incorporation).[14] Marginality and *liminality* have similar connotations of the transitional, or an experience of something between life and death: ambiguous, uncomfortable, indefinite—and apparently meaningless at times. Positively, the move needs to be toward life: working through a death-like struggle to a transformation of status and the beginning of new life—such as experienced in the *Rite of Christian Initiation for Adults (RCIA).*

Figure 14

PRELIMINAL, LIMINAL, AND POSTLIMINAL

PRELIMINAL	It is of short duration (days, not weeks). It represents hosts' duty of formal hospitality. It is highly indulgent of the guest, who is treated preferentially and with no obligations.
LIMINAL	It is of indefinite length but will end; can be irksome; a time of testing and scrutiny; the liminal person is expected to take some responsibility and initiative. It is a predictably unpredictable time, designed to lead to acceptance or rejection of the liminal person.
POSTLIMINAL	Is demonstrable inclusion and acceptance; long lasting and morally obliging to both. It is not full incorporation or assimilation, but authentic and respectful acknowledgment of difference.

These rites serve to move a person to a new identity in the community (and in the case of the RCIA, via submersion and symbolic death by drowning, to emergence to a new life in Christ). Traditional initiation rites, the original focus of Victor Turner's studies, place particular emphasis on new life through the ascription of a completely new status and incorporation into a new group. But if *liminality* is the technical term that usually emphasizes the positive (or movement in that direction), the word *marginalization* is most commonly used with negative connotations, signifying a gradual or dramatic fall from grace, a passage from life to social death. Yet while acknowledging the dreadful effects of imposed marginalization, it is particularly important missiologically to identify the potential benefits of positive marginalization, not only on the person who chooses it but also on the beneficiaries of that choice.

Margins: Problems and Possibilities

An exploration of margins or boundaries discloses that in fact they serve a triple function, each component of which has an essential purpose: to keep in, to keep out, and, critically for ourselves, to serve as contact points, bridges, or meeting places.[15] To consider not only associated problems, therefore, but also real pastoral possibilities, we can begin by noting that every person is situated in a particular place or center that is itself defined in relation to an edge, boundary, or margin. Each of us, as we saw in chapter 5, is a microcosm within a macrocosm, and we live in a series of microcosms nesting within their respective macrocosms. The microcosm of our body encapsulates something autonomous and sacred: our personal physical integrity. But the bodily microcosm is not an isolate; it exists in relation to a macrocosm, a bigger world beyond the boundaries of the self, in which other entities and other persons exist.

But if we started walking around blindly, we would either bump into each other or blunder into an immovable object. We exist, in other words, within a web of boundaries and margins. There are personal boundaries, visible and invisible, between each of us. There are structural boundaries—brick walls and closed doors—between ourselves and the world beyond a particular room. If these are negotiated appropriately, we can hope to live with dignity and harmony.

Then we can assume responsibility for maintaining our personal integrity and encounter others—or "the other"—in a wholesome and mutually respectful manner. Then, boundaries or margins, personal and interpersonal, serve a positive function of protecting human dignity and enabling wholesome interaction. But whenever something or someone inhibits the appropriate negotiation of personal and social boundaries or margins, people's lives are endangered and their human dignity impugned. Then, either people exploit others' physical integrity by failing to respect mutual boundaries or margins, or they constrain or restrain others within spatial or territorial boundaries, as in a prison or custodial area. Then boundaries become the locus of rank injustice and oppression.

In such a situation, it has often been assumed that a truly altruistic person can both embrace and rehabilitate the marginal "other," thus drawing him or her closer to the center (of respectability, influence, power, and so on). That is certainly within the bounds of possibility. But there is also another possibility that is often overlooked: that the person from the center now becomes truly marginal. This may happen by "contagion" or "stigma": simply by being located among the people already identified as marginal themselves. But there is a much more intentional possibility, and it describes the ministry of Jesus. People said disparagingly, "He eats with tax collectors and sinners." He not only chose to do that but, in effect, challenges each of his followers to do precisely the same thing.

To talk appropriately about margins and marginal ministry, we must acknowledge that our ministry is not simply "at the margins" or "to the marginalized." Such phrases reduce people to a category and can depersonalize and even dehumanize them, as do phrases like "the homeless," "the poor," or "prostitutes." Because there are no generic people (only particular people: women, men, and children), we cannot talk generically. Our language needs to become sensitized to human persons as individuals and agents. "Homeless woman," "unemployed man," or "marginalized people" is a more appropriate way of identifying our sisters and brothers. After all, ministry is, first and last, communication and relationship with real flesh and blood people, some of whom happen to be marginalized and live, or subsist, at the margins.

Nor are we ourselves typical of such people—though each of us can almost certainly identify some situations in which we are, or feel, marginalized, relative to church or society in general, or even to some of our own community members. Therefore, the marginal ministry we undertake implies and entails outreach across—or indeed at—whatever margins or boundaries separate or insulate us from those who are marginalized. But before returning to ask whether or how we ourselves might be or become marginal, we might reflect that, just as we can identify ourselves as both central and marginal in different circumstances, so each person in any community should strive to be *both* a giver and receiver. If the world were only composed of marginalized people, there would be no center; and if there were only givers, there would be nobody to receive, and vice versa. In a world of interdependence, we must become both.

Jesus: Marginal by Choice and by Example

Many people at the margins are victimized and treated sinfully. But others, including most conventional missionaries, are not forced into anything; and Jesus himself exemplifies one who chooses marginality precisely as a way of doing mission and as an example to those who presume to follow his missionary example. It always strikes me as curious and deeply saddening that, having read the words of Jesus, "I was a stranger" (Matt 25:35), we have concluded that what they mean or imply is that we should in turn embrace and show hospitality to the stranger. That is true. But that is only one implication and not perhaps the most important. Applying those other words of Jesus at the Last Supper, "I have set you an example, that you also should do as I have done to you" (John 13:14), we would need to conclude that Jesus is asking us to be like him in *actually embracing* the role and status of a stranger ourselves. To show hospitality to the stranger is to identify *the other* as stranger and oneself as host—a position of superiority and control. But the stranger, by definition, is in an inferior position and not at all in control; which is perhaps why we have been considerably quicker to opt for the role of host than to embrace the role of stranger. The letter to the Philippians is memorable here: "Though he was in the form of God, [he] did not regard equality with God as something to be exploited, but emptied himself, taking the form of a slave, being born in human likeness. And being found in human form, he humbled himself and became obedient to the point of death—even death on a cross" (2:6-8).

To do this is precisely to embrace the role and status of a stranger, the palpably marginal person! It would seem that, as Jesus' disciples in mission, we have, as Jesus did, two tasks: first, to acknowledge that we do indeed have a choice and that we must make that choice and undertake to learn to become marginal; and, second, to focus on the margins themselves as places of exploitation, committing ourselves to an active marginal ministry with the people to be found there. The whole life of Jesus was poured out in marginal ministry or ministry at the margins. Born outside the city and raised in marginal circumstances—of poor, migrant, and later refugee parents—he lived continuously in such circumstances "with no place to lay his head" and at odds with authorities. He died outside the city, having been branded variously as out of his mind, a blasphemer, Beelzebub, and a criminal. But at every step, Jesus made choices in favor of the margins and the women and men caught there because of circumstances economic, political, or religious. This was his preferential option for the poor. And he warned his disciples explicitly that to follow him would lead them to commit themselves to, for, and with the dregs of society: people living either on the margins of society or even beyond and even marked, as many were, by various forms of "social death." The Twelve, slow learners looking for privilege and seats on his right and left, were warned of the persecutions to come (Mark 10:30) and told that what he asked was "impossible" for them, but not for God's grace (Mark 10:27). As descendants of those disciples, we are instructed as they were, to reach out to the margins and the people who live there. That is our first task. But there is a further question: how, from the margins themselves, will we relate to those who occupy the centers of power and influence?[16]

The Missionary Potential of Marginal People

Those who live on the margins can learn and teach valuable lessons. They have agency or they would not survive for very long. They can often see things that from the center are out of view. But people on the margins cannot be restricted to those actively marginalized by social or religious forces; they also include people—like Jesus himself and every disciple—who choose some form of marginal living as a faith commitment. Sociologically they are "strangers," the very word Jesus applies to himself. Assuming that they remain with the people they serve over a considerable period of time and with due commitment to their well-being, they can make a unique contribution in half a dozen significant ways:[17] from the sharing of lives and histories to the pooling of their respective resources; from a commitment of solidarity and moral support to a mutual opening up of microcosms and discovery of alternative possibilities; and from mediating factional hostilities to forging bonds of real fraternal interdependence.[18] Engagement between people marginalized by circumstance or by choice—as outsider-participants in a world and community in which they can never and need not become fully assimilated or incorporated—can be lifesaving literally and figuratively. As a missionary commitment, chosen marginality creates a new space where, in encountering the other, we encounter a hitherto unknown and unrecognized face of God.

This brings us back to Jung Young Lee. An ever-present danger is that we lose our bearings as we struggle at and with margins and marginalized people. Then we would become *liminal* in a negative or pathological way, leaving us "in-between" worlds. But if we are truly committed to Jesus' mission and the people we meet at the margins, we can learn to live integrated and healthy lives, as Lee says, "in-both" worlds. We must always remember though, that as outsider-participants we cannot be fully "at home" with those in whose home we find ourselves—any more than we can ever become fully at home even when we return to the home we left. If we are intentionally marginal people for the kingdom or realm of God, we will come to realize that indeed we have here no abiding city. Theologically, that is to live "in-beyond."

Every person should learn—though some fail to do so—to identify and respect a range of margins: social, personal, interpersonal, religious, or national; the list can easily be extended. Self-abuse, in whatever way we choose to understand that term, bespeaks a breakdown of *self*-respect, just as the abuse of others, whether sexually, physically, or by neglect, is a desecration of the physical or moral integrity of individuals or groups of people. And the abuse of other things—of property, of space, of earth, air, fire, or water—is a social sin of structural proportions. But tragically, self-respect, mutual respect, and respect for nature are at a premium in many human communities and cultures today.

Respect for boundaries or margins, however, is only part of our responsibility to each other. It must always serve a greater and explicitly apostolic purpose: committed outreach, human contact, engagement and solidarity with "the other." People must discover new ways to reach out, to encounter, to engage at their respective boundaries, in order to establish authentic human connections of appropriate intimacy. Then they can build amicable and loving relationships and create new communities, lest human society break down and people become isolated and antisocial. True intimacy is intrinsic to true humanness; and margins are precisely the points of contact between individual persons.

Christians, since we are talking in a particular context here, must therefore identify various margins, understand their functions, and then learn whether, how, and under what circumstances to attempt to bridge or cross them in order to connect with whoever or whatever is just on the other side. Those who lack such finesse will fail to honor or claim their personal integrity or to respect that of others. Then people may overstep appropriate margins, causing grave harm, or they may become so fearful of encounters that they withdraw and cower within the margins of their own little world. Our challenge today is first to respect and then appropriately to cross or erase the boundaries or margins that mark our world and separate or segregate people who need each other. It is a huge challenge and it is vitally necessary that we meet it, as an expression of our faith, compassion, and solidarity.

An essential component of any lasting and authentic human relationship is mutual trust, which can only be established and maintained through actual face-to-face encounters and which in turn requires that people meet at their respective bodily or territorial margins. Regrettably, however, many human relationships crack and break because trust is shattered, as the church and religious communities should be only too aware. One reaction, on the part of people affected by the erosion of trust brought about by the scandals of some of their fellow Christian ministers, is to withdraw and refuse ever again to reach out for fear of compounding the felony. But mission is quintessentially a boundary-crossing outreach. Pastoral encounters always demand willingness to allow boundaries to become places for mutual encounter rather than the site of enmity and mutual destruction. Therefore we are—all of us—called not only to stand fast and faithful in our integrity but also to commit ourselves to erasing lines of division, to removing margins of discrimination or privilege, and to healing the wounds and scars caused by the abuse of trust. Standing fast and breaking through are, after all, two sides of a single coin, the currency of ministry and mission and the coin of community life.

Suggested Follow-Up

1. Identify some of the boundaries or margins that mark your community internally and in relation to who and what is outside. What is their significance?

2. In what ways have you chosen marginality? How does it help or hinder intercultural community life?

3. Can you identify with Jung Young Lee's vocabulary of living "in-both," "in-neither," "in-between," and "in-beyond"? If you aspire to living "in-both" and "in-beyond," what do you think it will cost you?

4. The marginal person or outsider can make significant contributions to "the other" or the insiders. Footnotes 17 and 18 point to some of these. Perhaps this could be a discussion point in community.

Chapter Nine

Psychological Responses to Intercultural Living

The Need for Mutual Adjustments

It is now appropriate to look more closely at the dynamic interplay between an individual who enters a preexisting intercultural community and the community itself. Much of what is said and suggested here, however, would be applicable to a not yet intercultural but international and multicultural community seeking to become intercultural. If all the members of that community commit themselves to the process of community making, all of them individually will be actively working to synthesize aspects of their own culture with the evolving demands of the intercultural community. But also, as we saw in the last chapter, when an entirely new community is constituted—as is sometimes done when a congregation or order takes on a new jurisdiction and assembles an international group—everyone in the community is initially and more or less equally marginal until a new organic unit is formed. This can create splendid opportunities for creativity and bonding but also produce the classical experience of liminality, during which there is inevitable confusion and lack of clarity.

Reciprocity through mutual respect and forbearance is an essential component of true intercultural living, and it requires two distinct but converging or overlapping commitments. First of all, each individual needs to endeavor to become a *cross-cultural* person, and that inevitably entails being "displaced" from one's own culture of origin and no longer to be living in one's "natural" environment. But this is not cross-cultural living in the conventional sense, where an individual lives among people of a homogeneous culture (all the members of which are "at home" themselves, while the cross-cultural person may be in a minority of one). Rather, in an intercultural community, there is no single homogeneous culture or society into which an individual outsider comes: an intercultural community is composed of people of several cultures, none of whom is entirely "at home" in one's natural environment. This is where the second commitment is required: a new culture, or an intercultural community, must be shaped and formed from the constituent cultures of the various group members; this requires a daily and never-ending commitment.

In time, this new culture will become a "standardized mode of coactivity," "the form of social life," and "a meaning-making system" such as we have discussed previously[1] among other exemplifications of culture. Thus each member brings his or her own cultural self to the community, where the various cultures will be challenged to mutual coadaptation. Then, as a result, and driven explicitly by the faith commitment of the total community, a new culture or way of life will emerge, leaving none of the community members without the responsibility of growing in knowledge, skills, and virtue. As emphasized more than once, this is a monumental and challenging task, and, to be perfectly frank, not everyone will be able to live in a wholesome and healthy way in an intercultural community. But unless there is a "critical mass"[2] of members of international communities, committed to building and sustaining their intercultural nature, the very future of international religious communities is arguably threatened with terminal decline.

As we well know, many international communities are very far from being intercultural; some have never really aspired to be so with appropriate intentionality, and some would simply not know where to begin. But insofar as there is ongoing commitment and daily effort, the intercultural community will develop an identity of its own—a culture that does not blend or melt or erase aspects of each individual's culture but becomes a "superorganic"[3]—something greater than the sum of its parts. It becomes more than simply a group of individuals living under one roof, for they will evolve a new way of interacting—verbally, nonverbally, and symbolically (through common rituals and conventions). The new culture they create will be a living, evolving reality that is continuously contested (challenged by innovators and dreamers, rule breakers and rebels, and consequently evolving) as its members work to claim their individual core identity and yet adapt to the physical and spiritual needs of the wider group. Thus, the latest arrival to a community will encounter a more or less established or standardized way of living to which he or she has not, as yet, contributed. But as new members are aggregated to the community, the community itself will continue to adapt and reconfigure as the individual community members themselves are challenged to adapt and reconfigure significant aspects of their own lives. How they do so is a matter for empirical study and psychological insight. But a schematic presentation might help identify some of the possible responses and their effects.

A Schematic Diagram of Psychological Adjustment

The diagram itself (figure 15) can first be applied to the initial cross-cultural encounter, as when an individual leaves home and becomes inserted into an unfamiliar and culturally different community. The individual in a cross-cultural context is the outsider in the midst of insiders, all of whom understand the conventional rules of the culture and the sanctions that underpin it; but the incomer, as yet, does not. Such are the dynamics of a cross-cultural encounter. But with reflection and adaptation, the diagram can also apply to a true intercultural situation, where the incomer encounters a preexisting community whose members know much more about each other and their common expectation than about the incomer and his or her previous experience. The "new kid on the block" syndrome is familiar to us all in one way or another. And among many possible responses, we can identify two extremes: clinging tightly to one's own familiar ways, or dramatically repudiating those ways and points of reference and endeavoring to accept everything that the others do. Most people will find themselves somewhere between these, and the diagram could help to identify their propensity.

Familiarity with a cross-cultural reality—and every member of an intercultural community will have such familiarity to some degree—

EFFECTS OF CULTURE CONTACT ON INDIVIDUALS AND COMMUNITY [4]

Figure 15

RESPONSE	TYPE	INITIAL EFFECT ON INTERCULTURAL COMMUNITY	LONG-TERM EFFECT ON THE INDIVIDUAL	LONG-TERM EFFECT ON THE COMMUNITY
(1) Reject one's own culture (*Culture 1*); Embrace the new culture (*Culture 2*).	*"PASSING"* Repudiation of one's own culture.	*Culture 1* norms lose salience. *Culture 2* norms become salient.	Loss of ethnic identity. Self-denigration and loss of self-esteem.	Assimilation. Erosion of features of *Culture 1* identity. Dominance of *Culture 2*.
(2) Reject *Culture 2*; Exaggerate qualities of *Culture 1*.	*"CHAUVINIST"* Aggressive enthusiasm for one's own culture.	*Culture 1* norms increase in significance. *Culture 2* norms decrease accordingly.	Nationalism, racism, bigotry, and crass or uncritical ethnocentrism.	Friction with the wider group. Resistance and resentment by "incoming" or minority individuals.
(3) Vacillate between the two cultures.	*"MARGINAL"* Indecisive and uncomfortable with both cultures.	Norms of both cultures are important but perceived as mutually incompatible.	Conflict. Identity-confusion and over-compensation.	Reform and social change impossible without coercion or dominance. Resentment or noncooperation.
(4) Synthesize both cultures in a healthy way.	*"MEDIATING"* Skilled at intercultural living.	Norms of both cultures are important and perceived as capable of integration.	Personal growth for committed and faith-filled individuals.	Harmonious and pluralistic community. Diversity accepted; preservation of individuals' cultural integrity.

will already have shaped and formed one's attitude, and the intercultural experience will cause previous habits and reactions—good, bad, and indifferent—to resurface. The following exercise in self-diagnosis or community discernment, or individual or group work with the diagram itself, can therefore be undertaken both in cross-cultural and intercultural contexts.

In this diagram, a person's own primary culture is identified as "Culture 1," and the cultural configuration or reality one experiences in a cross- or intercultural situation is named "Culture 2." Culture 1 will be affected by, and in turn affect, Culture 2 in a variety of possible ways. The diagram identifies four such ways as psychological responses.

Each one will affect personal and interactive behavior and may be used to gauge how well-equipped a person is for intercultural living. We should be aware that the significance attached by persons, whether the incoming community member or the preexisting community, to tradition, dogma, God's will, truth, and so on will all play a role in determining the outcome. Anyone attempting to work with this diagram should factor in these variables.

Also, the model on which this is based assumes a number of things: (1) that cultural contact can occur in mono-, bi-, cross-, or multicultural situations; (2) that "the cultural composition of the setting has a direct influence on the individuals in it,"[5] according to whether they resist or undergo changes toward other cultural groups; and (3) that people modify their environments so that even dominant cultures undergo change.[6] The model also implies why culture should be taken very seriously: changes of attitude, perception, or feeling signal a "re-ordering of individuals' cognitive structures, making them in a real sense different persons."[7] We saw the implications and applications of this when examining Milton Bennett's contributions earlier.

Reading across the top of the diagram from left to right are the criteria or parameters to be employed, and under them four vertically arranged responses, numbered one to four; four related types or names for the responses; four ways in which intercultural (and cross-cultural) living will be affected; and four ways in which the individual and the community, respectively, will feel the effect of the contact between an incoming person of Culture 1 and the current community (Culture 2). We begin with the first of the four responses.

Response 1: *A newcomer to community attempts to reject his or her own culture totally and to embrace the culture of the community unquestioningly and uncritically.*

This would be an extreme case: it is almost an "ideal type" except for the fact that it is far from an ideal or positive proposition. Nevertheless, it serves a purpose, if only by hyperbole or great exaggeration, because there are some people who actually imagine that they can repudiate their own culture and totally embrace another in a process sometimes called "going native" or "going bush." (A good analogy would be to imagine one could shed one's skin and somehow take on another person's skin.) This reaction, however, can also happen in an attenuated form, but since everyone's cultural identity is rooted in certain fixed points of reference and ways of interpreting and managing the external world, these points of reference cannot be totally rejected.[8] If they were, the person would become utterly insane. Therefore, even though people may appear to reject their own culture, they still retain a basic interpretive framework that they apply to decision making and the interpretation of events.

This response can be called "passing," to indicate a radical shift from one's original cultural perspective to a totally novel one. As far as the preexisting community is concerned, this attitude does not constitute a direct threat to its established patterns of behavior because the incoming community member appears to be totally positive in adapting to whatever ways in which the community functions. It does bear repeating, however: this is an extreme case, because in reality such incoming members would be unable to sustain the attempt to mask or obliterate their true cultural identity. What would likely happen, though, is that the incomer's integrity would be profoundly compromised. In fact, that person's ethnic identity would become stifled and depreciated, with the result that the individual would fail to be appropriately assertive and quickly lose a sense of individual or personal worthiness or positive self-image. Ultimately, for as long as the individual remained in the community (and, for both individual and community, one would hope this would not be too long at all), he or she would either become assimilated into or quite marginalized within the broader community, while the community itself would be the poorer by not having benefited from different perspectives, knowledge, and wisdom that could have enriched everyone. Because the community would be minimally affected by the presence of the incomer, its ways would continue, unchallenged, since the newcomer's life experience and perspectives did not serve to "contest" the culture of the community or provide an opportunity for interpersonal adjustment, transformation, and ongoing conversion.

Historically (and sadly), this approach—in an attenuated form no doubt—did characterize a classical way of assimilating new members. The implicit philosophy, sometimes made explicit, was "leave your culture and ideas at the door." But the communities were at that time predominantly monocultural, and such an approach did allow the incomer to become steeped in the tradition and values of the community. On the other hand, individuality was not encouraged; uniformity and standardization were the norm, and potentially creative nonconformists were quickly removed.

Response 2: *A newcomer to the community resists and rejects the culture—the* modus vivendi *and* modus operandi—*of the community and insists that his or her cultural and individual perspectives should be accepted as enlightened.*

This is rather more common than the previous response. In this case, instead of rejecting one's own culture and embracing the community culture, a person rejects or seriously challenges the established culture of the community by assertively maintaining his or her own familiar ways. Members of well-established communities are probably quite familiar with this, at least as an incomer's initial, unredeemed, egocentric, and ethnocentric attitude. And it is arguably more likely to happen today than in the past. For one thing, many people coming to join a community today are considerably older than those who joined decades before and therefore considerably more formed in their own cultural and often well-tried ways. For another, when communities were large and new members plentiful, it was easier to socialize them into the community's ways by enforcing strict standards of behavior and conformity. Today—at least in cultures where new members are fewer and older—the community itself needs to adjust more to persons who are quite often articulate, opinionated, and willing to confront and contest whatever or whoever they encounter, partly because they are not segregated from the senior members as in days gone by, when novices and postulants were "seen and not heard" and operated with a significantly restricted speech code.

This response can also be seen in a more extreme form as the assertive and uncritical nationalism or ethnicity of an incoming member and may be characterized as "the Ugly American" syndrome, although it is certainly not restricted to people of that nation. If not modified, such an attitude of national or cultural superiority quickly becomes quite objectionable. It not only trumpets the assumed qualities of one's own culture but also implies a corollary in that it does not spare criticism of the host culture: that is, of the established community. But since criticism of a person's culture is often understood as personal criticism too, someone with this attitude will become a constant source of irritation, friction, and confrontation within the community. Not inappropriately, this attitude is labeled "chauvinist." It goes far beyond reasonable patriotism and manifests itself in a combination of arrogance and ignorance. The extreme chauvinist is incapable of seeing difference as worthy of dialogue or even respect. Rather, such a person is quick to judge, inflexible, and intolerant of other ways. Moreover, the chauvinist gives virtually no thought to the possibility or desirability of his or her personal behavior modifications, yet constantly finds fault with the established ways of the community. Even worse, the chauvinist's demeanor betrays a refusal to adapt or accommodate to the daily routine. Some of the words applied to such chauvinism are "racist" or "bigoted"; and in Bennett's term,[9] ethnocentric in a quite extreme and unacceptable way. The whole community can thus be adversely affected by a single individual, while the individual him- or herself fails to adapt and grow in relation to the community. So long as they remain in the community, persons with such chauvinistic tendencies will create an atmosphere of simmering or explosive unease in the wider group and mutual resentment between themselves and the broader community.

Response 3: *The incomer fails to maintain a consistent attitude toward the community and constantly vacillates between attachment to his or her primary culture and to the cultural norms of the community.*

As we consider the third type of response, we may note that both from the perspective of the incoming member and that of the broader community, it represents—potentially at least—a significant improvement over both the "passing" and the "chauvinist" responses, though it is by no means a mature and integrated response as of yet. For it to become acceptable, its potential must be realized. If not, a chronic vacillating attitude will lead to ongoing difficulties, deterioration in interpersonal relations, and, consequently, a serious threat to the integrity of community life itself. The response is characterized by a degree of uncertainty, lack of full commitment, and at least intermittent vacillation by the incoming member attempting to negotiate or juggle with two realities. The question to be asked by both individual and community is whether vacillation is a chronic condition or something that is being actively addressed.

On the one hand, an individual's familiar, taken for granted way of living, relating, and evaluating is an intrinsic part of that person's makeup or socialization, and as such it is by no means easily discarded or modified. On the other hand, the broader community, with its history and established customs and rituals, is a hard reality, a social fact of life, and a challenge that needs to be faced and negotiated. Uncertainty can be very difficult to live with, both for the individual and the community as a whole, and as long as it remains unaddressed it will seriously inhibit the possibility of creating an atmosphere of mutual trust and thus destabilize any community. Nevertheless, as we saw when considering liminality, an intrinsic part of the transition into a new community is uncertainty, predictable unpredictability, and undergoing a certain testing of one's mettle. Therefore, so long as the novice or incomer is able to trust the process and the mentors and to understand that the period of uncertainty will eventually end, all should be well. But what would be counterproductive for all would be chronic indecisiveness and vacillation that persists long after the initial period of transition.

Though this response is identified as "marginal," it must be understood not as healthy liminality but as something to be carefully monitored lest it turn into a full-blown pathology. The individual who exhibits this third kind of response will show signs of persistent discomfort or "dis-ease," both with certain significant aspects of his or her own primary culture and with significant aspects of the community culture: its social organization or conventional behaviors and expectations. Essentially, the conflict is born of the desire or urgent need to cling to certain values and features of a precommunity existence and yet at the same time to embrace certain values found in the community. It seems to the individual—and to the community—however, that there is no satisfactory or virtuous way of doing so.

Such marginality might express itself in a variety of ways, particularly in repeated inability to make permanent commitment to the community and its mission. For example, the individual continues to value the freedom of choice and movement enjoyed prior to joining the community, but stability, the Rule, and a community schedule or *horarium* are also valued. Or again, cultivation of romantic and monogamous relationships has become a significant feature of a person's life experience, yet he or she is also attracted to a life of celibate chastity. Both the individual and the wider community will continue to be conflicted unless such a person succeeds in moving in a timely manner through the "marginal" response or stage and either leaves the community or reaches a much more stable and consistent way of life and commitment to it and its charism.

Two issues must therefore be addressed: the individual's commitment to resolving the conflict and the community's tolerance or acceptance of certain patterns of behavior. As far as the individual is concerned, unless he or she is willing, probably with appropriate guidance from a trusted wisdom figure, to confront and address the two conflicting sets of values or options, the internal conflict will likely fester until it results in increased anxiety and total inability to live an integrated community life. Alternatively, that person will attempt to live a double life, which will degenerate into secrecy, deceit, and hypocrisy.

As far as the wider community is concerned, it may, through appropriate leadership, take a positive yet confrontational stance and issue an ultimatum or impose sanctions in an effort to resolve the untenable situation. In fact, if the community, and specifically the leadership, hopes to change the individual for the greater good, then appropriate authority must be invoked and applied. If that fails, the situation needs to be resolved in a more radical way by the removal of the individual for the sake of the community and perhaps for the sake of the "marginal" person as well. But without strong leadership, or without a clear policy, there is a serious risk that everyone will become the loser, gaining nothing from their relationship but generating active or passive aggression, mutual resentment, and a breakdown of the spirit of community.

Response 4: *The incomer, by a concerted and enlightened effort, and with prayer, reflection, and accumulating experience, is able to live in harmony with self and others, true to his or her core self and values, yet adapting in a wholesome way to the different cultures and persons in the community.*

Looking at the psychological effects of cross-, multi-, and intercultural contact on individuals and communities, we can now identify the optimum outcome whereby the individual is enriched by intentional, daily, faith-based contact with persons of different cultures, and in turn the wider community is enriched by the presence, perspectives, and lived faith of the incoming person. If this is happening, then the organic, evolving community is actually becoming, over time, a culture (or subculture) itself: "a meaning-making system"; an expression of "rule-governed creativity"; and "the form of social life." By virtue of this happy condition that we call "mediating," a person joining a community is able to live wholesomely, integrating significant personal values, skills, and perspectives, while at the same time embracing the values and virtues of the community. This is to live "in both," to use the terminology of Jung Young Lee; but because intercultural living such as we are discussing is essentially a faith-based undertaking, it is also an ongoing attempt to live "in-beyond." If this does happen, however, it will be due in no little part to the receptivity of the community as a whole and will in turn act to stimulate and affirm to the community that such an intercultural way of life is more than a theoretical possibility. But it does not come without the cultivation of mutual respect; this takes time and does not occur easily or without mistakes.

In the scenario labeled "marginal," an individual is conflicted because he or she is not at all convinced that his or her previously constructed worldview and its constitutive values and aspirations are compatible with the demands of the new community culture. By contrast, the "mediating" person is able to identify some different but compatible elements both from a previous way of life and from the life of the community.[10] There will inevitably be some giving and taking, some losses and gains, but the "mediating" person is able to make appropriate, healthy, and holy choices and sacrifices, the outcome of which is to promote ongoing formation and transformation in faith and commitment to the community and its charism. If this is accomplished as a sustained process, then the individual and the community will continue to grow in harmony and pluralism. Diversity will be accepted in theory and practice as potentially good and mutually enriching. At the same time, the individual's integrity—cultural and spiritual—will not only be safeguarded but also be made to flourish.

From Theory to Practice: Authentic Intercultural Living

Cynicism is the deadly enemy of fraternal coexistence, but so too is romanticism. We must try—by commitment and repeated efforts—to live by faith and not simply by sight, sound, or kitchen smells. To repeat: Jesus said quite explicitly to disciples who imagined that the road would be easy and the journey full of affirmation and kudos, "[F]or [you] it is impossible; but not for God; for God all things are possible" (Mark 10:27). Peter expostulated that he and the rest had "left *everything*" (romantic hyperbole, when what they had in fact left was daily drudgery, body odor, sunburn, the smell of dead fish, leaky boats, tempest-tossed nights, and so much more) in the vain hope of preferential treatment from Jesus. Even when they had been humored by Jesus' promises of later rewards, they were again brought down to earth when Jesus said, "and with persecutions" (Mark 10:30). Though some translations attempt to soften this to "and not *without* persecution" or "and with (some) persecution," Jesus' words are unequivocal: there *will* be persecution of one kind or another, as anyone used to community living knows well.

So what should any of us expect when we attempt to transform an international, *de facto* multicultural community into a faith-based, missional, intercultural reality? Early romanticism will certainly be in danger of turning to cynicism, just as early and superficial *camaraderie* will sooner or later be threatened by mutual misunderstandings, irritations, and recriminations. If goodwill alone is palpably insufficient, tenacity and fierce faithfulness will only be possible where there is a consistent and focused attempt to deal with the unavoidable challenges of intercultural community living. And that requires individuals' application to systematic and directed learning from and about each other and real study of culture rather than mere "cultural sensitivity"—which is nothing but empty words unless it is realized in concrete circumstances.

In chapter 2 we identified certain characteristics of a community that is truly committed to intercultural living, and they included not only appropriate correction but also a forum in order to vent appropriately, attention to overload and burnout, and the fostering of mutuality and trust. These should be powerful antidotes to any threats to authentic community living. So, if we struggle against cynicism (which finds fault everywhere and operates out of a cloud of perverse negativity) and romanticism (which strives to hide faults and wrinkles and often to avoid confronting reality), what might be some further wisdom for the road that we could ponder and perhaps acquire?

Each person will probably have his or her own sense of priorities here. That is as it should be, but it is also good to remind ourselves that our priorities are *our* priorities and not necessarily identical to everyone, or indeed anyone, else's. This of itself can be a helpful reminder to each of us: if I personally feel the need for and would appreciate more sharing or mutual interest, affirmation, or encouragement, it is most likely because I currently feel deprived of these things to some degree. Likewise, if I would look for more privacy and silence, I am identifying my own personal wants or needs. But one person's privacy is another person's isolation, and one person's silence is another person's hell on earth. Each of us will have to negotiate some cultural expectations and be sensitive to those of others. Nevertheless, there will be some virtues or attitudes that many or most members of a community will and indeed should share, since without that, the very idea of a community would be impossible to realize.

Genuine fraternal interest in other people in the community—though not everyone in equal measure, since temperaments and personal attractions vary—should not be at the cost of the development of a true *esprit de corps* or attitude of solidarity and support for the community project.[11] Again, the context we are concerned with is a community of *people of faith*, united in a common undertaking, and notwithstanding each person's different contribution.

Conversation is of course crucially important to communication; but much conversation in community can become banal or superficial, at the cost of authentic communication about critical issues of common concern and commitment. To outsiders, apprised of the reasons for a faith community, faith sharing would seem to be an obvious and important component of community life. But some communities may perhaps be accused of using occasions for common prayer—the Divine Office, liturgy, or other devotions—almost as an alternative to, or a way to avoid, real faith sharing. And some men's communities are, arguably, much less proficient or committed to this than are many women's communities, with the result being that it is possible to live amicably with people for decades and yet have little or no idea (or interest?) in how they live or struggle with their faith, and what wisdom they may have accumulated over a lifetime. It would appear *prima facie* that members of an intercultural community should make faith sharing a real priority, delicate though it is to organize with subtlety and respect for all. But simply failing to attempt to discuss the matter with a view to some concerted action on the issue can leave members isolated, deeply lonely, and hungry for one of the very crucial things that drew them to the community in the first place.

Lectio Divina, in common or in small groups, is another way for an intercultural community to mature in faith. Likewise, the very practice of silent meditation in the company of other people can be enormously encouraging. Cardinal Basil Hume once said that his own daily meditation was sustained by his belief that he was not entirely alone, and that God was in the same room—even though he could neither see, nor hear, nor even feel God's presence on very many occasions. But if we gather to pray when other people are silently but physically present, though we do not speak or even open our eyes, we do *know* of their real presence and of our common commitment to meditation and contemplation as our primary soul food.

It is not only the sharing of faith that is important, however, but also the sharing of at least some glimpses into each member's cultural background and experience. In chapter 5 we looked at the importance of social location and geography, embodiment, health and sickness, and attitudes to time and space. And yet it is still commonplace for members of a single community to have virtually no understanding of exactly whom they are living with. Conversation, whether informal or of a more formal kind, intended to allow for sharing of very different lives, can be enormously beneficial to everyone.

Years ago, a colleague and I used to team-teach a course called "Marriage and Family in Cross Cultural Perspective," he as a pastoral care professional and myself as an anthropologist, but both of us from a faith-and-theology perspective. Rather than attempting to identify or describe a perfect, or normal, or average family, my colleague always said we would be looking to identify what he dubbed "the Goodenough Family" from culture to culture: a hypothetical—imperfect, struggling, failing, and persevering—family, but nevertheless recognizable to people in whatever culture, and thus not only hypothetical but also very real. I believe that it is neither possible nor desirable to try to define or describe the perfect intercultural faith community, for the simple reason that it does not exist in nature. But, in our many and varied contexts, we can perhaps strive to become a "Goodenough Community," though never settle for what actually is, since this is the lifelong task of fallible human beings: always on a journey in faith and a work in progress.

Another colleague used to sketch a bumblebee on the board and explain that, *in theory*, it was quite unable to fly: the wings were wrong for the body weight, their angle of tilt was insufficient to propel it forward, and the extra weight of the pollen would make it impossible for the bee to take off from the flower. Then he would remind his students that in spite of the theoretical impossibility, "amazingly, the bumblebee does fly, and perfectly well!" It's an image for those committed to doing the impossible: making a multicultural, perhaps multilingual, and even multigenerational community into a functioning and frankly "good enough" intercultural community of faith and mission.

The last words of this chapter are from St. Paul, encouraging his community in Philippi to commit to the challenge in the name of Jesus: "If then there is any encouragement in Christ, any consolation from love, any sharing in the Spirit, any compassion and sympathy, make my joy complete: be of the same mind, having the same love, being in full accord and of one mind. Do nothing from selfish ambition or conceit, but in humility regard others as better than yourselves. Let each of you look, not to your own interests, but to the interests of others. Let the same mind be in you that was in Christ Jesus, who, though he was in the form of God . . . emptied himself . . ." (Phil 2:1-5).

We all know the rest well enough; but knowledge is only part of it and of itself insufficient. As Samuel Johnson put it: "Integrity without knowledge is weak and useless" (which is at least arguable); but "knowledge without integrity is dangerous and dreadful" (which is certainly very true). We have been given knowledge of great theological and spiritual truths, but more than that, we are invited—indeed we are co-missioned—to try to live what we know: our attitude should be the same as that of Jesus Christ.

Suggested Follow-Up

1. It would probably help the whole community if each member were to sit with and reflect on the diagram (figure 15) in an attempt to identify his or her current state and current efforts to come to terms with the bigger challenges.

2. Likewise, the person(s) in leadership might be able to use this advantageously to help and challenge individual community members.

3. Can you identify some of your expectations of your community members? Can you share them candidly with others, and hear their expectations of you?

4. There needs to be give and take in each community. What would you be prepared to "give" and what would you most like to "take"?

5. Do you share your faith—and other aspects of yourself—with people in community? Is there something your community could undertake that would facilitate the process?

6. Is yours a "Goodenough Community"? How might it be even better?

Chapter Ten

Cultural Responses to Intercultural Living

The Grip of Culture

We must now complement the discussion of psychological responses to the challenge of intercultural living by looking at culture and cultural influences affecting community. We already identified culture in general terms and described some ways in which it can be approached, understood, and reckoned with. Now we shift the focus and look at how some specific cultural influences shaping enculturated individuals will assert themselves in a community striving to become intercultural. Together, these should help throw further light on how and why individuals respond to particular social situations. If we seek explanations for various psychological responses in the individual makeup, the cultural responses in turn might tell us more about certain trends shared by people of the same culture.

But we need to be aware of two things. First, neither psychological nor cultural responses are absolutely determined or programmed: we can change, mature, modify, be transformed, and be converted, no matter how our psychological or cultural makeup may have played a formative part in shaping the person we are. The so-called "selfish gene" theory has been roundly discredited, and human cooperation and altruism are once more affirmed.[1] Jesus called people to change: "Unless you change and become like children [that is, aware that they have a lot to learn and must be willing to try], you will never enter the kingdom of heaven" (Matt 18:3). Cardinal Newman said pointedly, "To live is to change; to be perfect is to have changed often."

Second, it bears repeating yet again that we must resist the tendency or temptation to "play the culture (and psychology) card," hoping thereby to deflect incoming criticism or to claim special privilege or exemption from challenge. Quite often these are excuses, as anyone with an insight into that person's culture or psychology can tell immediately.

Human persons are not monads: we are not isolates, autonomous, or answerable only to ourselves. We are social animals who exist in a relational way with other people and the rest of creation. But as we saw in chapter 8, there are boundaries between people that serve several purposes, by no means all of them bad. These boundaries help us classify the world by processes of distinction or separation. Every verbal definition places a kind of boundary or limit around a word, specifically to identify it and to distinguish it adequately from other things. So an apple is defined both intrinsically (what it is) and by distinction (what it is not) as a species of *malus silvestris*, and as *different* from an orange, just as a particular kind of apple (Jonathan) is *distinguished* from another kind of apple (Granny Smith). Similarly, man and woman, whether healthy or sick, good or bad, and so on, need to be defined and classified, because the ability to do so provides us—specifically the person with language—with a way to bring the world under our control in some measure. In principle, the power to name and classify represents a fine human capability, without which the external world would appear random and chaotic rather than relational and connected. There is, however, a problem: human beings, and not only by means of language, show a disturbing propensity not only for defining and differentiating but also for demeaning and discriminating. It is then that this potentially creative power can wreak havoc in human relationships. We will first elaborate this notion and then consider the implications for intercultural living.

The Dignity of Difference

Chief rabbi and public intellectual Jonathan Sacks named one of his many excellent books *The Dignity of Difference*.[2] Having first identified the contemporary "search for common values" approach," which he judges completely inadequate in today's world, Sacks offers an alternative paradigm, urging us actively to create space for the flourishing of differences. In the context of a would-be intercultural community, however, we must be careful. Differences distinguish one individual from another, even identical twins. But pushing differences too far—that is, by defending our right to be different—might easily cause us to fall into an unhealthy and destructive individualism. Consequently, a community united by charism and commitment must not be divided and destroyed by the unchecked cultivation of rabid egoism. There has to be a balance between pluralism and common commitment, and Jonathan Sacks offers many insightful ideas to help us in this. His starting point is simple and profound: it is God who created the vast range of difference within creation, and therefore difference is godly and very good. Mere tolerance or disinterested pluralism on our part, or a detached "live and let live" philosophy, is simply insufficient. We need to recognize that the unity of God the Creator is actualized and expressed quite clearly—and indeed ostentatiously—in the diversity of creation, without claiming thereby a license to defend our differences at the expense of community living and a community project or commitment.[3]

Fifty years ago, Jacques Derrida famously spoke about "différence" and "différance," two words that sound exactly the same in French, but the second of which was coined by Derrida himself to point up the meaning of the verb "différer," which means both to differ and to defer.[4] In our context, when we aspire to respect individual and cultural differences, this can be a useful reminder to defer graciously to the other whenever possible. It is a helpful counter to a sometimes spontaneous tendency toward intolerance of differences and to defending our own position rather than deferring to another person. As Sacks says: "If our commonalities are all that ultimately matter, our differences are distractions to be overcome. This view is profoundly mistaken,"[5] because it would inhibit each individual and stifle the creativity a community needs in order to live the mission. So let us explore the contemporary challenge to intercultural living against the background of the dignity and critical importance of difference.

As we try to deal with our human diversity, we tend to apply one of two hermeneutical criteria: relativism or universalism. With the former, we would simply acknowledge diversity wherever it exists but without any attempt to act in order to standardize or reconcile obvious differences. But applying a universalistic perspective, we would first identify every difference and then feel the need to pass judgment on it from the conviction that there is only one way and only one universal and eternal truth. People with this perspective tend to resolve the challenge of differences through a dialectical either/or verdict rather than try to find a more tempered and compromising both/and resolution.

Sacks identifies Judaism with an attempt to respect the both/and approach, while Greece and Rome, Plato and Aristotle—and subsequently Christianity and Islam—espoused the either/or perspective. David Tracy[6] and Andrew Greeley,[7] among others, however, have argued that Catholic Christianity has a history of being more analogical (allowing for a both/and approach), whereas Lutheran Christianity developed a more dialectical approach. In the former case, creation is a manifestation of God in disguise but close (both far and near); typically, for Protestant theologians, God is not only disguised but also hidden (far). The most important implication for us is that God is encountered in creation and in human beings and, therefore, the better able we are to relate to creation and community, the more we may hope to encounter God. This is one of the implications and challenges of intercultural living. Christianity in general, however, has a tendency to fear or be suspicious of relativism as compromising or abandoning commitment to a universalistic perspective of one, single, absolute, unchanging, everlasting truth. In this view, if I know myself to be right or correct, and you are of a different opinion, it logically follows that one of us is wrong, and since it is not me (because I *know*), it must be you. "From this," says Sacks, "flowed some of the great crimes of history, some under religious auspices, others under the banner of secular philosophies."[8] We have by no means always succeeded in dealing in a human and Godly way with social and religious diversity.

There are billions of people in the world today, tens of thousands of cultures, and thousands of languages, but there is only one single human race within all this diversity and one humanity common to all; and the astonishing fact is that with all this, it *is* nevertheless possible for us to communicate with and among people of any language or culture under the sun. One reason for our xenophobia and less than human approach to diversity is what can be illustrated as the "cultural flaw": our human tendency to divide and conquer, to oppose and confront, to separate and discriminate. But another may well be our tendency to religious intolerance, self-righteousness, and the aggressive defense of "my truth" against all comers.

From Paradise to Brokenness: "The Cultural Flaw"[9]

The twin Genesis creation myths paint a picture of initial chaos transformed into order, essentially by God's creative and life-giving separation and discrimination: light from darkness, sea from dry land, male from female. But God and all creation—including the man and the woman, created different but equal because equally in the Divine image (Gen 1:27)—live in peace and harmony; "and God saw that it was very good." In the second creation story, God brought animals and birds to the man and permitted him to name them: "And whatever the man called every living creature, that was its name" (Gen 2:19). This power—astonishingly and gratuitously granted by God to the man—will also become a measure of human control, discrimination, and sinfulness: it represents the "cultural flaw." The ability to use language to name and define gives the user great power, and the author of the Genesis story attributes that power, first and foremost, to God. "Light!" says God, and there *was* light! (Gen 1:3). But similarly, "I name this ship *Invincible*," says the queen, and it becomes reality; "I declare you husband and wife" says the minister, and the words actually make it happen. This is the "performative" power of words, as J. L. Austin demonstrated brilliantly in his classic *How to Do Things with Words*.[10] When we use language to define something or someone, we do so by distinction as well as by inclusion. Tragically, this creative power can also be used destructively and disastrously.

In the second Genesis creation story, we are first reminded of the mutuality or complementarity of the couple: together they are one body, one flesh (Gen 2:24). But it is disobedience—eating the fruit of the tree of the knowledge of good and evil—that brings disaster, disharmony, and dispersal. And yet, there are two critically significant and positive by-products of the Fall: first, "The Lord God said, 'See! The man [that is, male *and* female] has become *like one of us*, knowing good and evil' " (Gen 3:22, my italics); and second, though the human ones were dis-graced, they did not lose grace entirely. These two things, conscience and moral knowledge, contain the potential both for humanity's greatness and its shame.

In the mythical harmony of paradise, there was inclusion and a community of "we"; after the Fall, there was exclusion, confrontation, discrimination, and polarization: the original inclusive community ("we") is opposed, polarized, and antagonistic: the man against the woman, and each against God: a world of "we" is henceforth split into a world of "us" and "them." This is the universal and pervasive "cultural flaw" (figure 16).

Figure 16

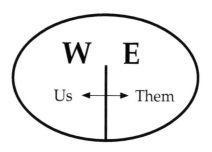

Every culture and language, by naming and taming, labeling and bringing under verbal control, distinguishes, separates, opposes, and excludes every bit as much as it includes, joins, or harmonizes. God's multiform and diverse creation is good, but the cultural flaw is the perverse tendency to see difference through the distorting lenses of discrimination, distinction, dissimilarity, divergence, discord, or disparity. Culture is what humanity does to the world in which it lives. And every culture produces, to some degree, the sundering of nature, creating the very separation and division that Genesis warned about.

Explicitly or not, from the raw materials in Genesis and the gospels, from "be masters" or "have dominion" (Gen 1:28), from "they become one flesh" (Gen 2:24), and from "what God has joined together, let no one separate" (Mark 10:9), human cultures have remade the world and often ridden rough shod over the earth and its people. As soon as "we" is opposed, split, ruptured, riven, and then renamed as "me" and "you," "mine" and "yours" or "us" and "them," the cultural flaw or tendency to reconstruct by deconstructing, and to advance by avoidance or competition rather than encounter and collaboration, is revealed. Left unchecked, this will of course undermine any efforts to create and maintain a healthy intercultural community.[11]

Insiders and Outsiders, Participants and Nonparticipants

The diagram below is intended to illustrate a universal *cultural* reality or social fact. In the present context it may perhaps serve three purposes. First, it can highlight the social conditions in the world of Jesus of Nazareth and show his pastoral-mission strategy. Second, it can, with due modification, help to identify some points of inclusion, exclusion, authority, and power to be found in every culture, including that of intercultural communities. And third, it might help to identify a particular intercultural community's outreach to "the other" whether within or beyond its own boundaries. So here is a general *cultural* description of society against which to measure our own individual and community responses.

In order to create and maintain an inner identity or social order, a culture or community will define itself first by drawing a real but vertical line between itself and the other (figure 17) so that "insiders" ("us") are clearly distinguished from "outsiders" ("them") or natives from foreigners. In some cases the line may be as concrete as the Berlin Wall, as massive as the Great Wall of China, or as ugly as the monstrosity that forms the border between the United States and Mexico; but it may also be a natural feature like an ocean, a large lake, or a mountain range. In other cases, the line may be invisible but no less real, marked for example by differences of language, ethnicities, or cultures within the borders of a single nation, as in the United States and many other countries. The more porous or permeable the line, the more likely it will have both a conjoining and a separating function; the less porous and the more tightly patrolled, the more its exclusionary function becomes evident. But within the "insider" community itself, every society draws another line or apartheid, and sometimes less obvious but no less real, as with gender discrimination or homophobia.

Figure 17

THE FOUR QUADRANTS

INSIDERS	OUTSIDERS
ADULT MALES/"VIPs"	**RESIDENT ALIENS/"STRANGERS"**
Holders of *authority* (legitimated authorization) and *power* (strength, capability, dominance)	Opposed, tolerated, and perhaps protected when appropriate
• **SIGNIFICANT OTHERS/ LEGITIMATORS**	• NOT SELF-IMPORTANT
○ HEADS OF HOUSEHOLDS	• VULNERABLE, AMBIGUOUS
○ MEMBERS OF PROFESSIONS	• DEFINED, IN PART, BY OTHERS
▪ *Physicians*	• TOLERANT OF MARGINAL ROLES
▪ *Financiers/Bankers*	• NOT INITIALLY "ON THE AGENDA"
▪ *Lawyers*	• FULL OF POTENTIAL
▪ *Clergy*	
▪ *Teachers*	• **JESUS THE STRANGER**
○ APPOINTED/ELECTED LEADERS	
• **THOSE WITH POWER OF SANCTION**	• DISCIPLES, LEARNERS (Greek: *mathētēs*)
○ MILITARY FORCES	• ALL RADICAL CHRISTIANS, SERVANTS,
○ CIVIL DEFENSE/POLICE	
○ RELIGIOUS AUTHORITIES	"OUTSIDER PARTICIPANTS"
○ POLITICAL/LEGAL AUTHORITIES	
①	④
②	③
NON-ADULT MALES/"NOBODIES"	**INTERLOPERS/TOURISTS**
Those without *authority* (social status) and with limited *power* (but not completely *powerless*)	• NON-CONTRIBUTORS: "PARASITES"
	• PASSERS-BY: "ONLOOKERS"
• **THE IMMATURE**	• SEASONAL VISITORS
○ *The unborn (lack viability)*	• SHORT-TERMERS
○ *Infants (lack language)*	○ *Employees of multinational corporations*
○ *Children (lack sexual maturity)*	○ *Those with diplomatic immunity*
• **THE DEVIANT**	○ *Socially insignificant/exploitative or dangerous personnel*
○ *Physically: cripples, the sick, paralyzed*	○ *Some volunteers or short-term missionaries seeking an "experience" or "immersion" on their own initiative?*
○ *Mentally: the insane, possessed, crazy*	
○ *Morally: criminals, murderers, prostitutes—"sinners" in general*	• INTRUSIVE "BUSYBODIES"
• **WOMEN**	• OCCUPYING FORCES
• **NONPARTICIPATING MALES**	

The left column is labeled vertically **PARTICIPANTS** (top) and **NON PARTICIPANTS** (bottom).

The horizontal line separates "insider participants" ("VIPs") from "insider nonparticipants" ("nobodies"); and different societies create and maintain it in such a way that it divides these into two equal or unequal groups. In some cultures, the "insider participants" are the majority, while the minority, substantial or not, are "insider non-participants." But if that horizontal line were projected to cut across the vertical line, it would create a figure of four quadrants: Top left (1) would be "insider participants" ("VIPs") and bottom left (2) insider nonparticipants ("nobodies"). Bottom right (3) would be "outsider nonparticipants" ("interlopers, tourists"); and top right (4) "outsider participants" ("resident aliens, strangers"). The diagram illustrates this social construct, created by the insiders and—implicitly, but very dangerously—from the patriarchal perspective, facts that are of enormous importance for our understanding of society and communities. Human cultures are patriarchal. There is no record of a truly matriarchal culture in which women alone would exercise authority and control and men would be subordinated.[12]

Quadrant 1: *Insider Participants.* This quadrant is occupied by the holders of authority who, cross-culturally, are usually adult males, but not invariably so.[13] Some have moral and/or legal authority (not only the authority to impose sanctions but also the discretion to appeal to another person's sense of honor or duty rather than to punish), predominantly at the domestic or local level; and some have authority associated with public sanctions—rewards and punishments—designed for the maintenance of law and order, such as military or religious figures. Others constitute the professionals skilled in medicine, politics, education, and theology. Together, these are the "participant insiders," VIPs, responsible for the maintenance of domestic and public order and services in the broader society. But sometimes they exceed and abuse their legitimate authority by wielding the brute power that can enforce sanctions but without the legal and moral authority to do so. It is important to identify when this happens.

Quadrant 2: *Insider Nonparticipants.* This quadrant is occupied by the people regarded in a particular society—by, of course, the VIPs or "number ones," and there will be variation here from one society to another—as expendable, useless, or without authority.[14] There are three primary groups: first, the immature (as yet unborn, infants, and children); second, those regarded as deviant (physically, mentally, or morally); and third, women. Some of these "have their uses" as is sometimes said: the unborn ("nonviable") can be brought to term, be born, and grow to maturity; infants (literally, "those without language") can acquire language; and children ("those lacking sexual identity") can become sexually mature adults. Likewise, criminals might reform, and some others, deemed "deviant," may become rehabilitated. But those who do so can only graduate into quadrant 1 if they are, or if they become, adult males. Throughout history, women have never—or only very rarely and under socially prescribed conditions—been able to cross from quadrant 2 to quadrant 1.

This portrayal—especially my identification of many women and other "nonparticipants"—is simply an attempt to sketch *"la condition humaine"*—the cultural lot of people down the ages and across the cultures: it is the "cultural flaw," the "original sin," the universal cultural bias; and its existence or reality poses a direct challenge to anyone committed to intercultural living.[15] And this brings us to the right side of the diagram containing people—viewed from the insiders' perspective—as "outsiders."

Quadrant 3: *Outsider Nonparticipants.* Although identified as "nonparticipating outsiders" in those cultures whose boundaries or borders are nonporous and exclusionary or whose members are extremely xenophobic, there may be virtually no such people; they are either irrelevant or simply unknown. Even today, there are some small social groups virtually cut off from contact with, or concern about, who or what might exist beyond their own little world: people such as the Amish; enclosed communities of monks, nuns, or hermits; or some small communities living in inaccessible parts of Amazonia. But in today's globalized world there are three categories that deserve mention. One includes outsiders who are social parasites and perhaps transients and even some who may pay their way but do not intend to contribute anything to the community. Most tourists are clearly nonparticipating in the sense that their purpose is entirely self-interested, if relatively harmless. They may be said to be important contributors to local economies, but that is certainly not their *raison d'etre*: they arrive, remain, and leave, entirely on their own terms. But there is a third category we can identify as unwanted outsiders: invaders, imperial agents, or interfering busybodies, including some perhaps well-intentioned but woefully inadequate and morally culpable religious and missionaries.

It is also important to acknowledge another category of people who are often treated as marginal and located between quadrant 3 and 4. Such are, for example, Asian Americans who often find themselves marginalized and treated as "forever foreigners" or "honorary whites." One can identify empirically how such people are treated—sometimes like other people in quadrant 3 ("nonparticipating") and sometimes like people in quadrant 4 ("participating").[16]

Quadrant 4: *Outsider Participants.* Looking more closely at this quadrant, we can identify their specific purpose and intention as contributing to—*precisely as outsiders and with their particular perspectives and the gifts they bring*—the well-being of the insiders, especially the "nobodies" or "number twos" (in quadrant 2), the "nonparticipant insiders." Such people can become champions of the poor and the nobodies when many insider participants exploit or ignore this underclass. Here the operative words are "outsider" and "participant" or "participating"; these two descriptors are held together in tension, as each component contributes something very particular to the interaction between insider and outsider, "us" and "them." Sociologically, the classic outsider participant is the person initially identified by the insiders as one of "them" (a rank outsider) but who, through a discernible and chartable process, passes, by structured stages, to a new status.[17] No longer simply "the outsider," nor an interloper or tourist, he or she now has the new ascribed sociological status of "stranger."

"The stranger" here is different from the sojourner or "bird of passage." He or she now has the status of permanent resident and as such fulfills prescribed and appropriate roles that are both clearly delimited and structurally and socially different from any role or status occupied by the insiders. Biblically, this is the stranger or "resident alien" (*gēr*) with specified rights and duties, in contrast to the biblical *nokri*, the sojourner or transient, who is accorded safe passage but who must not tarry and who has no permanent social status. But would-be strangers or resident aliens (*gēr*) cannot force or foist themselves on the community and must pass through the period of trial and testing before becoming accepted. One very significant reason for the insiders' caution is that although the stranger's contribution can be life-giving for the community, experience shows that strangers can also be deadly. ("I fear the Greeks bearing gifts" is Virgil's well-known line from *The Aeneid*.[18]) Both insiders and the stranger must, for a long time, act with caution; and the stranger lives in a state of some ambiguity precisely because of not being entirely integrated, never an insider, and thus inherently marginal. And yet the potential of the ambiguous or marginal stranger is enormous.

The stranger is not only identifiable as someone from outside but also as ourselves, for when we approach other communities through our apostolic ministry, we very often do so as outsiders in their communities. We should not imagine ourselves ("us") as insiders and others ("them") as the outsiders. Jesus identified his own *kenotic*, self-emptying role and status: "*I was a stranger*" (Matt 25:35). Because he became a stranger himself, this puts Jesus squarely in quadrant 4 or on its margins, whereas if he were only and always the host, he would be only and always in quadrant 1. This has profound implications for his way of doing mission and for our way of imitating him.[19]

The propensity to separate, divide, allocate, and stratify people is visible or lurks just beneath the surface of any culture or social group, even the most enlightened and committed. Jesus was only too familiar with a religious world like this and was at pains not to get rid of every rule but to subordinate rules, or law, to the legitimate needs and rights of individual people: "[T]he [Law of] the Sabbath was made for humankind" (Mark 2:27). It is by carefully identifying Jesus' approach to community living against the backdrop of his own culture that we, in turn, may hope to build an intercultural community out of the raw material of several cultures and many diverse people.

The Jesus Solution: Removing the Barrier[20]

As Paul says so lyrically, "[T]he law was our disciplinarian until Christ came, so that we might be justified by faith. But now that faith has come, we are no longer subject to a disciplinarian, for in Christ Jesus you are all children of God through faith. As many of you as were baptized into Christ have clothed yourselves with Christ. There is no longer Jew or Greek, there is no longer slave or free, there is no longer male or female; for all of you are one in Christ Jesus" (Gal 3:24-28 = Col 3:11; 1 Cor 12:12-13).

This revolutionary talk obviously does not remove the gender distinction between men and women any more than it removes the ethnic distinction between Jew and Greek or the social distinction between the slave and the free person: but it does abolish the moral and legal distinctions that taint every culture on earth and allow people to use simple differences to justify discrimination. From now on, Christians are called to be decidedly countercultural in relation to their fellow human beings. But this will prove almost overwhelmingly difficult because of the cultural flaw and our sinful propensity to separate and discriminate where God has gathered and blessed. After two thousand years, we have not developed a very good instinct for managing diversity, and yet Jesus' way and his example have been staring at us, challenging us, since the beginning.

The last chapter ended with the well-known quotation from Philippians 2, but on the subject of nondiscrimination and mutual cooperation, Paul says much the same thing, in different words, to the Romans, Galatians, and Corinthians. He instructs the Romans: "We who are strong ought to put up with the failings of the weak, and not to please ourselves. Each of us must please our neighbor for the good purpose of building up the neighbor. . . . May the God of steadfastness and encouragement grant you to live in harmony with one another, in accordance with Christ Jesus, so that together you may with one voice glorify [God]" (Rom 15:1-2). Immediately prior to that, he had warned them: "I say to everyone among you not to think of yourself more highly than you ought to think. . . . Let love be genuine; hate what is evil, hold fast to what is good. Love one another with mutual affection; outdo one another in showing honor" (Rom 12:3, 9-10).

To the Galatians he is more succinct: "Let us also be directed by the Spirit. Let us not become conceited, competing against one another, envying one another" (Gal 5:25-26). And he begs the Corinthians: "Now I appeal to you, brothers [and sisters], by the name of our Lord Jesus Christ, that all of you be in agreement and that there be no divisions among you, but that you be united in the same mind and the same purpose. For it has been reported to me . . . that there are quarrels among you" (1 Cor 1:10-11).

Evidently Paul felt the need to instruct his various communities frequently in this matter: the cultural flaw is pernicious and pervasive. But he does not only give criticism or encouragement; he also offers a full-blown explanation for the difficulties communities face and for the answers they seek. Paul is perfectly aware that the fruit of a common purpose and a common heart is not to produce clones; evidently diversity must be compatible with unity. But in the letter to the Ephesians,[21] written when he was under arrest in Rome in the final years of his life, he is able to articulate his mature insights and his thesis in some detail, showing precisely how Jesus approached the diversity that produces divisions in society and opposes people. He begins by highlighting the "us"/"them" polarization in his society. "You were dead," he says, "following the ways of the world." In other words, these Ephesians were "them," literally opposed to "us" (and Paul counts his former self among "them" prior to his conversion; see Eph 2:1-3). But it was precisely through Christ that God restored people to life: "God was pleased to reconcile to himself all things" (Col 1:20). Developing this theme, Paul now identifies the neophytes as newly reassigned from "them" to "us" because in Christ there is no longer division. The Jews themselves had classified pagans as "them," the uncircumcised, but Jesus himself reclassified them as among "us" through baptism into the Christian community: "Remember that at one time, you Gentiles by birth, called 'the uncircumcision' by those who are called 'the circumcision'—a physical circumcision made in the flesh by human hands—remember that you were at that time without Christ, being aliens from the commonwealth of Israel, and strangers to the covenant of promise. . . . But now, in Christ Jesus, you who once were far off have been brought near by the blood of Christ" (Eph 2:11-13).

Paul then shows how this cultural dividing line between "insiders" and "outsiders" no longer exists for those who belong to the Christian community—though he knows perfectly well that it does continue perversely to exist and to harden in civil society. The next verses are crucial, and the *Jerusalem Bible* translation begins well: "For *he is the peace between us* and has made the two into one and broken down the barrier . . . actually destroying in his own person the hostility" between us (Eph 2:14, my emphasis). And this was so that "he might create in himself one new humanity in place of the two, thus making peace, and might reconcile both groups to God in one body through the cross, thus putting to death that hostility."[22] Paul concludes that because Jesus literally put his life on the line of separation and discrimination, the "us"/"them" distinction no longer obtains; he has once again joined what humanity divided: "You are no longer aliens [*gēr*] or sojourners [*nokri*, "them,"] but fellow citizens like all the saints ["us"] and members of the household of God" (Eph 2:19).

This brings us back to the kind of community God had in mind at the beginning: a community of "we" in which the "us" and "them" opposition is resolved and the division is healed. It is a magnificent exposition of how Christianity has the capacity to promote the dignity of difference and use diversity in order to build rather than to destroy people and society itself. But it remains an impossible dream unless people—and Christians *a fortiori*, since we publicly profess it—strive to make it a reality. One of the primary tasks of people in intercultural communities therefore is carefully to identify what separates and divides its members and then, with equal care, to attempt to do precisely what Jesus gave his life for—the reconciliation of humanity and the creation of communities where difference could flourish for the common good. As Paul reminded and encouraged the community at Corinth: "Just as the body is one and has many members, and all the members of the body, though many, are one body, so it is with Christ. For in the one Spirit we were all baptized . . . and we were all made to drink of one Spirit" (1 Cor 12:12-14).

The common responsibility of members of intercultural communities is to bring this closer to reality by identifying our cultural differences and seeking to heal them in the spirit of Jesus.

Suggested Follow-Up

1. Identify some obvious differences among people and discuss criteria of acceptability within your community.

2. Can you accept to be a "stranger" and identify some of its potential advantages?

3. Discuss how it is possible for a community to marginalize some of its members.

4. Use Ephesians 2 (with several translations) as a discussion point within the community.

Chapter Eleven

Community, *Communitas*, and Living Fully

The Point of It All

Realists should not have a romanticized understanding of how good and joyful it is for brothers and sisters to dwell together in unity (the oft-chanted opening line of Psalm 133: "*Ecce/O quam bonum et quam jucundum habitare fratres in unum*"); it should be obvious to all—from experience or from reading—that to live in this way demands a great deal of work and commitment. As noted repeatedly, it is essentially a faith-based undertaking: we are not "colleagues" in a multinational corporation but members of one family attempting to live together as mutually indebted disciples. So our best aspirations must find their *raison d'être* not in simple pragmatic considerations but in much deeper personal and pastoral needs: we are driven by corporate fidelity to God's mission through the community in which we live.

At an individual level, intercultural living is demanded as constitutive of our life commitment, as members of international communities, to our ongoing conversion or transformation in a globalized and multicultural world. Pastorally, it is demanded by virtue of the intrinsic requirements of the ministry to which we are committed. Given that what used to be largely monocultural communities (even within international congregations or orders) are now increasingly multicultural and multiethnic, it is simply impossible to operate as in former times: a new form of religious living is struggling to be born. Today, when local communities within international congregations comprise people of several linguistic and ethnic groups, the "assimilationist" model of recruitment is less than inadequate: it is harmful both to individuals and to the broader community.

In the future, therefore, it seems that the development of international religious orders will proceed either by fission or by fusion. In the first case, if certain linguistic or ethnic groups are strong and members believe they can manage better independently, then fission—or "separate development"—is a likely outcome. Signs of this are already visible in parts of the world within and beyond the largely European cradle of religious life, where forms of tribalism, ethnic divisions, and historical enmities are not forgotten. Such signs are an indication and reminder of just how challenging it is to live together and how much easier and attractive the fission option can appear. But that would amount to a betrayal of our common commitment. Beyond these reasons, however, there is another: where members lack some vital skills or simply do not have the tools to deal with the contemporary challenges presented by personal, ethnic, linguistic, or historical differences, fission is almost inevitable. The purpose of this book is to locate and provide some of those tools.

It is ironic and scandalous that as the number of Euro-American religious continues to decline precipitously and most growth occurs in the other continents, particularly Africa and Asia, some of the ethnic tensions that plagued Europe are revealing themselves in these territories too. The result is that in some international, multicultural communities signs of rupture or fission are addressed by multiplying provinces or regions even within a single national or linguistic area. Where this occurs, communities may remain "international." But without a commitment to intercultural living, they will inevitably fragment as the demands of different cultures and ethnicities are addressed at the expense of an evolving international spirit of cooperation and *esprit de corps.* Santayana was right: "Those who cannot remember the past are condemned to repeat it";[1] not condemned perhaps, but they are clearly compromised if they have failed to learn.

This brings us to the second case: the alternative to community fission is fusion, or building the future on the solid foundations of intercultural living, which requires a mentality of and dedication to "integral development." In the previous chapters, we have explored various challenges facing members committed to intercultural living. The primary and essential purpose for intercultural living should never be for institutional survival. Rather, communities should commit to intercultural living so as to enable members to be more focused on and committed to the "missional" aspect of their charism. "Missional"—a word coined by American Presbyterians as a contrast to the word "missionary" as noun and adjective—can help us here. Classically, "missionary" denoted both a rather elite group of "specialists" working far from home and their "special" ministry of preaching and bringing the Gospel to people without it. But that tended to leave the people at home simply to concentrate on their own parishes or domestic scenes. They largely lacked a sense of mission because the word itself was invariably pluralized and attached to the word "foreign," as in "foreign missions," while "mission" itself was often understood very narrowly as focused on extending the church and making converts. But as many parishes went into steep decline because their focus was turned inward and concerned mainly with their own survival while current membership was dying, the understanding of mission itself was changing. "Missional" was coined in order to denote any person or parish, empowered by baptism, with a passion for outreach and inclusion, however far away or close to home it might be.

When the emphasis was placed more squarely on outreach rather than simply "inreach," on opening up the boundaries rather than protecting them, many dying parishes began to experience a new lease on life and sense of purpose: they discovered a deeper *raison d'être* which actually revived many moribund communities. The axiom then became, "we must all become missional," or we will die out and fail in our responsibility to those on the margins: homeless, indigent, excluded, despised people who nevertheless remain our brothers and sisters. Pope Francis has the same message with the old terminology: he says that *everyone* is called to be a "missionary disciple": there is no other kind of disciple of Jesus.[2] Intercultural living, then, must also have a missional focus or it risks the sclerosis of overinstitutionalization. To indicate how and why we have a moral and baptismal responsibility to choose this focus, we explore the formation, nature, and long-term prospects of community.

Community and Institutionalization

We can identify three kinds of community or stages of community development: spontaneous (or *communitas*), normative (or institutionalized), and mechanical (or moribund) community.

Spontaneous community is a condition or situation that actually precedes an established and structured community; it is almost a precommunity or paracommunity. Three examples may help. First, the "Pentecost moment": a multicultural group of devout Jews gathered for a Jewish feast with no possible anticipation of an unexpected outcome (see Acts 2). But then they were "amazed and astonished" (2:7) and unable to explain what was happening or what it could mean: wind, noise, something like tongues of fire—and people speaking and understanding foreign languages (2:2-4). While some of their number simply "sneered" (2:13) and accused their fellow Jews of intoxicated delusion, Peter addressed the crowd and declared this to be a mighty act of God, and three thousand were added to the fledgling Christian community (2:41). Here, we have a spontaneous community that will gradually become structured and organized.

Second, consider "founding moments" in religious communities: the (sometimes less than scrupulously exact) accounts passed around years or centuries later tell stories with many common features. Like those who "sneered" at the "Pentecost moment," some people at the "founding moment" would (and did) say that the group members were mad, deluded, or hopelessly romantic. Nevertheless, a small group—with an impossibly ambitious dream, little or no finances or resources, and often no support or even outright opposition from ecclesiastical authorities—inspired by a dream, commits itself totally, heart and soul, to its realization. This is spontaneous community, without structure or organization, united by a dream and very little else.

Third, if we strike a match and the phosphorous ignites, there is a very brief moment of combustion and a burst of incandescent energy. That initial flash is all flame and power, very much like the early moments of a spontaneous community. But immediately afterward, the matchwood or compressed paper catches fire, and the initial burst of energy settles into a steady flame as it begins to burn the length of the match. The spontaneous flare is prolonged into a steady or flickering flame only because of the match that sustains it. If there were only a drop of phosphorus but no match, the incandescence would be momentarily alive and immediately die. This too is an example of the characteristic or "spontaneous" energy in spontaneous community.

Normative community begins, as it were, *when the fire is harnessed or brought under control,* just as the flame of the match settles after the initial incandescence and burns as long as there is combustible wood or material: a six-inch match will burn for much longer than a two-inch match, though the initial phosphorous is the same in both cases. But a continuous moving and rotating of the match is necessary in order to catch the available air needed to sustain the flame. Left untended, a six-inch match would not burn its full length but would die long before the flame burns beyond half its length; it must be dipped and gently coaxed to keep the flame alive (recall St. Paul reminding Timothy to "fan the flame" [2 Tim 1:6]). If spontaneous community is generated with the initial combustion, then normative community begins when the flare settles into a steady flame. How does this happen when people, rather than matches and fire, are involved?

The beginning of normative community can be identified as the moment when, for the first time, someone utters the words, "we need to have a meeting!" There is truth in this frivolous-sounding statement because before there were any meetings, schedules, routines, or assignments, there was not simply chaos but real spontaneity. People worked until they were exhausted, ate—if there was food—when they were ravenously hungry, and slept where and when they were able. In that early phase of spontaneous community, resources were very often minimal and rational organization or "routinization" had not yet occurred. A permanent dwelling and a steady income were far from a reality and numbers were few. The movement from spontaneous to normative community develops in response to the increase of numbers and the development of a clearer and community-wide focus. The growing community now needs some order and a more standardized way of life. No longer can people work until exhausted and simply throw themselves at every perceived need: meals and personal space, prayer and the allotment of various jobs must be organized for the smooth running of daily life. By the time a rule and constitutions are approved, a community has already become normative, that is, adapted for long-term survival.

There is a mutual relationship between spontaneous and normative community; but before exploring this, a third kind of community must be named.

Mechanical community can be identified in several ways. Sociologist Emile Durkheim distinguished *mechanical* and *organic* community. An example of the former might be a brick wall: each brick is a constitutive part, but there is obviously no commitment or relationship between individual bricks. Organic solidarity requires an intentional expression of "one for all and all for one," dedicated to an end beyond and greater than what any individual can achieve alone. Mechanical solidarity might be seen in the instinctive behavior that unites a school of fish. Otherwise put (albeit less attractively), it may also describe the people at a parish liturgy. The fish might at least be said to have a common purpose, even though none of them individually is aware of it; but the same cannot always be said for people who forgather for some liturgies. By contrast, organic solidarity is expressed in the teamwork of a group of football players. "It is manifested by a group of people acting in unison; and though each person has a different responsibility, the outcome of the whole group depends on the commitment of each individual."[3] There is a "big picture" which is made explicit and embraced by all. The unusual strength of organic solidarity is that it can produce great breakthroughs and astonishing creativity.

But there is another way to describe purely mechanical solidarity: a group of people living under the same roof and accepting some formal responsibility but lacking any real sense of mutual commitment or accountability; this is much closer to mechanical than to organic solidarity. The history of monastic orders offers myriad examples of this lack of fire and enthusiasm (or the extinguishing of the fire) and an inexorable slide toward death. In the sixteenth century, the abbot's kitchen (not the whole community's kitchen, but the kitchen that served only the personal and social requirements of the abbot) at Glastonbury Abbey in England was big enough to spit roast four oxen simultaneously and up to a hundred swans, geese, or ducks: a sure indication of depleted religious zeal and a betrayal of the principles of monastic community life.

Communitas: "Community with a Task"[4]

Another name for spontaneous community is *communitas*; but the word is not self-explanatory, and an easy way to remember it is as "community with a task"—as distinct from any other community that might have lost its way. In that burst of spontaneous energy, that fusion of visions, that mutual commitment—to each other and to the ideal itself—there is absolutely no doubt that the small community knows *what* it is dedicated to, though not precisely *how* it will proceed or achieve its aim. It is clear about the end, though not about the means or the resources it will manage to generate. *Communitas* is sometimes described as "antistructure": it can be an ambiguous or interstitial stage on the way to more formal social organization. But its very "antistructure" (whether consciously resisting tendencies to create structure or simply struggling to find its way forward) is, paradoxically, predictably unpredictable. The novitiate experience—when novices are tested and not always clear about the way ahead—can generate *communitas*, a real bonding of people undergoing a common experience they believe to be worthy and valuable but the control of which is not entirely in their hands.[5] But such bonding is not automatic, and the process may not be positive for some or all participants. Assuming, however, the *communitas* experience continues to inspire and attract the participants, we can identify a number of features that makes it powerful and life-changing, and not only for them but also for future beneficiaries.

Communitas is marked by the highly charged energy of those involved: everyone is alert and alive. It evokes imaginative rather than simply rational responses to unpredictable situations. It resonates with questions that arise from the experience, asking "what if?" and "why not?" rather than being satisfied with responses like "we can't do that" or "that's impossible" ("because we can't afford it/don't have enough personnel/it hasn't been done before"). Above all, those involved in the *communitas* experience are utterly dedicated, both to each other and to the distant, invisible goal.

Communitas is the very opposite of organized routine; it inspires true heroism and it always faces a task significantly bigger or more challenging than ordinary or "normal" people would think of undertaking. Far from settling for what seems reasonably possible, the *communitas* ethos is idealistic and utopian in its dreams. But this can also make certain kinds of *communitas* both highly volatile and dangerous. One only has to think of Jim Jones or David Koresh—or some Jihadists and groups identified as fanatical—to know that people can bond and be driven by a common and dangerous mission that is also utterly destructive and quite the opposite of a noble or godly undertaking. And tragically, there have been fanatical, driven Christians motivated by—literally—crusading zeal or proselytizing fever.

So *communitas* might be generated in a Pentecost-like transformation, a founding moment of a religious community, an initiation process in a traditional society, or the insights, the *mystagogia,* and the bonding produced by the Rite of Christian Initiation (RCIA). Apart from the Pentecost accounts, we may think of the sending of the seventy disciples (Luke 10:17-20), the transfiguration (Luke 9:28-36), the post-Pentecost church (Acts 2:42-47), or an account in the *Letter to Diognetus* of the second century which describes Christians in the following way:[6] as "admittedly extraordinary. They reside in their respective countries but only as aliens. They take part in everything as citizens and put up with everything as foreigners. Every foreign land is their home, and every home a foreign land. . . . Christians are shut up in the world as in a prison, yet it is precisely they that hold the world together. . . . Christians, when penalized, show a daily increase in numbers on that account. Such is the important post to which God has assigned them, and they are not at liberty to desert it."[7]

Normative Community:
Institutionalization of Charism

As a match, once struck, produces a surging ignition and a brief moment of incandescence and then continues to burn with a steady or flickering flame, so the initial energy burst creating the first flaring of *communitas* cannot last indefinitely: it can continue to generate heat and light, but quite quickly the incandescence will turn into a steady flame. So it is that spontaneous community or *communitas* will settle into or become normative or *institutionalized* community. As a raw community becomes organized, structures are necessarily produced in order to ensure smooth running, efficiency, division of labor, and long-term stability, or at least survival. This is institutionalized living:

much more ordered and predictable than *communitas* living, its essential purpose is the maintenance of the community over time. If we make a rough contrast here between mission and maintenance, *communitas* focuses on mission while *institutionalization* tries to ensure maintenance. Just as mission and maintenance should be held in tension, so with *communitas* and *institutionalization*: both are necessary. Unless the initial burst of *communitas* energy is sustained over time, a fledgling community will simply burn out—like an ignited match deprived of air.

So *communitas* actually needs *institutionalization* if the community and its mission are to survive. But normative, or institutionalized, community also needs to be inspired by periodic bursts of *communitas*-energy, lest it settle into a comfortable but uninspired routine and the energy and commitment of the members become diffused and drained of the passion and conviction that marked the original *communitas* moment. Institutionalized community can be very effective in ensuring an efficient distribution of labor, but without the animation, inspiration, and imagination that mark *communitas*, it will become overcautious, unduly prudent, judiciously balanced, and commonplace rather than bold and open to risk and to the Spirit. Many features of normative or institutionalized community life are themselves designed to evoke *communitas*-energy: provincial or general chapters, annual retreats, or the celebration of jubilees or centenaries.

Spontaneous community (*communitas*) has the ability to generate the kind of thrust required for an airplane to take off, while sustained, level flight is like the smooth running of normative community. But long-term community renewal always requires the rediscovery of *communitas* energy because of entropy: a community with no *communitas* energy will become like a fire that loses its flame and gradually cools. Unless, therefore, the spark of *communitas* can be struck again from the flint of community, the group will run out of creative ideas and generosity of spirit. Spontaneous community (*communitas*) is to normative, institutionalized community as the flame is to the coal, as the spark is to the flint, or as the fuel is to the rocket. "Both are necessary, but the active agent is *communitas*. When the flame dies, when the spark fails, when the fuel is depleted, no coal can produce heat, no flint, flame, no rocket, liftoff"[8]—and no normative community can generate the passion and conviction necessary for it to remain faithful to God's mission and its own. The question then is: how much *communitas* is necessary to ensure that periodic bursts of energy are adequate to keep the community focused on mission rather than simply maintenance?

Mechanical Community

Little more need be said about mechanical community; our topic is building and strengthening intercultural communities, and our underlying assumption is that anyone reading this book brings a positive attitude to the enterprise. Mechanical community is a pathological condition that describes a community heading in the direction of terminal decline. Nevertheless, by identifying some dangerous symptoms that might develop in an intercultural community, this direction might still be reversed; it is not inevitable, and conversion is always possible.

The first, most obvious symptom would be a breakdown in interpersonal communication. The community might seem to be functioning effectively, but certain formalities would begin to replace authentic mutual interest. Notice boards might ensure the efficient flow of information but at the expense of real communication. Liturgy and common prayer might continue but with increasing recourse to standard formulae and creeping ritualism rather than creativity and life-giving ritual. Second, there would be a noticeable turning within, rather than a reaching out in ministry at the margins, with and for the people who live there.

Years ago, sociologist Georg Simmel identified this as a tendency, especially, he claimed, for old[er] people, to live "either in a wholly centralized fashion, peripheral interests having fallen off and being unconnected with his essential life and its inner necessity; or his center atrophies and its existence runs its course only in isolated petty details, accenting mere externals and accidentals."[9] He has a point, although its applicability is surely not limited to the old or to males; and what he calls "peripheral interests" refers to those things that were once vitally important (what would be central to our vocation) but are no longer so. In fact, in that same essay Simmel wrote that adventure is something that starts on the very periphery of our life but works its way to the very center, which seems to apply quite well to the experience of members of an intercultural community. Moreover, he puts his finger unerringly on one characteristic of those whose community has become sclerotic and pathological: the concentration on "externals and accidentals" like playing too much golf, watching too much TV, reading too many novels, and chronic self-indulgence. How much amounts to "a concentration" on, or "too much" of these things, is a matter of judgment and discernment. But any community whose members fail to direct their energies centrifugally toward the mission is a community moving inexorably toward its own death.

How Much *Communitas*-Energy Is Needed?

Every automobile requires fuel and every fire needs a spark. So what can we say about the *communitas*-energy needed to keep a community faithful to the mission and living a purposeful life? I offer little more than a possible heuristic device or "discovery procedure," and certainly not a finely calibrated scientific model, as a way to identify whether there is sufficient energy, drive, or commitment ("critical mass") to sustain a community in its faithfulness to charism and mission.

In order to answer the question—vitally important for the future of any community, whether numerous or few, young or old—each person must be asked to state his or her position on the common or community project and his or her commitment to it.[10] Then imagine a community of one hundred persons (figure 18) in which up to twenty are passionate, committed, and actively promoting the mission of the community. It then becomes important to identify the dispositions of the rest of the community. There are probably some members who are "free riders,"[11] "foot draggers," "abbey lubbers," or "resisters,"[12] but if they are relatively few, they need not seriously compromise the mission. If each community member has been asked personally, it should not be too difficult to gauge the numbers. So, if we identify up to 20 percent of the community as positively, avidly, and actively engaged, and up to a corresponding 20 percent who generate negative energy, alienation, resistance, or noninvolvement with the community project, this still leaves the majority (60 percent) whom we can designate the "pivotal group." The diagram looks something like this:

Figure 18

SEEKING THE "CRITICAL MASS"

POSITIVE ENERGY	PIVOTAL GROUP	NEGATIVE ENERGY
20 percent	60 percent	20 percent

The people in the pivotal group are in a real sense critical to the community enterprise and survival. Some of them, and perhaps most, may be aged, infirm, or incapacitated, but they will also be among the most dedicated and faithful community members. Assuming that a community can identify three-quarters of this pivotal group (three-fourths of 60 percent = 45 percent of the whole) as zealous and committed to the community's mission, that leaves the other quarter (one-fourth of 60 percent = 15 percent of the whole) who, though not alienated or actively resisting, are lukewarm, torpid, procrastinating, or unreliable, or like the son who told his father that he would go to the vineyard but then failed to do so (Matt 21:30). Then we are left with a rough and ready calculation (figure 19). The figure of 65 percent positive energy is made up of the 20 percent positive energy plus three-fourths of the 60 percent (the pivotal group); the 35 percent negative energy is made up of the 20 percent of resisters or free riders, plus one-fourth of the 60 percent in the pivotal group. So, with virtually a two-thirds majority of the community either generating great energy or supporting those who have it, through prayer, moral support, and real approval, it would look like the community certainly has a "critical mass" of *communitas*-energy with which to remain committed to the mission.

Figure 19

CALIBRATING THE "CRITICAL MASS"

TOTAL POSITIVE ENERGY	TOTAL NEGATIVE ENERGY
20 percent + 45 percent = 65 percent	20 percent + 15 percent = 35 percent

If, however, the aggregate of positive energy fell below 50 percent of the whole community, it would be doubtful whether there is a critical mass; then people will make decisions, some leaving the community to join one with more energy and focus, others "retiring" and no longer being accountable to legitimate authority. This effectively signals the demise of any community.

This is a simple and approximate way of identifying the "critical mass." Originally the phrase itself referred to the minimum quantity of radioactive material which would enable a chain reaction to proceed, but it serves very well to identify the minimum amount of missional commitment needed to ensure that a community is alive and faithful. Although these are approximate figures, any community can make more precise calculations on the strength of which to shape future policies. Evidently, the higher the percentage of positive energy above a threshold of 60 percent (or the lower the percentage of negative energy below a threshold of 40 percent), the more vital a community will be and the more committed to the mission.

The importance of the support of the majority of the "pivotal group" cannot be overemphasized: that a community is depleted in numbers, and ailing and aging is of itself no impediment to the community's faithfulness to the mission. Many people, infirm or inactive, are a tremendous blessing and resource for the whole community and beyond because of their missional zeal and fierce faithfulness. Their commitment can be an inspiration to the positive 20 percent with the physical energy but very much in need of the moral support of the community. Some of the oldest members were their former mentors, remain respected figures, and are dedicated to prayer—the dynamo of individuals and communities.

A conundrum remains. Younger community members may not be culturally free to make important future decisions while the elders remain alive; afterward, they will have no choice. But if it is unclear what directions will be taken in twenty years, how will today's younger members live faithfully in the meantime? The conundrum must be addressed by current leadership.

Communitas, Liminality, and Creativity

Communitas-energy is an imperative for survival and places serious responsibility on community members, but the deep connection between *communitas* and *liminality* must also be acknowledged. *Communitas* refers both to a group with a common vision and the energy it generates—and by extension, to the community with a critical mass of commitment to the challenge of a noble cause. Its classical manifestation is the adventure of an initiation process whose outcome is unclear but whose value is unquestioned: a novitiate experience, expedition, retreat, or life commitment. During that process, the adventurers or neophytes constitute a group separated from the wider community, and though they will later reconnect, they are for an unknown period of time marginal or *liminal*, betwixt and between a previous and known situation and a subsequent but currently unknown one.

Liminality or marginality applies to those who are deemed not to be mainstream, typical, or even normal. Theirs is a heightened and intense experience but may be unknown to, or of little concern to, some of the majority. Some highly zealous members may be marginalized by others who feel threatened or jealous: such is the lot of the prophet. Insofar as they are marginalized or ignored, they are often seen as, or know themselves to be, vulnerable, afflicted, and weak. Our tradition is full of examples of such weakness and suffering. Jeremiah cries out: "Ah, Lord GOD! Truly I do not know how to speak, for I am only a boy" (Jer 1:6); God says about St. Paul: "I myself will show him how much he must suffer" (Acts 9:16); and countless saints and founders speak of their personal experience of vulnerability or unworthiness in the face of a mighty task. *Liminality* or marginality is, therefore, more than simply fragility or infirmity; it is also potential strength and creativity, or what we might call *creative marginality.* To pursue this line of thinking would take us back again to the work of Jung Young Lee.[13]

Liminal people can form invisible bonds of support as a community of equals committed to an inspiring endeavor, united by a common vision and mutual trust. Though they cannot know the future, they are passionately committed to the journey. But if their endeavor is to bear fruit, the creation and maintenance of trust is crucially important.[14] If trust is broken, whether between leadership and the broader community or between community members at large, it is extremely difficult to repair; but since intercultural living is a *faith-based* commitment, the repair must be attempted as an urgent priority. *Communitas* is not the experience of a single individual but thrives on the mutual support of a fragile group or a group of fragile people. But individuals who are creative, innovators, visionaries, and pioneers are themselves in need of *communitas,* as was Jesus. Although *communitas* tends to lack structure, if it lacked all structure to support and sustain it, it would be rather like wine without bottles. In a similar way, normative or institutionalized community with plenty of structure but without the infusion of *communitas*-energy would be like bottles without wine. Wine and bottles can exist independently; but each is enhanced by the presence of the other. St. Paul expresses this relationship vividly when he urges Timothy to fan into a flame the gift from God or "rekindle the gift of God that is within you" (2 Tim 1:6). Without that, the original incandescence will fade and fail.

Fanning the Flame

Almost forty years ago, Lawrence Cada and colleagues wrote of the "vitality curve," a way of identifying changes and stages of growth and decay in religious life.[15] Like its members, a community is mortal. It may wax, wane, and die, but if it is refounded and reinvigorated at a critical point, it may flourish again, provided periodic bursts of *communitas-energy* are generated. Beatrice Bruteau, like others, has insightfully picked up this theme. She speaks of institutional growth or decay rather like the seasons of the year, "culminating in 'winter' when they are on the verge of collapse."[16] This would be due, in effect, to the shift from normative to mechanical community. At that point, she believes, there are four possible outcomes: "muddling through, descent into chaos, increasing authoritarianism, and transformational change."[17] In the terminology used here, this transformational change would be the result of a new infusion of *communitas,* without which, one of the other three possibilities would materialize.

As we consider the longevity of intercultural community living, we should also be encouraged by remembering that *communitas* is the lifeblood of community life, and that it requires the commitment of people who embrace a degree of marginality and vulnerability—for the kingdom of God. In fact, permanent liminality, as we noted, marked the whole of Jesus' life: he lived on the margins of society, experienced misunderstanding and condemnation, was abandoned by his friends, and gave his life for others. The challenge of intercultural living is the challenge of radical discipleship, which is neither easy nor painless. Jesus told the Twelve unequivocally, "For [you] it is impossible, but not for God: for God all things are possible" (Mark 10:27); "No one who puts a hand to the plow and looks back is fit for the kingdom of God" (Luke 9:62); and "Heaven and earth will pass away but my words will not pass away" (Matt 24:35). It is because we take these words very seriously that we commit to intercultural living for the sake of the future of international religious life and the mission it serves.

Suggested Follow-Up

1. Can you identify, in your own community, aspects of spontaneous (*communitas*), institutional (normative), and even mechanical (sick/dying) community?

2. Does your community have a "critical mass" of energy and focus with which to continue the mission?

3. There is a connection between *communitas* and *liminality* or marginalization. This is indicative of prophets and creative dreamers, people who ask "what if?" and "why not?" How blessed is your community in this respect, and how do creatively marginal or *liminal* members remain focused and faithful? Are there problems?

4. "Permanent liminality" marked the life of Jesus. He also had a community (who virtually abandoned him at a critical moment); and he had his prayer life to sustain him. So it must be for us. Where do you find community support, and how does your personal prayer life sustain you for the challenge of God's mission?

Chapter Twelve

From Invitation to Radical Welcome

Realizing Intercultural Community

In this book, each of the individual chapters—and perhaps some separate sections within a chapter, as well as each of the five appendices—might be visualized as pieces of a jigsaw puzzle. Each of them can represent the work that every community member committed to intercultural living is required to undertake in order to build the new cultural entity. And just as when a jigsaw puzzle is assembled, the finished picture that is revealed represents what the puzzler was attempting to re-create, so too if a community commits itself to the task, the day will come when a new, real, existential way of living becomes clearly identifiable.

But no puzzle solver would ever buy a jigsaw without first seeing and being attracted by the beautiful picture on the box cover, revealing what the completed puzzle can look like; this becomes both an incentive and a guide when nothing seems to fit and no clear picture has yet emerged. Just so, having attempted to identify various pieces and indicate their interrelationship, before concluding the present book we need to provide an overall image of what a mature intercultural community—not perfect, always in process, yet grounded in a clear vision—might actually look like.

Everything we have explored in the previous pages has been with a view to articulating not only how an intercultural community can

Figure 20

FROM INVITATION TO RADICAL WELCOME

	INVITATION	INCLUSION	RADICAL WELCOME
THE MESSAGE	*"Come and join us and share the riches of our cultural and religious tradition."*	*"Come and join our community and help us to diversify internally and internationally."*	*"Bring your cultural and religious values, your voice and yourself: help us to become an intercultural community."*
THE PURPOSE	*ASSIMILATION:* *We invite new people to become one of us as part of our community.*	*INCORPORATION:* *Marginal "others" are welcome but the community's style and practices remain.*	*INCARNATION:* *The community will be transformed by each person's talents and faith commitment.*
THE COST	*Little cost to the community: structures are set and newcomers incorporated into them. Resisters are marginalized or removed.*	*Some cost to the community: it preaches inclusivity but does not practice power analysis or self-analysis. Individuals sink or swim.*	*Significant cost to the community, striving to practice real inclusion and be mutually enriched through the infusion of new and culturally different ways of living the faith.*
THE OUTCOME	*Encouraging numbers, but the community is very monocultural. Those who are different are marginalized or overlooked.*	*High turnover of members. Whoever is not mainstream is muted or made to leave. Community remains largely monocultural, with few exceptions.*	*The community evolves organically. Difference is dignified and valued. Authority does not dominate but respects all. There is a common spirit and missionary commitment.*

actually exist but also, critically, how it can best fulfill a purpose greater than its own survival: the mission, the apostolate, the ministry it serves and to which each member is dedicated. The "model for"[1] such a community that I offer in this concluding chapter derives, in large part, from a grid produced by Stephanie Spellers, the author of a very helpful book for multicultural congregations.[2] In a way somewhat similar to Eric H. F. Law, she explains how churches can better welcome outsiders or "others" with their various differences and thus expand the cultural mix of their congregations. Her three stages, from invitation to radical welcome, fit very well with what is being discussed here (figure 20).

There are three vertical columns named "Invitation," "Inclusion," and "Radical Welcome," respectively, used to describe three different types of community, from the least to the most effective in the context of faith-filled and inclusive community building. Down the left side of the grid is a set of parameters that specify, first, the message conveyed by each of the three community types, and then the end in view, the means to the end, the cost, and the eventual outcome. So we can first visualize three contrasting communities: a community of invitation, a community of inclusion, and a community of radical welcome. Then we can analyze their specific features.

Three Types or Styles of Community

1. *A Community of Invitation*

The *message* conveyed here, implicitly or even explicitly, is that the community is already well established, secure in its identity and purpose, and open to new membership under certain well-specified conditions. Prospective community members will be made to understand the conditions for membership and then evaluated accordingly.

The *purpose* of the community is to be regenerated and to grow by assimilating new members. They will be socialized (acculturated to the existing community culture) and assessed according to their malleability, adaptability, and conformity. They must be both able and willing to fit into the community, but they will not constitute a challenge to it, nor will the community take them very seriously, at least in the early years. One of the features of the formation period will be to iron out, minimize, or even erase their cultural and personal variations from the community norms, and the corollary: to establish and inculcate those norms and expectations.

The *cost* to the existing community will be very small, but to the prospective recruit, the experience is perhaps traumatic. "Rules are rules" in the community and are not to be tampered with or challenged. "Keep the Rule and the Rule will keep you." Those who can conform may join; those who do not conform will not remain or will be marginalized. Should they persevere and want to stay, their conformity will come at great cost to their cultural integrity and the legitimate expression of their faith.

The *outcome*, for as long as this situation prevails, may be that significant numbers are initially attracted to the community (and here one would need very carefully to evaluate the "attractors" to see if they are compatible with the spirit of the community: educational and travel opportunities, upward mobility, or freedom from parental or kinship constraints may be significant contributing factors here). Nevertheless, if the community itself were to remain predominantly monocultural, with only token acknowledgement of other cultures (occasionally varied foodstuffs, dress, or liturgies), then the individuals would either sacrifice significant elements of their cultural identity (modes of praying, celebrating, mourning, socializing, and so on) or, if in the numerical minority, would be marginalized, overlooked, and effectively "muted."[3]

2. *A Community of Inclusion*

The *message* here has shifted from "you join us and we will teach you everything you need to know and do" to a much more accommodating "come and join us so that you can bring much-needed new blood, new perspectives, and new ways for everyone to approximate more closely to the community of inclusion envisaged and taught by Jesus." The message here is particularly attractive to outsiders aware of their differences but seeing them as strengths and not simply as deviation or deficiency. And to the insiders it is also attractive because it suggests that their longevity might be extended and thus the mission might be continued but with some new personnel, energy, and ideas.

The *goal* is no longer assimilation, which smacks of absorption and—for those being assimilated—loss of identity. "Incorporation" is intended to convey the notion that the existing community would willingly modify its own structures and procedures in order to receive people of diverse cultures, as a host would prepare to show respect for a guest or stranger by anticipating some of his or her real needs. This attitude also implies that the host community is an attentive listener, willing to accommodate to the guest's needs wherever possible, *for the sake of the mission and the community's ability to serve it faithfully.* It is not a matter of the insiders compromising principles nor of the incomer manipulating the community but rather a deliberate policy of realistic compromise in situations that have changed significantly since the "monocultural" era and the monolithic practices of religious community life—but always for the sake of the mission, the apostolate, and the needs of the recipients of a community's outreach.

The *effort* tends to be top heavy: explicitly focused on greater inclusivity and diversity, yet significantly less sensitive to the needs for structural change in the community, which would entail primarily a careful assessment of power distance and power analysis.[4] The rhetoric sounds attractive but the reality proves less so. The clash of expectations when people from high-power-distance cultures engage with those from low-power-distance cultures can cause enormous confusion and mutual misinterpretation. Again, members of a stable, and particularly a monocultural, community might be perfectly at ease with how authority is exercised. But add some new members from different cultural backgrounds, and resistance, misinterpretation, and simmering hostility can erupt into resentment and even rebellion.

How power (and authority) is distributed in the community is a matter that needs to be reappraised with great delicacy and finesse if a previously stable community is to be able to function when new people with different experiences and expectations enter it. Unaddressed misunderstandings can be the seedbed for raw and racist responses from community members that could have been anticipated and perhaps avoided if the topic of power and authority had been addressed at community level. That is certainly not to say, however, that every negative eventuality can be headed off simply by inviting everyone to sit down and calmly discuss issues. Nevertheless, many of our misunderstandings are due to implicit cultural understandings and attitudes that would not be contested in a monocultural environment but produce significant confusion, leading to negative judgments in a multicultural community.

The danger faced by a community ostensibly committed to inclusion is that the power and authority holders take too much for granted and do not listen to other voices. A general appeal by leadership to all members to be tolerant and loyal may foreclose on a much-needed open discussion. And if those in positions of leadership feel under threat, the original warm welcome offered by the community may well cool rapidly, and incomers of cultures different from that of the leadership may be left to fight a lone battle against overwhelming odds.

The sad *outcome* (sad because, among other things, it was avoidable) is a constant stream of two-way traffic: people are attracted by the promises and the prospects but the reality is not what they expected or can deal with. Consequently, some will leave and some will stay for a shorter or longer period while they assess their position. If they feel consistently overlooked or marginalized, they may leave. And if one person who was their anchor or moral leader should decide to leave, often several more may do likewise as a consequence. The community, however, fails to understand the dynamics involved; and despite tokenism in respect of minority individuals or cultural differences, the institutional mind-set and organization remains resolutely monocultural and apparently unable to imagine a future different from its own past experience.

3. *A Community of Radical Welcome*

Such a community can only come into being as a result of a previous moment or process of conversion among the members. Sometimes this happens as a result of an initiative within the community, as when it reflects seriously on the call of Vatican II to return to its roots and undertake a process of *ressourcement*: both a reexamination of its hidden or overlaid tradition or foundational *sources* and a renewal brought about by discovering new *resources*. The most obvious new resources that have been identified, particularly in the past half century, are the personnel themselves, increasingly drawn from many diverse cultures and seeking to be part of the church's mission in the context of international and intercultural communities. A simple "return to the sources" of a monocultural eighteenth-century foundation is obviously not sufficient without a "turn to the subject" or acknowledgement of the challenge and opportunity afforded by the new personnel resources themselves.

For as long as the classical "assimilationist" model dominated, even though there might have been a trickle of people of diverse cultures, they were certainly not allowed to modify old ways of community organization and old understandings of "The Truth" as a commodity held proudly by the community. In today's church, however, the insights of people of diverse cultures must be truly appreciated as adding new and intrinsically important elements to the Body of Christ. The church needs to be open to and appreciative of new ways of living faith through culture, new understandings of truth not as a commodity but as a treasure still being discovered. Consequently there must be new approaches to mission itself. Without such discoveries and approaches, there will be no radical reimagining and restructuring of community living that would equip it to engage with contemporary challenges, much less to measure up to the future.

Increasing openness to people of different cultures, though stimulated by Vatican II, did not originate within the church. Rather, in many ways, Vatican II was a response to a changed world and church as much as it was an initiative. And the most obvious stimulus for community conversion though was ultimately the fact that people from different cultures—formerly recipients of the Christian message but now commissioned by their own baptism—now wanted to take a more active and even lifelong part in God's mission. These two sets of stimuli—the call to retrieve the best insights and practices from the founders and the call to respond to and collaborate with people of different cultures and experiences—are the prerequisites for the formation of intercultural communities. Where each of them is taken equally seriously, there is a potential for the evolution of communities of radical welcome.

The *message* proclaimed by such a community is that there is an open invitation for people to come, without hiding or minimizing their own cultural identity and their own mature self, and to see if, between the existing community and themselves, a way can be found for everyone to celebrate one's common faith and vocational commitment, specifically in the context of a community of diverse individuals committed to developing a relationship of respectful interdependence and mutual respect, tolerance, and forbearance. Evidently this is a very tall order, but that is the nature of the invitation and the expressed desire of a community of radical welcome. It presupposes of course that the members of the current community are also actively seeking to develop some of the skills and virtues we have identified, and that they can show appropriate patience and mentoring to anyone who is relatively new to or just entering the community.

The *goal* of such a community is neither the assimilation of new members nor the assumption of their successful incorporation without appropriate adjustments from the current members. Rather, the goal must always be greater fidelity to their individual and common call and to the mission they serve as a community. This requires, on the part of everyone, a thoroughgoing attempt to listen, defer, encourage, and change, rather than simply to build on the assumption that incoming members will obey, conform, accept, and change themselves. A successful intercultural community will be measured by the attention of each member to the several "others" who constitute the total community. And such attention will generate in the spirit of each person a call to ongoing and continuous conversion, to be more conformed to Jesus Christ and more informed about and respectful of the differences encountered daily.

The *effort* required here demands that the community members prepare appropriately, not merely socially but psychologically and spiritually, to welcome the similarities and differences encountered in each interaction between persons. Particularly necessary is sensitivity to those from very different cultural backgrounds and to those who constitute a cultural minority of one in the community; but this must not mean treating other adults like helpless children. There is always a tendency either to be intimidated by, and consequently to withdraw from, "otherness," or to be attracted by its novelty and want to domesticate or control it. Therefore real maturity is required if people from very different backgrounds and with very different experiences are to successfully bond and form mature relationships of mutual interdependence.

The *result*, it is tempting to say, would be a perfect community. But there is no such thing; and because communities are organic, changing, and evolving, the result will in fact be a community of persons committed to each other, the mission, and their own ongoing conversion. But its particular characteristic would be that it demonstrated the real possibility that people can be united rather than divided by their differences, and that the community is striving to see, as God sees, that differences can be profoundly enriching. God's creation itself is manifest in limitless differences and human society in unnumbered cultures. But God calls the whole human community to try to live as a family, and cultural differences are themselves part of what it means to be human. The prayer of Jesus, asking his *abba* that "they may all be one" (John 17:11, 21) is the reason for our efforts to make community, and St. Paul's hymn to unity in diversity ("For just as the body is one and has many members, and all the members of the body, though many, are one body, so it is with Christ" [1 Cor 12:12-27]) is our inspiration.

Of course, people have said, and some still maintain, that this is impossible, hopelessly romantic, or even wrongheaded, and that "separate development" is best for everyone. That kind of argument is only a step away from enforced *apartheid* or Hitler's "Final Solution," and as far away from the call of Jesus as one could imagine. His call to unity-in-diversity is the ideal for which we strive. Jesus never tried to hide the real cost: impossible for human beings, but still possible with God's help (see Mark 10:27). That is why any aspirations to forming intercultural communities—intellectual and moral commitment notwithstanding—are ultimately and unequivocally an act of faith, sustained by hope and strengthened by love.

Suggested Follow-Up

1. Can you—individually and as a community—identify the message, the purpose, the cost, and the outcome implicit in your own community?

2. Can you suggest possible improvements that would bring your community into greater conformity with the hope of your founders and the call of Jesus?

"Cultural Baggage"

For years I warned students never to use a dictionary definition when dealing with theological words like "spirituality" or "hope." Theological language is specialized, and a typical dictionary cannot cope adequately with it. But now I am about to invoke a dictionary definition myself, partly because it is apt and partly because the word I want to explore is not exactly a theological word: it is simply "baggage."

Whenever we travel far from home we carry luggage or baggage. The words carry both positive and negative connotations. Positively, they identify whatever is necessary for our journey and sojourn; negatively, the *Random House Dictionary* definition is "things that encumber freedom, progress, development, or adaptability," with an added reference to "intellectual baggage," or whatever "keeps one from thinking clearly; [or] neurotic conflicts that arise from struggling with too much emotional baggage." This provides us with a helpful topic for reflection: what do we carry with us on our cross-cultural and intercultural experiences? Is it necessary and helpful or could some of it be left behind? We can hardly travel far or for long periods without any baggage at all, yet much of what we do carry often proves superfluous or useless in the situations we encounter. With these thoughts in mind, we consider some "cultural baggage" that we may carry and assess its appropriateness in the circumstances in which we find ourselves.

As cultural beings, creatures formed and shaped by culture, we simply cannot abandon every feature of our (enculturated) cultural identity and travel culturally naked toward a cross-cultural encounter. But we are hardly even aware of, or simply take for granted, some items of our cultural baggage until confronted by a situation in which they seem quite out of place or in striking contrast to the styles and fashions that surround us. We briefly consider a handful of such items and see how necessary or disposable they may be, starting with ethnocentrism, already mentioned.[1]

1. Ethnocentrism

The human propensity to see things and form opinions initially from a subjective viewpoint is perfectly normal and natural; but left "unredeemed" or not counterbalanced by a serious attempt to see things rather more objectively or from other perspectives, it can be pernicious and destructive. Unredeemed ethnocentrism is synonymous with bias, prejudice, and condescension—all the way to racism, sexism, clericalism, and many of the other poisonous "-isms." From the brute fact that I am not the center of the universe and that there are myriads of other people with their own subjective views, it follows that if there is to be any authentic communication between people— and *a fortiori* between people of diverse cultures or ethnicities—there must be a conscious and mutual attempt to identify their respective ethnocentric biases and to strive to see or appreciate other possible perspectives too. This is not at all to say that everyone must immediately abandon the principles they live by, but at least that they should put them to the test of dialogue. Ethnocentrism gives us a narrow and myopic view of reality that is simply not good enough to serve us adequately in novel situations. As a piece of cultural baggage, it needs to be replaced by something much more suitable: binocular vision and balance.

2. Relativism

At its most simple, relativism refers to any theory or criterion of judgment that is subject to revision as circumstances vary. This would be a "live and let live" approach to human differences—in food, fashion, furnishings, and all the rest. But there are degrees of relativism that need to be identified. Extreme or "absolute" relativism would hold that "anything goes" and that there are no universally applicable standards: everyone is free to do whatever one chooses and nobody has the right to interfere. This of course is a recipe for total anarchy or lawlessness.

On the other hand, people who encounter certain things (much easier to see in cultures other than their own), such as maltreatment of women through sexual trafficking, domestic violence, slavery or restraint of freedom, child labor or child pornography, the imposition of the death penalty, or preemptive military strikes, and so on, are understandably upset and even outraged. For the most part, these people are "relative" relativists: they believe that mutual tolerance and freedom are necessary but not unlimited, that some things are relative or optional—but not everything.

In an intercultural community, the cultural baggage each person brings, including tolerance or intolerance of relativism, will be put to the test. Extreme or unnuanced relativism (complete lack of any moral standards, sheer arbitrariness about them, or assertion of one's entitlement to do what one pleases) is evidently totally unacceptable. This cultural baggage has no place in an intercultural community. On the other hand, since each person may well have some practices or behaviors that others might find difficult or even objectionable, everyone together will have the responsibility of determining what constitutes suitable "baggage" to be brought into the community. It will fall somewhere between the extremes of absolute uniformity and complete self-interest.

3. Romanticism

A person may come to a community with an open mind and heart but also be very naïve. Such romantics are "fanciful, impractical, and unrealistic," as the dictionary aptly puts it. They believe, with Molière's *Candide*, that they are living in "the best of all possible worlds." They are not, and none of us is. Consequently, romantics will find community life difficult at times and will probably make it difficult for others unless they become much more realistic (but without degenerating into cynicism): romantics tend to see everything as good or to make-believe everything is good, whereas cynics perceive the opposite and become embittered and selfish. The romantic is forever an optimist, always looking at, or for, the good in everyone and everything; but the realist is aware of the imperfections in human beings and their cultures, and the virtuous realist is appropriately tolerant and forgiving. The difficulty for the romantic will become apparent when something does go badly wrong or when personal bad news arrives. The difficulty for the community is that the romantic's *naiveté* grates on everyone else after a while. Romanticism should have been grown out of before one leaves home and joins a community. It is baggage that should not have been brought, but it is possible that a person can gently and gradually lay it aside.

4. Pessimism

Where the congenital romantic tends to overlook or simply not see certain significant imperfections, the habitual pessimist seems to be programmed to see nothing else. If the romantic is "eternal sunshine" and the pessimist is "eternal gloom," then reality and the realist can be found somewhere in between. The realist does not come to a situation with mind made up but weighs the evidence before making a judgment. Chronic pessimism and the inveterate pessimist contribute nothing to the community and have no place in it. To be pessimistic, however, is not to be without hope: pessimism is a tendency to anticipate undesirable outcomes, and it has its place; sometimes there is very good reason to expect a difficulty or failure. But the habitual pessimist expects nothing else. Hope, however, is a theological virtue and a nonnegotiable for Christians. Therefore, it might be perfectly appropriate at any given time to be pessimistic *and* still hopeful. No matter how pessimistic we might be, we should never abandon hope. But the congenital pessimist will create negative and depressing emanations that will ultimately require nothing less than total eradication from the community setting. As a piece of cultural and temperamental baggage, intractable, habitual pessimism has no place in community.

5. The "-isms": Tribalism, Racism, Sexism, Clericalism

Those who protest the loudest that they are not tarnished by any of these may be among the most at fault. Sometimes it might be best for everyone, as we engage with a new reality, inwardly to acknowledge that we are indeed prone to some of the above—and more besides. Tribalism, in one form or another, can corrode friendships and alienate friends, even though it can be harmless enough sometimes, as when one cheers for the home team. But if this is done often and loudly enough, it can become highly irritating to other people in the community: moderation rather than extreme chauvinism in any mixed group is usually called for. But there are also much more serious forms of tribalism or racism, sexism or clericalism that manifest themselves in rudeness, intolerance, or injustice toward people of other tribal or ethnic groups, another gender, or anyone outside the ranks of the clergy. In general, all of the "-isms" represent sinful excess or unacceptable bias: they constitute dangerous cultural baggage that the traveler should not be allowed. These things are toxic and quite antithetical to the spirit of a faith-based community.

6. Muted Groups and Representation

These last two items can only be loosely identified as cultural baggage: they are social facts or realities that are the *result* or *effect* of a person's cultural insensitivity rather than characteristics of that person's personality or disposition alone. But these results are certainly not acceptable, and insofar as they owe their origin to an outsider who comes to a community, they are among the baggage or impedimenta that ought to have been left at home. They represent the power that one person wields over another due to culpable insensitivity.

"Muted groups" are victims, those people whose legitimate voices are silent or silenced. They are included here because they may exist even within a religious community due to other community members who carry a certain attitude as part of their own cultural baggage. Some people subscribe to the principle that "children should be seen and not heard" but then generalize that principle. So they may apply it to junior community members, religious brothers in a clerical community, or people in initial formation—thereby not listening to them or even not giving them an opportunity to speak and to be heard respectfully. When this happens, there are muted individuals or groups within the community itself. Highly egocentric people may be the most culpable in this respect, particularly if they also operate with an elaborated speech code: together these two tendencies can lead to dominance over others who may be from a more sociocentric background and who operate with a more restricted speech code.[2] They then feel bullied into silence or simply not listened to when they do speak.

Two factors contribute to the creation or perpetuation of muted groups: cultural and interpersonal. Culturally, some people do not dominate a conversation, are respectful listeners and receivers of information and communication, and do not think of themselves primarily as dispensers of personal opinion or intellectual capital. If a conversation is dominated by articulate and opinionated persons, these listener-receivers can be isolated from any community decisions and considered as without voice or opinion. Eric Law has a very effective suggestion: he speaks of "mutual invitation" as a way of ensuring that nobody is silenced or excluded, but each person is invited to speak and contribute to conversations and decision making.[3] In any intercultural community, this could become a standard procedure, for community meetings and elsewhere, that would significantly address a situation in which there might be a muted group of individuals.

"Representation" is also not strictly part of one's cultural baggage—it is a personal trait. If a politician opens an address with a lofty, "I am speaking on behalf of all of my constituents," one should be able to determine to what extent this is true. But how can one person represent the view of "all," especially when the "all" represent a wide variety of people? Even more unacceptable would be for a cleric to say: "I speak on behalf of women, or the poor, or homeless people." It is easy to fall into this habit. The American bishops once tried this approach, proposing to write a pastoral letter about women—until they were reminded by women themselves that clerics had no idea of the circumstances, concerns, or emotions of the women on whose behalf they presumed to speak. A similar response was heard quite loudly at the 2014 Synod on the Family. In the future, these "muted" voices need to be heard, and people in various cohorts need to speak for themselves and be respectfully heard. If one person or group presumes to speak "on behalf of" others, the obvious question should be: "why can they not speak for ("represent") themselves?"[4] Too often, the true answer would be that they belong to a "muted group." For that reason such representation will always and ultimately be unacceptable.

These topics might offer food for thought and stimulate everyone to identify changes that might need to be made, attitudinally and behaviorally, in the context of a flourishing intercultural community.

Appendix II

Skills and Virtues for Intercultural Living

Perhaps ad nauseam, the affirmation "goodwill is not enough" has been reiterated in the previous pages, usually attached to the equally strong affirmation that intercultural living demands skills that must be acquired or worked at assiduously and continuously if people are to live harmoniously and remain committed to the mission. It is now time to identify some of these in specific terms. But rather than tabulating them, I will use the terms employed by several authors, though some of these are virtually synonymous.

Two prominent contemporary authorities, Wolfgang Messner[1] and B. H. Spitzberg,[2] created checklists[3] that I combine, gloss, and apply to our context. Two criteria are invoked: *appropriateness*, which requires that the values of each party be respected; and *effectiveness*, judged according to whether the aims and hopes of each party are fulfilled by the interaction. In our context, "each party" can be an individual and the community or a person in ministry and the people being served. We look, then, at skills of particular relevance to people in intercultural and faith-based communities.

Identifying a Skill Set

Self-Awareness: Sometimes referred to as reflexivity or introspection, it is the ability to assess the effects of one's behavior and attitude on others. It requires a degree of sympathy or empathy: the ability to project oneself into the situation faced by someone else. The self-aware person is conscious of his or her prejudices and limits as well as of his or her talents and personal qualities. Aware also of one's moral influence or standing in the community, the self-aware person is careful not to abuse personal power.

Appropriateness is sensitivity to different social situations, such that one can adapt dress, demeanor, or speech accordingly. Some people, otherwise perfectly competent, seem to have no or very little sense of what is appropriate and sometimes refuse to acknowledge the importance of respectful sensitivity to contexts and persons.

Self-Confidence shows itself in a person's trust in one's own ability to handle challenges (and awareness of limitations). It is not to be confused with brashness or reckless and foolhardy disregard of danger or convention.

Effectiveness is simply the ability to achieve what one sets out to achieve. But it requires realistic self-confidence and the ability to learn from mistakes. People who learn from mistakes will be more realistic about what they should and should not undertake and whether or not they can be effective.

Motivation or commitment to a goal is a prerequisite for successful intercultural living. Our assumption ought to be that anyone who voluntarily seeks to belong to an intercultural community has appropriate theological and pragmatic motives or a sincere willingness to change and sharpen one's motivation to bring it into phase with the broader group.

Flexibility is the capacity to change perspectives during the give-and-take of community life and to be appropriate relativists rather than either absolute relativists (lacking any core values or principles) or absolutists (inflexible and wanting to impose their own values on everyone else). Those who acknowledge several valid insights or perspectives rather than only one will more likely change perspectives appropriately. The flexible person is both autonomous and collaborative: grounded and rooted in personal values yet open and adaptable to the values of others, being respectful of their otherness.

Open-mindedness: When people of different cultures meet with the intention of forming real bonds of collaboration, the open-mindedness of each is crucial to the outcome. Each one must find a balance between the principles and practices they need to hold on to and those that can be adapted and even abandoned. Compromise that does not impugn a person's integrity is necessary, but bullying or coercion of any kind will sour and then destroy authentic relationships.

Communicative Competence: Some people's frustration builds like a pressure cooker when they are unable to express their feelings or thoughts adequately. This is either because they feel intimidated or they lack the ability to express themselves clearly and without making personal attacks. Communicative competence is a skill that can be developed by those who genuinely seek and ask for assistance and who are patient with self and others. Impatient or threatened people are unlikely to achieve the level of competence required for harmonious intercultural living.

Tolerance is the ability to identify irksome persons or circumstances and yet refrain from attack or condemnation. Tolerance is not uncritical acceptance; that would amount to an undiscriminating relativism. Key to authentic tolerance is forbearance, which is patient acquiescence in what may sometimes irk or irritate. It is a much-needed virtue or skill for intercultural living.

Sensitivity, or an intuitive sympathy for another person's feelings, first of all requires that a person be aware of being one among many rather than the center of everything or the sole agent. It resonates with the moods and motivations of other community members and is able to affirm and console appropriately.

So much for a list of skills and values: an analytical presentation that isolates and separates. But in real life, people tend to synthesize or integrate, so we should supplement the list with some indication of overall attitudes that would produce whole clusters of skills and values—or indeed the opposite: incompetence, irresponsibility, or fecklessness.

So here is a more synthetic picture of skills and accompanying virtues that derive or grow from an underlying attitude or *habitus*—a mature mind-set or disposition that characterizes a person as an integrated whole. This picture is composed of "clusters" of several components in the list above, and the total picture is the aggregation of all the clusters. The selection and explanation offered here is not set in stone but might serve as a discussion opener that would, in turn, lead to additions and modifications in particular contexts.[4] Because these skills are not innate, they must be identified and worked for; this is part of the purpose of (religious) formation. By the time a person actually joins an intercultural community, some of these skills should have already been acquired. The actual skill level will vary among individuals, but skills always need continuous sharpening and refining in the actual circumstances of a person's life.

Forming a "Habitus" or Disposition

The following are more than individual, isolated skills; each specifies an attitude or state of mind lying beneath or behind specific efforts at skill acquisition. If the skills themselves identify *what* we need or seek, then these dispositions say more about *why* we seek them.

Respect for the Human Person and for Human Cultures. Ethnicity, as we mentioned, identifies who people are; culture specifies what they do and how they live. To attack other people's culture is to assault their spirit. A highly self-focused person will be insensitive to the ethnicity and the culture of others and indeed unresponsive to other people as subjects and agents. The level of sensitivity (or its lack) will determine whether sustained intercultural living is possible. The arrogant chauvinist—at the national, ethnic, or cultural level—has no place in such a community.

Commitment to Search for Truth through Respectful Dialogue. Some people believe truth is a commodity to be grasped and owned, possessed only by some. Then they either show scant respect for the other or they attempt to persuade others—by various means—of the error of their ways. But others see truth as a scattered treasure to be identified and uncovered through a collaborative enterprise of dialogue or mutual truth seeking. Three characteristics of dialogue might serve as a self-administered test. First, dialogue changes both parties. Second, the outcome of dialogue cannot be known in advance. And, third, from a structural perspective, dialogue and hierarchy are incompatible: they cannot occupy the same ground at the same time. If any these criteria are not met, there is no authentic dialogue but some degree of intransigence, manipulation, dishonesty, or blindness. Because an intercultural community needs authentic dialogue, its members need appropriate skills.

Cultivation of a Learning Posture. The word "disciple" (Greek: *mathētēs*) simply means "a learner." In an intercultural community,

although there are different people and a variety of roles, it is important that everybody becomes a learner and accepts this role. Some
may indeed be "teacher," since it is impossible to have a learner
without a teacher, or *vice versa*; but as Jesus said, role reversal is always necessary: in some situations the first must become the last and
the teacher becomes the learner (see Mark 10:43-45). Everyone has
something to learn, and only the arrogant and ignorant fail to understand this. They have no permanent place in an intercultural community and therefore must have, or seek to acquire, the necessary
skills, and urgently.

Learning "Downward Mobility" and Accepting Marginality. As the
gap between rich and poor (or the "haves" and "have nots") widens,
any increment in a person's upward mobility widens the gap between
them. If the purpose of intercultural communities is to serve God's
mission and God's preferential option for the poor, we must learn
from Jesus' example and choose "downward mobility" in order to
encounter those we purport to serve. This has been dealt with elsewhere; but since the only way to learn a skill is to practice and practice, members of intercultural communities must commit themselves
to a specific course of action in order to acquire the skill of *truly* encountering people through downward mobility and of *seeking* the
people who are marginalized by frequenting the margins themselves.
A great danger is that an unhealthy hierarchy is formed in a community and certain people (particularly the leader or those with
authority) have no time to reach out to the margins while other people
(typically the juniors or those in formation) are given assignments
that bring them into contact with people on the margins. But unless
everyone in a community is seeking downward mobility and a certain
marginal status, the community itself will fail to demonstrate a clear
commitment to the poor (*not* "The Poor," but specific flesh and blood
persons), community spirit will be adversely affected, and certain
people will become a countersign, claiming that their responsibilities
actually prevent them from encountering the *anawim*—which of
course is the very purpose of the community.

Cultivating an "Ecumenical" Approach. The word "ecumenical" is
used here in a broad sense to indicate openness to, and collaboration
with, people of diverse cultures and personalities. Everyone is aware
how challenging it is simply to live in a monocultural community
and to acknowledge and respect everyone's differences. To live in an

intercultural community is much more challenging, but one hopes that "forewarned is forearmed." People should be prepared in advance to work constructively with their cultural as well as personal differences. Without this sensitivity, it would be impossible to build a healthy community. But sensitivity alone will not take people very far; it is necessary to cultivate more skilled interpersonal relationships by practicing and fostering some of the attitudes already itemized.

Learning the Wisdom of the Midwife.[5] As a person with a distinctive social role, the midwife has much to teach us. The word itself comes from "mid," meaning "with," and "wife," meaning "woman": a midwife, interestingly, is a "with-woman" but need not necessarily be a woman. Persons with, attending to, and professionally supportive of a woman in childbirth have multiplex and critically important roles which include the following characteristics and skills: they literally have another life in their hands; they are life sustaining; and society cannot manage without them. Furthermore, midwives need both creativity and credibility; their job is neither to give birth themselves nor to interfere but to facilitate, to guide and affirm the birth mother. Midwives have always worked "on the edge" and proved particularly effective among the fearful, oppressed, and needy. The French term is simply *sage femme*, "wise woman." This can be an encouragement for everyone in formation, whether they are "midwives" (leaders) or "mothers" birthing new life.

Learning from the Social Sciences. A fundamental justification or rationale for this book is to offer and blend insights from the social sciences—psychology, sociology, and social/cultural anthropology in particular—with the accumulated wisdom provided by our theology and our religious tradition. Just as no adult can learn another language simply by being among people who speak it but must be intentional, motivated, and systematic in studying it, so many skills required for successful intercultural living cannot be acquired simply by living in a community for a certain time: real commitment and dedication to the task require specific steps—which can be taught by actively learning some of the wisdom of the social sciences. But since readers of these pages and members of intercultural communities need not become social scientists, information and recommendations are offered here in an attempt to share what might be relevant to a person seeking to grow into an intercultural community. Folk wisdom reminds us that whoever seeks or desires the end must seek and desire the means to it; the social sciences and their practitioners can offer the fruit of experience and practical wisdom.

Learning from Theology and Tradition. Without a firm theological base or rationale, we will not achieve any degree of honest intercultural community living. Since ours is a faith-based undertaking, we must return frequently to our theological roots and particularly to the life and teaching of Jesus: he is "teacher," we are "disciples," and the gospels are full of examples of what this implies, from "it is enough for the disciple to be like the teacher" (Matt 10:24) to "I have set you an example, that you should also do as I have done to you" (John 13:15).

Forming Virtuous People

Skills can be impressive, but our objective is not to impress but mirror and exemplify some of the qualities that marked the mission of Jesus and led people to follow him. First and last we are his disciples; we are not the Teacher, as he reminded us: "You are not to be called rabbi [teacher] for you have one teacher, and you are all students [learners, disciples]" (Matt 23:8). So we look at some of the virtues we should seek to cultivate for the sake of the community and the mission.

The formation of a moral character is incumbent on anyone who presumes to minister to others, which includes calling them to develop their own moral character. Sanctity and humanity must come together in an uncommon blend. There will always be something of a disjunction between what we proclaim and who we are, but we must be committed to closing the gap between the two. This requires virtue—specifically, a virtuous life. Here are five clusters of virtue that would seem to be particularly appropriate to anyone committed to apostolic intercultural community living. Some of them are included above, and it would be helpful to refer back to that list of skills. But specifically as virtues, they are products of God's enabling grace and our cooperation with that grace.

Patience, Longanimity, Tolerance: Virtues of the Servant. Patience includes a capacity to suffer and persevere. "Longanimity"—one of the Twelve Fruits of the Holy Spirit—is patient forbearance (from *animus*, soul, it means "soulfulness"). Tolerance is the capacity to endure.

Each is associated with a long-term commitment, and each is particularly needed in a community, a home that exists over time and is neither a motel nor a temporary residence. People who emphasize "self-actualization" and high personal achievement may need to acquire greater patience if they are to adjust to the demands of community. And endurance has the root *dur-*, meaning hard, hardened. We must become hardened, not like flint but like high-tensile steel: not brittle but flexible. To cultivate patient steadfastness in the face of misunderstandings and real suffering is to offer a powerful witness of compassion and commitment to God, the community, and those among whom we minister.

Humility: Virtue of Earthiness and Fruitfulness. Many writers have commented on the etymology of the word humility. *Humus* is the dark organic component of soils, the source of fertility and life. It was from the earth, the *humus*, that the human one (*'adam*) was formed. Mary, the mother of Jesus, is called humble because from her fertile body Jesus was born. The *Magnificat* is her exultant praise of the God who can do wonderful things with and for human persons. Like Mary, each of us is called to be fertile and to produce a harvest from all that we are and all that we do. From our humility God finds a voice to speak and actions to heal. Consequently, one of the most important and creative virtues to be practiced and polished in community is humility: fruitfulness. Community living should never be demeaning or destructive of people's self-respect ("humiliation" is being treated like unproductive dirt rather than allowed to be productive). A community should be a seedbed ("seminary") in which each one can strive to reach his or her full, fertile potential and not become sterile and unproductive. A community of authentically humble members will never become withered by destructive competition but will thrive like a garden of flourishing blooms.

Wisdom: Discernment and Insight. Wisdom is a rare combination of knowledge and experience. If knowledge alone were enough, all graduates, teachers, and professors would be wise; if experience alone were sufficient, all older people would be wise. But neither of these is true. Wisdom is revealed when just judgment is added to knowledge and experience. One of its components is "common sense"; but common sense is far from common currency, because not everyone possesses mature or appropriate judgment, one of its essential constituents. But wisdom—a gift of the Spirit—is vital for passing on the faith; without it, the best we can do would be simply to pass on what we have received. Wisdom helps a person to distill knowledge and transmit it in appropriate ways and circumstances, which requires discernment and insight. But without a base of common sense, there would not seem to be sufficient moral character for wisdom to root in; and without the flourishing of wisdom, our ability to live and work within and beyond an intercultural community would be seriously inhibited. Wisdom is not given to everyone, but every community needs it. It can be prayed for and, if given, can be cherished and practiced.

Commitment to Personal Conversion. Who will evangelize the evangelizer; who will convert the one who seeks to bring others to conversion? These seem like rhetorical questions, but they urgently require a response, an answer, from each of us. As St. Paul said rather dramatically, "I punish my body and enslave it, so that after proclaiming to others I myself should not be disqualified" (1 Cor 9:27). If each of us is a lifelong learner as well as a teacher, we must be committed to our personal and ongoing conversion. At no point in our life can we know who may yet be instrumental in that process (or how we might contribute to others' conversion); but our community should surely be a place in which our conversion is actually happening. If we are truly open to the Spirit of God working in our lives, we should pray that opportunities within the context of our community should not be overlooked or minimized. Part of our commitment to our personal conversion, therefore, should be a real willingness to engage with those among whom we live: they may be among the most immediate agents of our conversion.

Trustworthiness and a Trusting Heart. Recently, the scandal of sexual abuse of minors has massively compromised trust between many people and the clergy and religious. But it has also affected relationships within communities and among their members. Trust is rather like porcelain; if it shatters it is effectively beyond repair. And yet trust is the very cornerstone of relationships, so it *must* be repaired. Whoever lives by double standards is not worthy of trust, but whoever does not trust the kith and kin with whom one lives is not worthy of trust either. Therefore, all community members have a moral responsibility to seek to become trustworthy and also strive to trust those with whom they live. Without that underpinning, a community cannot survive, much less remain faithful to the mission. In chapter 2 we identified some characteristics of an intercultural community. Among them must be the availability of mechanisms for addressing mutual suspicion or the erosion of intracommunity trust. But such mechanisms will never be sufficient unless each person undertakes to work on trust issues and to cultivate the virtue of trust.

Intergenerational Living

The Challenge

Intercultural living is a *challenge* but not a *problem*, which is not to say that it is always easy to negotiate. But if we visualize it as positively, as an invitation or a challenge rather than a vicissitude or a problem, we will be much less likely to look for blame and might even find it more engaging. Problems (suggesting difficulty, hardship, and uncertainty) deter many people and can often and easily be blamed on someone else; but challenges (suggesting the need for courage and boldness) can appear much more attractive to many others.

But one of the challenges of intercultural living is concerned as much with individuals as it is with cultures. Because individuals are undoubtedly shaped by culture, we have explored some of the effects of culture on individuals;[1] but another characteristic of individuals needs to be explored here, and one less obviously grounded in one's cultural identity than it is part of every person's identity (though culturally handled or interpreted): namely, age. Members of every community can, in principle, be gathered in cohorts or age groups and separated in generations or age grades. But how people within and between such groups relate to each other, and how this affects the community as a whole, is intrinsically interesting—perhaps especially so in some contemporary communities.

Same, Adjacent, and Alternate Generations

Here are some generalizations that will not prove true in every instance but will provide a rule of thumb or helpful approximation. People of the *same generation* as oneself (often identified as peers or a peer group) may offer or be called on to provide peer support and encouragement and often do so very effectively. But they can also exercise considerable power: the power to bring peer pressure, disapproval, or sanctions on others of their peers, also to great—and sometimes very painful—effect. During the period of secondary socialization (roughly speaking, adolescence), individuals can be particularly influenced by their peer group.[2] Indeed, gangs are shaped, sustained, and motivated by it. So in the context of a community, it would be helpful to identify peer groups and their significance.

Adjacent generations are any two adjoining or contiguous generations: that is, people related as parent and child. But more than children and their parents, this also applies to adult children and their aging parents, as well as to younger parents and their own growing children. Very different social dynamics characterize each of these configurations. Typically, however, we can say that the relationships here are marked by stress, struggle, ambiguity, and structural friction: they rub against each other, sometimes lovingly and harmoniously, but at other times contentiously and antagonistically. This characteristic seems to fit the experience of people from widely different cultures and might be a cultural universal. The relationship between people of adjacent generations is very often volatile, at least until there is some mellowing and forbearance on the part of each.

Contrast that situation with the relationship between people of *alternate generations,* in which there may be little or no struggle over authority, collaboration rather than competition, and structural ease rather than structural friction.[3] Alternate generations are any two generations separated by at least one intervening generation, as grandchildren and their grandparents or great-grandparents. Grandparents are often (but not always or universally) much more relaxed with their grandchildren than they ever were with their own growing children, while grandchildren are typically indulged or "spoilt" by their grandparents in ways their own parents never demonstrated.

However interesting this might be, it is not our main point. When applied to community life, however, this information can be quite enlightening. If we had to choose between "the same," "adjacent," or "alternate" generations, how would we describe—in today's world, compared with that of half a century ago—the relationship between a novice and novice director, a superior and the community, and a small number of people of very different ages but professed on the same day?

Cross-Cutting Cohorts
and Mingled Generations

In my novitiate, half a century ago, we were more than fifty novices; the novice master was an "old" man well into his fifties; and with two very obvious and singled-out exceptions, we were all born within two years of each other. The novice master was clearly the parent figure in the generation adjacent to ours. Two of the confessors were unquestionably of a generation alternate to ours; they were our grandfathers. But the other confessor seemed hardly old enough to be ordained; he was more like a brother in age, but few people made him their confessor because they felt uneasy with him in the circumstances. All the novices were, of course, from the same religious community, and we were strictly men only.

Today I work with several internovitiate groups. These are clusters of half a dozen or more communities, male and female, clerical and lay, each with anything between none and half a dozen novices in a given year. When I go into the room, where there might be between twenty-five and fifty people, including novice directors, I have no idea who is who, apart from surmising that anyone who looks *really* young (of whom there are only a few) is not a director but a novice. So I always need to ask, because a sixty-year-old—formerly married, now perhaps divorced or widowed, perhaps a grandparent—might be one of this year's novices—or, indeed, the director of novices. And a person in his or her forties might just as well be either. Again, this is familiar enough to us, but the dynamics of interpersonal and intracommunity relationships can often become confused and confusing.

Can a novice under thirty without a great deal of life experience be a real peer to another novice in the same community who is over fifty and has enjoyed a career in teaching, banking, or law? And can a novice director who is much the same age as the only novice in the community ever be a peer or a buddy? It is sometimes as difficult for an older person to defer appropriately to a younger director as it is for a younger director to be appropriately directive with the novice.

Then there are "grandparents" in the community and also the "mentors" and "midwives." The grandparents are typically old enough to be part of a community that includes people of two or three—or four—generations, and the mentors or midwives are trusted personal guides who have proven themselves people of moral authority but not authoritarianism, who are gentle rather than stern, and as eager to support as they are able to correct without undermining their own or another's dignity. But mentors are rarely parents or peers, and neither parent nor peer can assume that status: it is up to the person being mentored to affirm that title. And a person may be a mentor in a community without being the superior. As for midwives, likewise not necessarily superiors of the community, their reputation will go before them and largely determine the response of those they attend or assist. And it might be very interesting for leaders in men's communities to know that in one of Plato's dialogues he quotes Socrates on the subject of *male* midwives. Socrates says: "My art of midwifery is in most respects like [women's]; but differs, in that I attend men and not women, and I look after their souls when they are in labor, and not after their bodies: and the triumph of my art is in thoroughly examining whether the thought which the mind of a young man brings forth is a false idol or a noble and true birth."[4]

In short, there are many and multiplex roles and statuses in any community today which create a delicate challenge in themselves. If we then complicate the challenge by identifying specific cultural differences between these various persons, then we are approaching the reality that obtains within an intercultural community. A novice director of a completely different culture to all the novices, and one whom they cannot see as an elder or mentor but only as a parental figure or disciplinarian, is going to find life as difficult as the novices do. And if the director does not have a peer to consult, loneliness and isolation can complicate an already delicate situation.

What Is Possible and What Is Not?

Some people in leadership positions try to be peers or buddies with as many people as possible, while others abdicate their responsibility because of personality clashes. Some affect being "grandparents" when that is quite inappropriate because the nature of the relationship is patently one of structural friction. And while some may try impossibly to be all things to everyone (peer, buddy, parent, grandparent, mentor, and midwife), others might opt, equally impossibly, to maintain one single status and role that would be adequate to meet every challenge of community living.

Each of us is challenged to examine ourselves and—preferably with a discerning friend or mentor—to identify our strengths and weaknesses, our aptitudes and ineptitudes for intergenerational community living and/or leadership. Then we would need to explore cultural variables such as the following half dozen.

First, check who are considered the wisdom figures in the cultures of community members and find out how one becomes a wisdom figure: by age, social role, gender, achievement, and so on. Then identify different roles and expectations between people in authority and their charges in other cultures. Third, identify how individual community members perceive the authority figure(s) in their religious community and discover what is and what is not considered appropriate behavior between a particular leader and the subordinate. Next, remember that reciprocity may be symmetrical or asymmetrical. Between peers it should be symmetrical and equal; between leader and charge, or superior and subordinate, it can be asymmetrically reciprocal or mutual but unequal, as between parent and child or grandparent and grandchild. See if you can clarify which relationships within a community can or should be symmetrical and which are or should be asymmetrical. Fifth, do not impose hierarchy on potentially dialogical situations or force dialogue in hierarchical situations. (Dialogue and hierarchy are structurally incompatible: we cannot have both at the same time, as we noted in Appendix II.) Finally, clarify personal and interpersonal aims and expectations in particular circumstances, then check back to see if these were realistic and/or fulfilled, and if not, why not.

SWOT Analysis Tool

The acronym SWOT stands for Strengths, Weaknesses, Opportunities, and Threats associated with an actual situation or proposed undertaking. A SWOT analysis or SWOT matrix is a way of identifying critical factors involved in an enterprise and analyzing them with a view to gauging the feasibility of an intended plan or strategy. It was initially developed as a tool to be used in the business field but has since proved helpful for nonprofit organizations and even small communities. It can help people identify both potential opportunities and problems and assess the likelihood of success or failure in particular undertakings. We cannot go into details here: it is enough to identify the tool itself and how it can be accessed.

In using the SWOT approach, the objective is to look for a *strategic fit* between the available resources and the proposed outcome. As each component of the SWOT is identified, future planning can be calibrated accordingly. The effectiveness of SWOT analysis in a community-wide consultation, or between a novice director and novice, will depend partly on being able to ask the most pertinent questions—about strengths, weaknesses, opportunities, and threats—that will produce useful answers that lead to action.

On the Wikipedia website for SWOT analysis, there is a simple diagram, similar to the one below (figure 21).

Figure 21

SWOT ANALYSIS

	HELPFUL	*HARMFUL*
INTERNAL ORIGIN *(Attributes of the community or individual)*	STRENGTHS	WEAKNESSES
EXTERNAL ORIGIN *(Attributes of the wider environment)*	OPPORTUNITIES	THREATS

For further information, simply Google SWOT analysis Template or SWOT analysis tool or go to www.smartsheet.com or www.business newsdaily.com/4245-swot-analysis.html.

Appendix IV

Preferential Option for "The Other"

The Stranger in Each of Us

"The concept of the stranger remains one of the most powerful sociological tools for analyzing social processes of individuals and groups confronting new social orders."[1] We have already looked at Jesus as a stranger himself and at the need for us not simply to reach out to the stranger who is "the other" but also to identify and embrace that status and role.[2] I have developed this theme more fully elsewhere.[3] The point of the present reflection is to remind us that "the other" not only is someone else but also, in the context of an intercultural community and commitment to cross-cultural mission, "the other" is the person in your mirror: yourself. Every one of us becomes the stranger or "the other," which means we have two roles: to act appropriately as the stranger, the not-at-home person, but also to treat others appropriately as strangers. If these two roles are properly understood and lived, there will, or should be, a progressive development of mutual relationships. As a result, everyone will be the stranger ("other" and "participating outsider") but also incorporated (not assimilated) as a true and full member of the intercultural community ("participating insider"). This will leave every member in a delicate or volatile situation, sometimes feeling very much as a stranger feels (not assimilated and not quite belonging) and sometimes very much "at home." Alternating between these two states is exactly what a marginal person does; and as each community member tries to live appropriately as a marginal person, so every member should attempt to empathize with everyone else as they too experience the ambiguity of the marginal or liminal person, living, as Jung Young Lee expresses it, "in-between," "in-both," and "in-beyond."[4]

As we saw in chapter 8, however, just as Jesus came not only to identify but also to actively remove or erase the boundary line between insiders and outsiders, "us" and "them" (Eph 2:14), so every member of an intercultural community is required to attempt the same feat.

Theological Reflection

In a brief appendix we can only mention some significant contributions to this topic and encourage people to undertake further reading. Here are some very helpful reflections from some significant authors.

In a brilliant and prescient article twenty-five years ago, Johannes Metz analyzed a situation that has become more acute with each passing year: the shift from a culturally monocentric (Euro-American) to a polycentric church.[5] The specific challenge is that of unity in diversity and whether it is met by a defensive, "safety-first" mentality or an "offensive loyalty" to God's, and the church's, mission.[6] This of course is the essential purpose of intercultural communities. Metz identifies the challenge or dilemma in four parts: cultural polycentrism is being rapidly eroded by globalization; non-European cultures are being pulled into a "Eurocentric whirlpool"; non-Western peoples are under intense pressure to conform to the processes of secularization; and the survival of cultural polycentrism in the face of a globalized world that seems to have lost its moral moorings. Given these currents, what hope is there of authentic unity in diversity?

Metz suggests that a culturally polycentric church (and for our specific purposes, an intercultural community) is possible on two conditions. First, it must be explicitly committed to seeking freedom and justice for all; second, it must be demonstrably "based on the acknowledgment of the other in their otherness . . . such as ought to be familiar to us from the primitive history of Christianity."[7] For this to happen, the church must "implement the biblical inheritance primarily as the basis of a hermeneutical culture: that is, a culture which acknowledges the other in their otherness." Such a "new" hermeneutical culture—one that interprets and explains reality in a new way by endorsing and defending "otherness," "alterity," or the dignity of difference—is precisely what we argued for in chapter 2 as "Culture E," a *new* intercultural community. Metz refers to it as a culture of acknowledgment. But acknowledgment is not enough; we must go further and create a culture of radical welcome and inclusion, as we saw in our final chapter. But Metz would also add to the classic phrase "preferential option for the poor" a second "option for others in their otherness."[8] Members of intercultural communities must surely embrace the same nonoptional option.

Wilhelm Dupré speaks in broader terms,[9] looking at a religious tradition itself at the national or diocesan level; but his remarks apply pertinently to a local intercultural community. He quotes Julia Kristeva, who speaks of a "contrasting community" that is "made up of foreigners who are reconciled with themselves to the extent that they recognize themselves as foreigners."[10] He goes on to say that such a community does not operate by assimilation but rather by "a partial integration with an optimum of self-identification. Anyone who wants to come and accepts the conditions which delineate this possibility is welcome. . . . It is the factual (and freely chosen) residence which determines the meaning of citizenship."[11]

Philosopher Emmanuel Levinas was a source of great insight into the relations between the self and the other.[12] For him, "the other" is, in the first place, the other human being who calls forth ethical responsibility"[13] from oneself. Theologian David Tracy echoes this: "The turn to the other is the quintessential turn of postmodernity itself. It is that turn, above all, that defines the intellectual as well as the ethical meaning of postmodernity. The other and the different come forward now as central intellectual categories across the major disciplines, including theology."[14] Elsewhere, in acknowledging that Levinas uses "other" as referring both to a human "other" and to the transcendent "Other," Tracy shows the relationship between them: "Surely, this ethical route to the Absolute Other only by way of the interrelationships of human others is Levinas's most original, and daring, and for Jewish and Christian theology, both promising and controversial move."[15] And Terry Veling adds: "Like the sensibilities of liberation theology, Levinas wants to keep the human neighbor between myself and God, such that we cannot too readily approach the invisible God without first encountering the height of our neighbor."[16]

Father of liberation theology Gustavo Gutiérrez wrote: "Rediscovering the other means entering his own world. It also means a break with ours. The world of inward-looking absorption with self . . . is not only interior but is socioculturally conditioned. To enter the world of the other . . . with the actual demands involved . . . is to begin . . . a process of conversion."[17]

It would be much easier of course—at least in the short term—to treat the other only as a guest or stranger, thus maintaining our own initiative and control; it is much more difficult, as Levinas says, to "emphasize instead the act of deference to the Other in his [her] alterity, which can only come about through the awakening of the Same [that is, oneself]—drowsy in his [her] identity—by the Other."[18] Veling pursues this thought in a way that challenges our own intercultural communities. He says that if we experience difficulty in adjusting to the other, at least we will be more aware of the other's actual existence, while the more comfort we feel, the more impervious to the other's very existence we will become. The task of revelation, he says, "is always to announce, command, perforate, rupture, unsettle—to break open our world and turn us toward the call and demand of the other in our very midst."[19] This is where we feel the call to conversion. "The face of the other breaks into my world and calls out to me. I am not an *I* unto myself, but an *I* standing before the other. The other calls forth my response, commands my attention, refuses to be ignored, makes a claim on my existence, tells me I am responsible."[20]

Living with Ambiguity

The other, then, is the stranger, the stranger is the other, and each of us is both of these: this is the challenge faced by those who undertake to create and live in intercultural communities. We recall the great opening verses of Genesis 18: "The LORD appeared to Abraham by the oaks of Mamre, as he sat at the entrance of his tent in the heat of the day. He looked up and saw three men standing near him."

We may also be aware that the rabbis taught that this is the longest verse in the entire Bible: the invisible space between the sense of verse one and verse two is where the epiphany takes flesh: God actually appears as the strangers. Here is Levinas again: "The Justice rendered to the Other,[21] to my neighbor, gives me an unsurpassable proximity to God. . . . One follows the Most High God, above all, by drawing near to one's neighbor, and showing concern for 'the widow, the orphan, the stranger and the beggar,' an approach that must not be made with 'empty hands.'"[22]

A final theological voice is that of David Power who, in a fine essay, speaks about respect for the otherness of the other and looks for signs of a common agreement by people of different cultures about the critical importance of this attitude.[23] He then identifies a "civic" (common to many or all people) and a "religious" (specifically for Christians) imperative.[24] The latter is to have abiding faith in Jesus Christ. But this Christian faith, he says, "has to be recovered as common beyond the particularities of the specific cultural expressions given to it."[25] This faith then must have three referents. First, it must draw us "to the memory of Jesus Christ as it comes to us first and foremost in the formulation of the gospels, whatever we have done in our particular cultures to seek to understand and read beneath or through that formulation, and as it is kept alive in Christian worship, in all its diversity."[26] Second, our faith must sensitize us "to the power of God's own Spirit . . . working through a variety of cultural forms."[27] And, third, faith must help us be committed "to the hope of reconciliation when overshadowed, or overwrought, by the denial of the other and the excess of evil which that brings with it."[28] Here is a rallying call to all people called to intercultural living.

And a final voice is from a secular social anthropologist who says this:

> In becoming intercultural we rise above the hidden grips of culture and discover that there are many ways to be good, true, and beautiful. In this process we acquire a greater capacity to overcome cultural parochialism and develop a wider circle of identification. . . . In a way, becoming intercultural is a process of liberating ourselves from a limited perspective on life—or becoming more fully human, with a greater awareness of and sensitivity to self, others, and the relationship between them.[29]

Power and Authority[1]

Clearing the Ground

A rather small child may have the power (physical capacity) to poke out someone's eye; the state may have the power (legitimated authority) to execute a criminal; a parent may have power (moral authority) to shape a child into a virtuous adult; and a nation may have power (military capacity) to obliterate a city. Clearly the word "power" is used in many ways and contexts, so we begin with a working definition from the social sciences. Power is the sheer capacity to act on something or someone, and authority is the entitlement to do so. I have the power, but not the authority, to do many things, from baking a cake to kicking someone, from offering assistance to a needy person to detonating a bomb. Authority is the authorization or legitimation of an act. So a judge has the authority to sentence a criminal and a parent has the authority to discipline a child. But sometimes authority is invoked when there is none. Sometimes it is invoked only as exercise of crude power, as in a preemptive strike on a declared enemy, a husband beating his wife, or a military person torturing a suspect.

The concept of power itself is morally ambivalent, ambiguous, or neutral, but once applied, it affords a context for moral judgment. To assert flatly that power corrupts is too neat; in any case, Lord Acton said that it *tends* to corrupt. Theologian and former bishop Stephen

Sykes produced a beautifully presented and argued treatise on theological approaches to power in which he identifies two main approaches.[2] Some people argue that the use of all power is antithetical to the life and spirit of Jesus; others that God is the *fons et origo*, the very source, of all power, and that humanity can exercise a derivative godly power. But, as Sykes shows clearly, legitimately derived or claimed power (that is, authority) has been dreadfully abused historically: God has often been invoked for some very ungodly purposes.

From a theological viewpoint, a problem relating to the use of power-as-authority is precisely the fact that we all act culturally: we are persons of culture, and culture provides the context for all our actions. But human cultures are myriad, and all notions about God, about the nature of God, and about the authority humans derive from God are culturally and linguistically coded and inextricably linked with more secular ideas of appropriate governance and sanctions. Human agents are always capable of invoking God as their ally or ultimate authority when they exercise their own authority, even when they have become corrupt and cause great physical or moral harm. So let us look at the use of power and authority in the context of intercultural communities.

Power Distance

Geert Hofstede defined "power distance" as "the extent to which the less powerful members of institutions and organizations accept that power is distributed unequally."[3] Here, "power" is understood as "power-in-authority" rather than the sheer capacity to effect an outcome, and Hofstede distinguishes high-power distance from low-power distance. We can show this in a table (figure 22), the total contents of which owe as much to Eric H. F. Law[4] as to Geert Hofstede, with some additions of my own:

Using "power distance" as a scheme, an explanatory model or hermeneutic, it becomes possible to add cultural variables, such as male or female, egocentric or sociocentric enculturation, ethnicity or age, to provide greater explanatory detail. For example, Law characterizes the French, Mexicans, Indians, Filipinos, and Brazilians as high-power-distance cultures, in contrast to the British, Germans, North Americans (United States and Canada), Australians, and

Figure 22

POWER DISTANCE

HIGH-POWER DISTANCE	LOW-POWER DISTANCE
• Individuals accept power (authority) as constitutive of ordered society	• Most people seek a minimization of hierarchical authority
• Hierarchy is built into the organization	• Power (authority) should only be invoked rarely
• Superiors and subordinates are distinguished and distinct	• Hierarchical power (authority) is acknowledged as an organizational value
• Leaders/superiors have a sense of entitlement and legitimate privilege	• Differences do not amount to moral distinctions
• Power includes the legitimate threat or use of sanctions	• Every individual has the same rights
• Parents/superiors expect obedience	• People value honest work as its own reward
• Students/subordinates value conformity and display authoritarian attitudes between themselves	• Knowledge, respect, and happiness are mutually shared and expected
• Strong supervision and fear of the superior produce lack of trust, both vertically and horizontally (between subjects)	• People have "social mobility," the capacity to move freely in the institution
• Discretion, tact, and subservience are valued by subordinates	• There is a real striving for mutuality and collaboration rather than competition
• Everyone has a place, but it is ascribed and people are unequal	• Power (authority) is understood as service
• Power (authority) is maintained by the superiors and rarely challenged	• Those with power are aware and inclusive of the less powerful

Scandinavians as low-power-distance cultures. This could provide an interesting talking point for an intercultural evening but immediately seems far too broad a generalization, and "Great Britain" and "North America" contain such a variety of cultures and styles that it would be impossible to use this scheme as anything more than a *very* crude tool.

Hofstede's scheme can be helpful when we contrast men's and women's communities. Summarizing his contribution, Gudykunst and Kim contrast high masculinity (or low femininity) with high femininity (or low masculinity) groups. The former emphasize things, assertiveness, power itself, separation and specialization of roles, and personal independence, while the latter value persons, nurture, and mutuality and are more concerned with the integration of roles within each person and with interdependence.[5] This rather polarizes and opposes women's and men's attitudes, whereas one would hope that in actuality there would be more overlap or drift of "male" and "female" attributes within specific communities. Nevertheless, Hofstede's scheme again provides food for thought and community conversation. But it does help to explain some gender-based and cultural differences. For us, how the stranger or "the other" is treated is very important, and perhaps high-power-distance cultures are less welcoming than low-power-distance communities. If incomers are consistently made to feel inappropriately isolated after a certain length of time within a community, perhaps attention needs to be paid to the power distance ratio operative within the community. Low-power-distance communities would be much more inclusive of outsiders and less likely to stand on ceremony or emphasize protocols for gradual integration.

The Example of Jesus

Jesus had a very strong and clear sense of his own identity and authority, but he did not lord it over anyone and explicitly warned his followers not to: "You know that among the Gentiles those whom they recognize as their rulers lord it over them, and their great ones are tyrants over them. But it is not so among you" (Mark 10:42-43). The Greek does indeed say, "It is not so," but the sense is "it is not to be so" or "it must not be so among you." But about his personal authority Jesus also reminded people: "You have heard that it was said . . . But I say to you" (Matt 5:21-22), as a result of which people questioned the source of this claim, evaluated his person and actions, and made their minds up about him accordingly. But he defined power as the capacity to love, expressed nonviolently as sacrificial service toward everyone, especially the most needy and exploited.

Power Analysis

Eric H. F. Law offers an insightful description and analysis of how power is distributed in any given group. He is talking about groups of mixed ethnicities, economic circumstances, and genders. Our focus would normally be narrower: mixed ethnicities and ages, of course, but the same gender and—in principle—economic circumstances characterize our intercultural communities. When we consider our missional outreach, of course, the situation would be different. In a high power distance community—or a low power distance community where people are highly independent—there may be a range of economic circumstances, with some members having much greater access to financial resources than others. So, with minimal modification, the questions Law poses can be very pertinent for any intercultural community. He spends a dozen pages on power analysis, identifying pertinent questions and offering a helpful case study;[6] here, we simply relate some of what he says to some themes from earlier chapters in the present book.

We looked at the four quadrants in chapter 10, first identifying insiders and outsiders and then participants and nonparticipants. This scheme could be used in a conversation about power analysis both within our own communities and between ourselves and those we serve. Eric Law poses questions like the following: How is power distributed in this particular group; between men and women; between different ethnicities; between groups with different levels of education; between the leadership and the membership; between the older/more long-serving members and the juniors? And so on. Having first identified who has power and who does not, and then enquiring whether there is a causal relationship between those two conditions, "we must determine where we stand in relation to others in the power continuum."[7] Then from personal experience and insight, Eric Law proposes this gem of a suggestion: "If I find myself in a powerless situation in relation to others, I must practice a spirituality of the empty tomb. If I find myself in a powerful place, I must practice the spirituality of the cross."[8] Here is solid food for very serious thought.

Leaders Must Lead

Having contrasted high and low power distance cultures and then power analysis, what happens to the legitimate exercise of authority, and how is the responsibility of leaders to serve their respective communities appropriately exercised? Since Vatican II, many communities have experimented with different authority structures with which we are now familiar—from the pyramidal or vertical to the almost-inverted pyramid or horizontal. But attempts to be less authoritarian and more inclusive have sometimes resulted in great confusion or near anarchy. Those in positions of authority—the legitimate use of power—have a moral responsibility to lead, though there are different and compatible styles of leadership that vary not only with persons but also with the nature of different communities. To conclude this reflection on power and authority, we might find it very instructive to return to a well-known and highly respected study of religious life that goes back twenty five years.[9]

Briefly, the authors identify four categories of leader, two leadership styles, and two grades of leader:[10]

Four Categories of Leader

1. Value-based: they see values but fail to see strategies

2. Visionary: they have a sense of direction and understand strategies

3. Conflicted: they are unable to address change: frustrated, angry, despairing

4. Incognizant: they are unaware of major issues and thus fail to address them

Two Styles of Leader

1. Transformational

   • They provide vision and a sense of mission

   • They instill a sense of pride

2. Transactional

   • They are administrators and operators; goal- or project-based

   • They monitor and sanction behavior

   • Some avoid decision making and abdicate responsibilities

Two grades of leader

1. Outstanding
   - They are explicitly dedicated to doing better than previously
   - They seek new ways to achieve goals
   - They attempt to better serve others
   - They take initiatives and deal with problems
   - They use their "power" to influence group decisions and behaviors
   - They attempt to build consensus
   - They often refer to God as leader

2. Typical
   - They threaten sanctions
   - They invoke formal authority
   - They get bogged down by individuals' problems
   - They seldom refer to God as leader

Here is rich material for reflection and conversation in intercultural communities in which people of different cultures have different understandings of authority and leadership, obedience and initiative, personal responsibility, and mutual accountability.

Suggested Follow-Up

1. Explore the notion of power distance as you experience it in community. Do you find the notion helpful in explaining some of your experiences?

2. Do you see possibilities for a shift to a more Jesus-like distribution of power in community?

3. Reflect on leadership qualities. What can you learn to help your own leadership style? How do Nygren-Ukeritis insights help you to communicate with, and experience, leadership?

Notes

Introduction (pages xiii–xxi)

1. Statistics from Mary Gauthier, "Catholic Ministry Formation Enrollments: Statistical Overview for 2013–2014," 11, 25, 31, http://cara.georgetown.edu /Overview201314.pdf.

2. Jonathan Sacks, *The Home We Build Together* (London: Continuum, 2007), 84.

Chapter 1 (pages 1–14)

1. A helpful compendium of articles can be found in *Verbum SVD* 54, no. 1 (2013).

2. S. M. Michael, "Interculturality and the Anthropos Tradition," in *Verbum SVD* 54, no.1 (2013): 62.

3. We must always be careful not to *essentialize* culture or Gospel: culture cannot "speak" to Gospel any more than Gospel can "speak" to culture. The agents are always human persons, *pace* Franz-Josef Eilers (*Verbum SVD*, 56) and others, including me, who sometimes write as if a culture or religion has a voice.

4. See Milton Bennett, "A Developmental Approach to Training for Intercultural Sensitivity," in Judith Martin, ed., *International Journal of Intercultural Relations (Theories and Methods of Cross-Cultural Orientation)* 10, no. 2 (1986): 179–96; William Gudykunst, *Bridging Differences: Effective Intergroup Communication* (Newbury Park, CA: Sage Publications, 1991); Edward T. Hall, *The Silent Language* (Greenwich, CT: Fawcett Publications, 1959); Edward T. Hall, *The Hidden Dimension* (New York: Anchor, 1966); Edward T. Hall, *Beyond Culture* (New York: Anchor, 1977).

5. But the terminology is still not standardized, and sometimes "multicultural" means "intercultural," especially as used by the very popular and widely read author Eric H. Law.

6. New techniques are necessary but not of themselves sufficient. As S. M. Michael observes, "Daily life together [among people of] different cultures requires constant and intense work to overcome one's own limits," *Verbum SVD* 54, no. 4 (2013): 61. The operative words are "constant" and "intense."

7. See Anthony J. Gittins, "Developing Mature Ministers for Diverse Cultural Contexts," *Reflective Practice* 29 (2009): 9–22; also van Thanh Nguyen, *Verbum SVD* 54, no. 4 (2013): 35.

8. Jonathan Sacks, *The Home We Build Together* (London: Continuum, 2007).

9. The classic resources on the nature of institutions, as well as the social relations that characterize these and other contexts are the whole *opus* of Erving Goffman. His books include *Asylums: Essays on the Social Situation of Mental Patients and Other Inmates* (Garden City, NY: Anchor Books, 1961); *The Presentation of Self in Everyday Life* (New York: Doubleday, 1959); *Strategic Interaction* (Philadelphia, University of Pennsylvania Press, 1969); *Stigma: Notes on the Management of Spoiled Identity* (Englewood Cliffs, NJ: Prentice-Hall, 1963); and others.

10. Sacks, *Home We Build Together*, 82.

11. Jonathan Sacks, *The Dignity of Difference: How to Avoid the Clash of Civilizations* (London: Continuum, 2003).

12. Francis, in interview with Antonio Spadaro, "A Big Heart Open to God," *America* 209, no. 8 (September 13, 2013): 28.

13. Sacks, *Dignity of Difference*, 8.

14. See David Tracy, *The Analogical Imagination: Christian Theology and the Culture of Pluralism* (New York: Crossroad, 1981), 408–20.

15. Rudy Wiebe, *The Blue Mountains of China* (Toronto: McClelland and Stewart, 1970), 215–16.

16. Identifying how we come to think as we do and the critical influence of culture in that process leads us into the field of the sociology of knowledge and authors such as Marx, Weber, Scheler, Durkheim, Mannheim, and the classic by Peter L. Berger and Thomas Luckmann, *The Social Construction of Knowledge* (New York: Anchor Books, 1967).

17. "Critical mass," or the minimum requirements for a well-functioning intercultural community, is dealt with in chapter 11, where we also note the valuable contributions of aging and infirm religious.

18. This is the topic of chapter 6.

19. Jonathan Swift (1667–1745) was an Anglo-Irish poet, satirist, and cleric who became dean of St. Patrick's Cathedral, Dublin.

20. Donal Dorr, *Spirituality and Justice* (Maryknoll, NY: Orbis Books, 1984), chap. 1.

21. Orlando Costas, "Conversion as a Complex Experience," in *Down to Earth: Studies in Christianity and Culture*, ed. Robert Coote and John Stott (Grand Rapids, MI: Eerdmans, 1980); Also in *Occasional Essays* 1, no. 5 (1980): 21–44.

22. Lewis Rambo, "Conversion," in *Dictionary of Pastoral Care and Counselling*, ed. R. Hunter (Nashville, TN: Abingdon Press, 1990).

23. Jim Wallis, *The Call to Conversion* (San Francisco: HarperSanFrancisco, 1981).

24. Orlando Costas, "Conversion."

25. Nikos Nissiotis, "Conversion and the Church," *The Ecumenical Review* 19, no. 3 (July 1967): 261–70.

26. Bernard Lonergan, *Method in Theology* (London: Darton, Longman & Todd, 1972), 132–33. It is only fair to point out, however, that this dream can turn into a nightmare: individuals and communities can also *lose* the faith from generation to generation, as has happened widely in Europe between the opening and closing of the twentieth century.

Chapter 2 (pages 15–31)

1. A good summary is in William Gudykunst and Young Yun Kim, *Communicating with Strangers: An Approach to Intercultural Communication*, 4th ed. (New York: McGraw Hill, 2003), 3–17, 246–67.

2. In the terminology of Jung Young Lee (1995), this is "living in both." See chapter 8, below.

3. Exceptionally, and usually as a result of war or enforced flight from home, a person who did not so choose, may in time become truly cross-cultural by intention and commitment. But not everyone living outside his or her original culture is cross-cultural, since many deliberately seek people of their own culture among whom to live ("the expatriate community").

4. There is a significant literature on the sociology and theology of the stranger. See Anthony J. Gittins, *A Presence that Disturbs: A Call to Radical Discipleship* (Liguori, MO: Liguori Press, 2002), 143–62; and *Ministry at the Margins: Strategy and Spirituality for Mission* (Maryknoll, NY: Orbis Books, 2002), 121–60.

5. Becoming a true cross-cultural person is never automatic, no matter how long a person remains in another culture. Again, Jung Young Lee (1995) identifies the problems associated with being "in-between" or "in-neither." See chapter 8, below.

6. Gittins, *Presence*, 96–107. We will consider this in more detail later, in chapters 8 and 10.

7. Gittins, *Ministry*, 135–41.

8. In fact, that same process—of biding one's time, scrutinizing others, and not being fully committed to offering unqualified acceptance and hospitality—applies to every single member of an intercultural community in the making, as will soon become clearer.

9. See Gittins, *Ministry*, 121–60; and chapter 8 below, on margins.

10. The connotations and denotations of the words "multicultural" and "intercultural" are not absolutely standardized. Eric H. F. Law, in his book *The Bush Was Blazing But Not Consumed* (St. Louis: Chalice Press, 1996), uses "multicultural" for a community in which no one culture dominates. He also includes the dynamic process I call "intercultural" community but speaks of such a process as consisting of "a constructive dialogue" (x). I would go much further. He also identifies intercultural dialogue as including "intergenerational, intergender, or

interreligious dialogue" (xi). He is addressing parish communities specifically, while I am exploring the social dynamics relative to the formation of permanent communities, stretching diachronically and embracing people who do not only collaborate and dialogue but also actually live together. Law's focus is on intercultural/multicultural collaboration and communication. Mine is on intercultural *living*.

11. A splendid resource for multicultural parishes (that is, *intentional* multiculturalism) is John Coleman, "Pastoral Strategies for Multicultural Parishes," *Origins* (2000): 497–505.

12. The "melting pot" theory goes back to the eighteenth and nineteenth centuries with people such as de Crevecoeur (1782), Emerson (1845), Robert Zangwill (1905), and Henry James (1908) but was refined in Robert E. Park's highly controversial theory of successful intergroup relations. Its four stages are competition, conflict, accommodation, and assimilation. He argued that different ethnic groups in the same area (what I am calling a multicultural society) would actually blend into a single community.

13. Liminality, or "betwixt-and-betweenness," can serve very positive social functions, as with pilgrims, retreatants, novices, or initiands. It is a stage leading to a new social status. Negatively, however, it can destroy people, as with prisoners in solitary confinement for an indefinite period.

14. Leadership is discussed briefly in Appendix V.

15. In many religious communities, including my own, the members of the General Council, living in Rome, must acquire fluency in Italian for everyday living, English for council deliberations, and either French or Portuguese for conversation, so that no single language is allowed to dominate and everyone has multilingual skills. This is particularly challenging for people from Africa or South America, who may need several new languages, and challenging enough for Europeans, most of whom will need to learn at least one new language, and in their middle years too.

16. The nature and status of participating and nonparticipating outsiders will be dealt with under the topic of "stranger" in chapter 10.

17. In figure 5, the vertical and horizontal lines bordering each of the cultures A, B, C, and D are broken rather than bold to show that the boundaries are not impermeable but open to mutual communication.

18. Homi Bhaba speaks of culture as "a contentious, performative space" in *The Location of Culture* (London: Routledge, 1994), 3.

19. *Spiritan Rule of Life*, 44.3; Pedro Fernandes, "Constructing Religious Community: A Spiritan Rereading," *Spiritan Horizons* 8 (Fall 2013): 25–38.

20. For more on "critical mass" in relation to a community, see chapter 11.

21. Francis, *Evangelii Gaudium* (On the Joy of the Gospel), par. 33, 259 (November 24, 2013); https://w2.vatican.va/content/francesco/en/apost_exhortations/documents/papa-francesco_esortazione-ap_20131124_evangelii-gaudium.html.

22. Quoted by *National Catholic Reporter* columnist Joshua Mc Elwee, *National Catholic Reporter* (January 1, 2014); http://ncronline.org/blogs/ncr-today/francis-tells-religious-wake-up-the-world-outlines-modern-struggles-church.

23. Eric H. F. Law has some helpful insights on the safe place when he talks about the "grace margin" as an extension of one's immediate safe space to a point where one can encounter "the other" and build a new community. See his *Inclusion: Making Room for Grace* (St. Louis: Chalice Press, 2000), 43–45.

24. See Appendix V for more on leadership.

25. Adapted from the Bernardin Lecture at Catholic Theological Union, Chicago, by Brian Hehir, in November 1988.

26. David Steindl-Rast, in *Fugitive Faith*, ed. Benjamin Webb (New York: Orbis Books, 1999), 112.

27. As noted in the introduction, however, many of these comments can equally well apply beyond intercultural religious communities. Dedicated ministers of all kinds will resonate with many aspects of intercultural living.

Chapter 3 (pages 32–45)

1. Raymond Williams, *Keywords: A Vocabulary of Culture and Society* (New York: Oxford University Press, 1985), 87, as quoted in Gerald Arbuckle, *Culture, Inculturation, and Theologians: A Postmodern Critique* (Collegeville, MN: Liturgical Press, 2010), 1. This book could be particularly helpful to religious communities seeking some of the skills required for intercultural living as it takes culture very seriously and shows how badly a deeper understanding is required in today's globalized and pluralistic world.

2. Anna Green, *Cultural History: Theory and History* (New York: Palgrave, 2009), 1–10.

3. Robert J. Schreiter, *The New Catholicity: Theology Between the Global and the Local* (Maryknoll, NY: Orbis Books, 1997).

4. This is the topic of chapter 5.

5. Schreiter, *Catholicity*, 29.

6. David Couturier, "At Odds with Ourselves: Polarization and the Learning Cultures of Priesthood," *Seminary Journal* (December 2003): 64–71. Members of intercultural communities could identify their own and others' preferred "learning style" (p. 71), in order to understand and manage their differences.

7. Note here that the historical record attests to "feral children," of whom there have been more than one hundred (many poorly documented or evident hoaxes). Born of human parents, they are raised with virtually no human contact or language. They thus lack a basic quality of humanness: sociality. Abandoned or abused, they have consequently not "learned" human culture—yet some may have the rudiments of animal culture, such as the capacity to eat and to groom. But they are a palpable exception; a striking anomaly. They are cultureless, and by any normal definition, which always includes the *social* aspect, cannot be said to be fully human. Even the famous "Wild Boy of Aveyron" could not be socialized (Harlan Lane, *The Wild Boy of Aveyron* (Cambridge, MA: Harvard University Press, 1975).

8. Enculturation, acculturation, and inculturation need to be carefully distinguished. See the next chapter.

9. These descriptive components are gleaned from many sources. "Culture" is a topic that has generated a vast amount of easily accessible literature. I offer a simplified but multifaceted description.

10. The literature on orality is vast and fascinating. Given that Jesus was operating in a largely oral culture and used the skills of orality, it would be helpful for members of an intercultural community to explore the psychodynamics of orality. For a brief treatment see Anthony J. Gittins, *Ministry at the Margins: Strategy and Spirituality for Mission* (Maryknoll, NY: Orbis Books, 2002), 85–100. A more extended discussion is Walter Ong, *Orality and Literacy: The Technologizing of the Word* (New York: Routledge, 2002, [orig. ed. 1982]).

11. We will expand on this in chapter 6.

12. Edward T. Hall, *Beyond Culture* (New York: Anchor Books, 1976), 74–123. Also see chapter 6.

13. A good introduction is Ronald L. Grimes, *Beginnings in Ritual Studies* (Waterloo, Canada: Ritual Studies International, 2013), or Catherine Bell, *Ritual Theory, Ritual Practice* (Oxford, UK: Oxford University Press, 1992).

14. A social institution is defined as "a standardized mode of coactivity," indicating both social interaction and relative permanence. For more on social institutions, any primer on social anthropology will help. A favorite and a classic is John Beattie, *Other Cultures: Aims, Methods and Achievements in Anthropology* (New York: The Free Press, 1964).

15. An excellent analysis of power in a theological context is Stephen Sykes, *Power and Christian Theology* (London: Continuum, 2006). And see Appendix V.

16. There was a long-standing argument about whether social control includes the legal system itself (B. Malinowski) or whether law should be defined as social control through the systematic application of force in politically organized society (A. Radcliffe-Brown). But because such arguments do not shed much light on the challenge of intercultural living itself, I offer here a much more straightforward description. See Tim Ingold, ed., *Companion Encyclopedia of Anthropology* (London: Routledge, 2002), 968; and Simon Roberts, *Order and Dispute* (Harmondsworth, UK: Penguin, 1979).

17. In order to avoid *essentialization* or *reification* (since cultures as such do not "act" or "think"), I will use "society" when referring to the actions of real people, and "culture" as a more generic term to describe achievements or failures not simply attributed to specific individuals.

18. For a fuller discussion of this classic anthropological theme, see Paul Sillitoe, "Why Spheres of Exchange?," *Ethnology* 45, no. 1 (Winter 2006): 1–26.

19. A classic reference here is Robin Fox, *Kinship and Marriage: An Anthropological Perspective* (Cambridge Studies in Social Anthropology: Cambridge University Press, 1988).

20. Anthony J. Gittins, "Belief and Faith, Assent and Dissent," *New Theology Review*, no. 3 (August 1989).

Chapter 4 (pages 46–61)

1. This is not an absolute requirement, but anyone who has not sufficiently encountered their personal biases and prejudices, the challenge of moving beyond their comfort zone, the experience of acute vulnerability, and the delicate interaction between stranger and host is not yet ready to move to an intercultural setting and may well find it personally traumatic and socially disruptive.

2. See Edward T. Hall, *The Silent Language* (Greenwich, CT: Fawcett Publications, 1959), 15, 128–45.

3. This will become clearer in the next section, culture as "a meaning-making system," and later.

4. Reflexivity combines self-reference (reflection), contemplative review (more reflection), and spontaneous (reflex) reaction, in an attempt to interpret and understand more deeply.

5. For a more detailed account, see Anthony J. Gittins, foreword in *Culture, Inculturation, and Theologians: A Postmodern Critique*, by Gerald Arbuckle (Collegeville, MN: Liturgical Press, 2010), xi–xvii.

6. "The person to whom I spoke" is grammatically correct, but most people say, and accept, "The person (who) I spoke to." But this also breaks the rule that one must not end a sentence with a preposition. Winston Churchill was once challenged for committing this solecism, to which he replied, "This is an insult up with which I shall not put," thus demonstrating that this perfectly grammatical usage was simply not the way people speak.

7. In his 1957 groundbreaking study, *Syntactic Structures*, Noam Chomsky identified a core of 150 rules in English. With this finite number of rules, a virtually infinite number of valid utterances (full or partial sentences, oral or written) could be generated.

8. Anthony J. Gittins, "Developing Mature Ministers for Diverse Cultural Contexts," *Reflective Practice: Formation and Supervision in Ministry* 29 (2009): 9–22. Skills identified here include: respect for persons and cultures; commitment to seek truth through respectful dialogue; cultivating a learning posture; learning "downward mobility" and accepting marginality; cultivation of an ecumenical approach; and learning the wisdom of the midwife (to facilitate without interfering).

9. Peter Berger and Thomas Luckmann, *The Social Construction of Reality: A Treatise on the Sociology of Knowledge* (New York: Anchor Books, 1967).

10. For enculturation and acculturation, see also Aylward Shorter, *Toward a Theology of Inculturation* (London: Geoffrey Chapman, 1988), 3–6.

11. Two classics on the subject are Berger and Luckmann, *The Social Construction of Reality*; and John Beattie, *Other Cultures: Aims, Methods, and Achievements in Anthropology* (New York: The Free Press, 1964); see also Anthony J. Gittins, *Ministry at the Margins: Strategy and Spirituality for Mission* (Maryknoll, NY: Orbis Books, 2002), 64–72.

12. Later (chapters 8 and 10) we will explore the sociology of the stranger, noting that each of us is, and must be, a stranger to some degree. We will iden-

tify some transitional stages and coping strategies. But if a willing outsider (stranger) is driven from a community before having a chance to become initiated, all the theoretical readiness will be in vain.

13. Shorter, *Inculturation*, 12.

14. Ibid.

15. This is the *ur*-definition proposed by Pedro Arrupe. See Arrupe, "Letter to the Whole Society on Inculturation," in *Other Apostolates Today: Selected Letters and Addresses of Pedro Arrupe SJ*, ed. J. Aixala (St. Louis: Institute of Jesuit Sources, 1981), 172–81.

16. Shorter, *Inculturation*, 11.

Chapter 5 (pages 62–79)

1. T. J. Gorringe, *Furthering Humanity: A Theology of Culture* (Hants, UK: Ashgate Publishing, 2004), 3.

2. "The split between the Gospel and culture is without doubt the drama of our time." Paul VI, Apostolic Exhortation *Evangelii Nuntiandi* (December 8, 1975), par. 20; http://www.vatican.va/holy_father/paul_vi/apost_exhortations /documents/hf_p-vi_exh_19751208_evangelii-nuntiandi_en.html; and Vatican Council II, *Gaudium et Spes*, develops a rather unnuanced understanding of culture in 53–62.

3. This is how St. Jerome (342–420) defined spirituality—a word he "invented."

4. Social geography focuses on the cultural significance of natural geographical features.

5. Apollo and Dionysius were sons of Zeus. Nietzsche famously spoke of Apollonian and Dionysian in *The Birth of Tragedy* (Oxford: Oxford University Press, 2008). An Apollonian character uses reason and restraint, while emotion and even chaos mark the Dionysian. Anthropologist Ruth Benedict, in *Patterns of Culture* (New York: Houghton Mifflin, 1934), identified the former with restraint and modesty and the latter with ostentation and even excess. My use is closer to Benedict than Nietzsche.

6. Vatican II, *Sacrosanctum Concilium* (Constitution on the Sacred Liturgy), par. 34.

7. In 2012, an undersecretary for the Congregation for Divine Worship announced that liturgical law "does not foresee the use of dance or drama within Mass, *unless particular legislation has been enacted by the* [national] *bishops' Conference.*" *The Catholic Herald* (London: October 12, 2012): 4.

8. Because African religious are structurally linked to extended family needs, they remain sisters or brothers, daughters or sons, responsible to the family especially at deaths. Some African religious feel that Euro-Americans completely misinterpret this. The latter, in turn, sometimes find it impossible to compromise or change long-established procedures, fearing that the families become a drain on community finance—a very delicate matter for all.

9. Chronemics is the culturally variable structure of time. See Nina Moore, *Nonverbal Communication: Studies and Applications* (New York: Oxford, 2010). In an intercultural community, "time" can be highly problematic. Some people are "clock watchers"; others seem unconcerned about timeliness. See Edward T. Hall, *The Silent Language* (Greenwich, CT: Fawcett Publications, 1959), 128–45.

10. Proxemics (a term coined by Edward T. Hall) is "the interrelated observations and theories of man's use of space as a specialized elaboration of culture." See Edward T. Hall, *The Hidden Dimension* (New York: Doubleday, 1966); and "A System for the Notation of Proxemic Behavior," *American Anthropologist* 65, no. 5 (1963): 1003–26. Here, we only consider some very basic issues relating to space.

11. Viktor Frankl, *Man's Search for Meaning* (New York: Pocket Books/Simon and Schuster, 1959).

12. For more on this, see Anthony J. Gittins, "Spirituality and Mission: Body, World, and Experience of God," *New Theology Review* 23, no. 4 (November 2010): 62–73.

13. As mentioned, we owe this word to American Presbyterians, to express the outreaching component of the life of every disciple; "missionary" proved too narrow. It has since circulated widely. See George Hunsberger and Craig Van Gelder, eds., *The Church Between Gospel and Culture* (Grand Rapids, MI: Eerdmans, 1997); and Darrell Guder, *Missional Church* (Grand Rapids, MI: Eerdmans, 1998).

14. Inagrace Dietterich, extracted from *The Gospel in Our Culture* 8, no. 3 (September 1996): 1–6. This section is indebted to this article.

15. Ibid.

16. Michael Paul Gallagher, *Clashing Symbols: An Introduction to Faith and Culture* (London: Darton, Longman & Todd, 1997).

17. Jon Sobrino, *Witnesses to the Kingdom: The Martyrs of El Salvador and the Crucified Peoples* (Maryknoll, NY: Orbis Books, 2003), 174–75.

18. Francis X. Moloney, *A Hard Saying: The Gospel and Culture* (Collegeville, MN: Liturgical Press, 2001), 209.

Chapter 6 (pages 80–97)

1. But see also figure 11 at the end of this chapter, illustrating another cultural, rather than simply individual, feature: high-context and low-context communication styles.

2. The elaborated/restricted distinction was originally formulated by Basil Bernstein in "Social Class, Language, and Socialization," in *Language and Social Context*, ed. P. P. Gigliolo (New York: Penguin Books, 1972). William Gudykunst and Young Yun Kim, *Communicating with Strangers: An Approach to Intercultural Communication*, 4th ed. (New York: McGraw Hill, 2003), 152–63.

3. Again, see figure 11 at the end of this chapter.

4. In chapter 5, "Cultural Understandings of Past, Present and Future."

5. Chapter 3, n 12. See also Franz-Josef Eilers, *Communicating Between Cultures: An Introduction to Intercultural Communication*, 4th ed. (Manila: Logos Publications, 2012), 116.

Chapter 7 (pages 98–114)

1. See Clifford Geertz, *The Interpretation of Cultures* (New York: Basic Books, 1973), 93–94.

2. Milton J. Bennett, "A Developmental Approach to Training Intercultural Sensitivity," in *Special Issues on Intercultural Training, International Journal of Intercultural Relations* 10, no. 2 (1986): 179–86; Milton J. Bennett, "Towards Ethnorelativism: A Developmental Model of Intercultural Sensitivity (revised)," in *Education for the Intercultural Experience*, ed. R. Michael Paige (Yarmouth, ME: Intercultural Press, 1993); Milton J. Bennett, "Becoming Interculturally Competent," in *Toward Multiculturalism: A Reader in Multicultural Education*, 2nd ed., ed. J. Wurzel, (Newton, MA: Intercultural Resource Corporation, 2004), 62–77.

3. See the work of Mitchell Hammer at *Intercultural Development Inventory*, http://idiinventory.com.

4. See also Franz-Josef Eilers, *Communicating Between Cultures: An Introduction to Intercultural Communication* (Manila: Logos Publications, 2010), 133–36.

5. See Appendix I.

6. This topic will be explained and discussed in chapter 10.

7. Bennett, "Becoming Interculturally Competent," 65.

8. Chapter 9, "Psychological Responses."

9. Bennett, "Becoming Interculturally Competent," 66.

10. Ibid.

11. Ibid.

12. Ibid., 67.

13. This is slightly reformatted from Bennett, "Becoming Interculturally Competent," 63.

14. Ibid., 68.

15. This does not mean that the "witchcraft mentality" can never change. Awareness of alternatives opens up closed worlds, and witchcraft explanation can give way to other explanations, as history demonstrates.

16. For more, see "liminality" and Jung Young Lee. Also Bennett, "Becoming Culturally Competent," 72.

17. This will be chapter 9, after we have examined some features of marginality/liminality.

18. M. Scott Peck, *The Different Drum: Community Making and Peace* (New York: Simon and Schuster, 1987), 59–72.

Chapter 8 (pages 115–30)

1. In illuminated manuscripts, including Bibles, margins are often filled with visual aids to the text. These "apostils" had an explanatory function but also drew attention to the text itself. In other words, margins can throw light on facts or surrounding territory.

2. This will be explained and explored in chapter 10, "Cultural Responses."

3. John P. Meier, *A Marginal Jew: Rethinking the Historical Jesus*, 4 vols. (New York: Doubleday, 1991–2009).

4. Amartya Sen, "Social Exclusion: Concept, Application, and Scrutiny," *Social Development Papers, 1*, Office of Environment and Social Development, Asian Development Bank, Manila, 2000.

5. Ibid., 14–15.

6. Georg Simmel, "The Stranger" (1908), in Donald N. Levine, ed., *Georg Simmel: On Individuality and Social Forms* (Chicago: University of Chicago Press, 1971), 143–49.

7. Everett Stonequist, *The Marginal Man* (New York: Russell and Russell, 1961), 8.

8. Jung Young Lee, *Marginality: The Key to Multicultural Theology* (Minneapolis: Fortress Press, 1995), 45.

9. Ibid.

10. Ibid., 4.

11. Ibid., 62.

12. Arnold van Gennep, *The Rites of Passage* (London: Routledge & Kegan Paul, 1908 [repr. 1977]); Victor Turner, *The Forest of Symbols* (Ithaca, NY: Cornell University Press, 1967).

13. Gennep, *Rites of Passage.*

14. See also Anthony J. Gittins, *Ministry at the Margins: Strategy and Spirituality for Mission* (Maryknoll, NY: Orbis Books, 2002), 131–33.

15. Another reference worth pursuing is Eric H. F. Law, *Inclusion: Making Room for Grace* (St. Louis: Chalice Press, 2000). See especially his thoughts on "boundary function" (pp. 16ff.), and "grace margin" (pp. 43ff.).

16. This is the topic of chapter 10.

17. Law, *Making Room for Grace*, 121–60.

18. Ibid., 135–41.

Chapter 9 (pages 131–46)

1. See chapters 3 and 4.

2. The notion of a "critical mass" is discussed in the context of *communitas* in chapter 11.

3. This now rarely used term, coined by anthropologist Alfred Kroeber (1876–1960), can point to a useful way of visualizing a culture or society as greater than the sum of its parts. Inorganic matter is inert; organic matter is living entities

composed of inorganic elements, but the "superorganic" refers to human cultures that have developed complex modes of communication that are not only genetic but also constitute systems external to individuals. Human social activity is cultural and symbolic rather than instinctive or genetically programmed.

4. Adapted from Dawid Venter, "Mending the Multi-Coloured Coat of a Rainbow Nation," *Missionalia* (1995): 316–17, who used S. Bochner, "The Social Psychology of Cross-Cultural Relations," in *Cultures in Contact* (Oxford, Pergamon, 1982), 5–44. The diagram is modified from Bochner, "Social Psychology," 27.

5. Bochner, "Social Psychology," 23.

6. Ibid., 23–24.

7. Ibid,. 24.

8. Such cultural reference points would include aspects of social geography, body tolerance, attitudes to health, sickness, and death, and cultural perceptions of time and space, as seen in chapter 5.

9. See previous chapter on intercultural competence, for Milton Bennett's terminology.

10. In *The Dignity of Difference* (London: Continuum, 2003), Jonathan Sacks says that the "search-for-common-values" approach is completely inadequate in today's world and urges that we identify some of the differences—cultural, religious, and the rest—that people in a pluralistic society can mutually live with. As far as community life is concerned, of course, we do need to emphasize the common values, but at the same time, in intercultural communities we are challenged to explore together how to deal creatively and respectfully with some of our differences. The "dignity of difference" is a wonderful phrase to cultivate.

11. For this, see the important qualifications and description in chapter 2.

Chapter 10 (pages 147–61)

1. Richard Dawkins, *The Selfish Gene* (Oxford, UK: Clarendon Press, 1976). See Martin A. Nowak and Sarah Coakley, eds., *Evolution, Games, and God: The Principle of Cooperation* (Boston: Harvard University Press, 2013). Cooperation is defined as "a form of working together in which one individual pays a cost (in terms of fitness, whether genetic or cultural) and another gains"; and altruism is "a form of (costly) cooperation in which an individual is motivated by good will or love for another (or others)." These deserve a special place in intercultural living.

2. Jonathan Sacks, *The Dignity of Difference* (London/New York: Continuum, 2002).

3. Partly excerpted from the front cover of Sacks, *The Dignity of Difference*.

4. Jacques Derrida, "Cogito and the History of Madness," in *Writing and Difference*, trans. A. Bass (London: Routledge, 1978), 75.

5. Sacks, *The Dignity of Difference*, 48.

6. David Tracy, *The Analogical Imagination: Christian Theology and the Culture of Pluralism* (New York: The Crossroad Publishing Company), 1981.

7. Andrew Greeley, *The Catholic Imagination* (Berkeley: University of California Press, 2000).

8. Sacks, *The Dignity of Difference*, 50.

9. This is dealt with in greater detail in Anthony J. Gittins, *A Presence That Disturbs* (Liguori, MO: Liguori Publications, 2002), 94ff.

10. J. L. Austin, *How to Do Things with Words* (Oxford, UK: Clarendon Press, 1962).

11. In chapter 6 we noted the tension between egocentric and sociocentric norms. Unless addressed and resolved by appropriate compromise and collaboration, community members will become polarized.

12. This is a general principle of human social organization. A religious community in which the "no longer Jew or Greek . . . slave or free . . . male or female" (Gal 3:28) principle is espoused is thus "countercultural." Generally, intercultural communities are single sex, so some of this diagram is not applicable. The *cultural* tendency to dominance and subordination, however, will have to struggle with the *religious* commitment to service (*diakonia*) and servant-leadership. The diagram offers an insight into the "cultural flaw" that *opposes* insiders to outsiders and "VIPs" to "nobodies"—of which there are always traces in any community, however enlightened.

13. In a matrilineal society, descent is determined through the female line, and some women have significant authority. But men's authority (traced through a key woman's brother) is dominant. In a somewhat analogous sense, despite the legitimate authority of women leaders in religious communities, in the Catholic Church they are always deemed accountable to some men further up in the hierarchy, which, in the contemporary church, remains an ongoing problem. For a survey of gender equality/inequality and women's power and authority, see André Beteille, "Inequality and Equality," in *Companion Encyclopedia of Anthropology*, ed. Tim Ingold (London: Routledge, 2002), 1010–39, especially 1021–23.

14. Older members of religious/faith communities will recall being treated as children and reminded of the gulf between postulants or novices and professed or ordained members. In some communities, this created huge dependency on others (leaders) and some infantilization of adults.

15. In men's communities, if some members come from a *machismo* culture, this may create enormous tension with others, while in women's communities, members raised in a patriarchal and sociocentric environment may find a more egalitarian but egocentric community very difficult to negotiate. These cultural variables must be identified and factored in.

16. For the important issue of "hyphenated nationals" (Africans, Asians, and others), see Jonathan Tan, *Asian American Theologies* (Maryknoll, NY: Orbis Books, 2008), 41–56. Are they sometimes relegated to quadrant 3 or 4 and with what consequences?

17. See figure 14, chapter 8. This is also highly relevant to members in initial formation: *via* postulancy, novitiate, first vows, or theological studies, they pass from being outsiders/them to insiders/us.

18. Virgil, *Aeneid*, II, 49.

19. See K. Koyama, " 'Extend Hospitality to Strangers'—A Missiology of *Theologia Crucis*," *International Bulletin of Missionary Research* 82 (1993): 283–95; and Anthony J. Gittins, "Beyond Hospitality? The Missionary Status and Role Revisited," *Currents in Theology and Mission* (1994): 164–82.

20. A brilliant essay by Andrew Walls is "The Ephesian Moment" in his *The Cross-Cultural Process in Christian History* (New York: Orbis Books, 2002), 72–82.

21. The Pauline authorship of Ephesians is contested, but these sentiments certainly harmonize with Paul's.

22. I return to the NRSV for the second part of this passage.

Chapter 11 (pages 162–77)

1. George Santayana (1863–1952). The quotation comes from *The Life of Reason*, vol. 1 (Amherst, NY: Prometheus Books, 1998).

2. Francis, *Evangelii Gaudium* (On the Joy of the Gospel), par. 120, http://w2.vatican.va/content/francesco/en/apost_exhortations/documents/papa-francesco_esortazione-ap_20131124_evangelii-gaudium.html.

3. Anthony J. Gittins, *A Presence that Disturbs: A Call to Radical Discipleship* (Liguori, MO: Liguori Publications, 2002), 74.

4. This concept was explored and elaborated by social anthropologist Victor Turner in a series of major publications. Though its original application was to small-scale society in Africa, it has since been expanded greatly and is currently used widely by liturgists and missiologists as well as social scientists.

5. And see Franz-Josef Eilers, *Communicating Between Cultures* (Manila: Logos/SVD, 2012), 116–17.

6. Johannes Quasten and Joseph Plumpe, eds., *The Epistle to Diognetus*, Ancient Christian Writers Series 6 (Westminster, MD: The Newman Press, 1948), 135–47.

7. Ibid., 139–40.

8. Gittins, *A Presence*, 79.

9. "The Adventure" is one of Simmel's essays and available in many compendia, such as Kurt H. Wolf, ed., *George Simmel, 1858–1918: A Collection of Essays, with Translations and a Bibliography* (Columbus, OH: Ohio State University, 1959). This quotation is from section 22. It is differently formatted in Donal Levine, ed., *Georg Simmel: Selected Writings on Individuality and Social Forms* (Chicago: University of Chicago Press, 1971), 191–92.

10. The community project is identified in chapter 2.

11. Robert Dunbar has a very helpful chapter on the subject: Robert Dunbar, "Culture, Honesty and the Freerider Problem," in *The Evolution of Culture: An*

Interdisciplinary View, ed. Robin Dunbar, Chris Knight, and Camila Power (New Brunswick, NJ: Rutgers University Press, 1999), 194–213. Dunbar says that "freeriders (those who take the benefits that derive from social contracts while allowing everyone else to pay the cost) become a particularly intrusive problem" (p. 194). See also Rodney Stark, *The Rise of Christianity* (Princeton, NJ: Princeton University Press, 1995), 174–79. And in his famous *Dictionary*, Doctor Samuel Johnson famously describes an abbey-lubber as "a slothful loiterer in a religious house, under pretence of retirement and austerity."

12. "Resisters" is made up of "re" and "sisters." It is of course, by no means only sisters who become "re-sisters," but I cannot find a suitable word to describe the brothers or brethren who resist.

13. This can be found in chapter 8.

14. See some of the conditions for the survival of an intercultural community in chapter 2.

15. Lawrence Cada, et al., *Shaping the Coming Age of Religious Life* (New York: Seabury Press 1977), chap. 3.

16. Beatrice Bruteau, *The Holy Thursday Revolution* (Maryknoll, NY: Orbis Books, 2005), 114.

17. Ibid.

Chapter 12 (pages 178–86)

1. In chapter 7 we contrasted a "model of" and a "model for"; the former would be a scale model of something that already exists, while the latter is more imaginative but helps orient people to a possible outcome and shows how it might work. It can also accommodate creative ideas about how to create what needs to exist. And it is always open to development, modification, and inspiration.

2. Stephanie Spellers, *Radical Welcome: Embracing God, the Other, and the Spirit of Transformation* (New York: Church Publishing, 2006). The (modified) diagram is from the accompanying *Study Guide*, p. 1. I have used the structure of that model and some of the author's terminology but modified it for our present purposes.

3. See Appendix I for "muted groups" and "representation."

4. See Appendix V.

Appendix I (pages 187–93)

1. See chapter 7, "Developing Intercultural Competence," and the section on Cultural Baggage in Anthony J. Gittins, *Ministry at the Margins: Spirituality and Strategy for Mission* (Maryknoll, NY: Orbis Books, 2002), 14–21.

2. To refresh on these terms, see chapter 6, "Social Profiles and Social Interaction."

3. Eric H. F. Law, *The Wolf Shall Dwell with the Lamb: A Spirituality for Leadership in a Multicultural Community* (St. Louis: Chalice Press, 1993), 79–88.

4. A highly influential article is Gayatri Chakravorty Spivak's "Can the Subaltern Speak?" in *Marxism and the Interpretation of Culture*, ed. C. Nelson and L. Grossberg (Basingstoke, UK: Macmillan Education, 1988), 271–313.

Appendix II (pages 194–203)

1. Wolfgang Messner, *Intercultural Communication Competence: A Toolkit for Acquiring Effective and Appropriate Intercultural Communication* (Bangalore, India: Messner Consulting & Training Pvt. Ltd., 2013). Wolfgang Messner & N. Schäfer, eds., *The ICCA™ Facilitator's Manual: Intercultural Communication and Collaboration Appraisal* (London: Createspace, 2012), www.globusresearch.com.

2. B. H. Spitzberg, "A Model of Intercultural Communication Competence," in *Intercultural Communication: A Reader*, ed. L. A. Samovar and R. E. Porter (Belmont, CA: Wadsworth Publishing, 2000), 375–87.

3. For easy access: http://en.wikipedia.org/wiki/Intercultural_communication.

4. A fuller treatment is Anthony J. Gittins, "Developing Mature Ministers for Diverse Cultural Contexts," *Reflective Practice: Formation and Supervision in Ministry* 29 (2009): 9–22.

5. A fuller treatment is Anthony J. Gittins, "Mentors and Midwives: Images of Discipleship," in *A Presence That Disturbs* (Liguori, MO: Liguori Publications, 2002), 131–41.

Appendix III (pages 204–9)

1. See "Social Profiles and Social Interaction" in chapter 6.

2. See "The Need to Clarify Terminology," in chapter 4.

3. Where, however, grandparents are raising children due to some malfunctioning of the nuclear family, the grandparent-grandchild relationship may replicate the structural friction more typical of the parent-child relationship.

4. Edith Hamilton and Huntingdon Cairns, eds., *Plato: The Collected Dialogues. "Theatatus" #149–50* (Princeton, NJ: Princeton University Press, 1969), 855.

Appendix IV (pages 210–14)

1. W. Shack, "Open Systems and Closed Boundaries," in *Strangers in African Society*, ed. W. Shack and E. Skinner (Berkeley: University of California Press, 1979); quoted in William B. Gudykunst and Young Yun Kim, *Communicating with Strangers: An Approach to Intercultural Communication*, 2nd ed. (New York: McGraw-Hill, 1992), 19.

2. See chapter 10 and Quadrant 3, "Outsider-Participants" and "The Jesus Solution."

3. Anthony J. Gittins, "Strangers in the Place," chap. 7, and "Missionary as Stranger," chap. 8, *Ministry at the Margins* (Maryknoll, NY: Orbis Books, 2002), 121–41, 142–60.

4. Jung Young Lee, *Marginality*. And see chapter 8, above.

5. Johannes Metz, "Unity and Diversity: Problems and Prospects for Inculturation," *Concilium* 204 (1989): 79–87.

6. Ibid., 79.

7. Ibid., 82.

8. Ibid., 83.

9. Wilhelm Dupré, "Multiculturalism and Xenophobia: Reflections on a Common Dilemma," in *'Mission is a Must': Intercultural Theology and the Mission of the Church* (Amsterdam and New York: Editions Rodopi, 2002), 161–77.

10. Dupré, "Multiculturalism," 169, quoting Julia Kristeva, *Strangers to Ourselves* (New York: Columbia University Press, 1991), 195.

11. Dupré, "Multiculturalism."

12. Emmanuel Levinas, *Totality and Infinity: An Essay in Exteriority* (Pittsburgh, PA: Duquesne University Press, 1969).

13. Terry A. Veling, "In the Name of Who? Levinas and the Other Side of Theology," *Pacifica* 12 (October 1999): 275.

14. David Tracy, "Theology and the Many Faces of Modernity," *Theology Today* 51, no. 1 (1994), as quoted in Veling, "In the Name," 276.

15. David Tracy, "Response to Adriaan Peperzak on Transcendence," in *Ethics as First Philosophy: The Significance of Emmanuel Levinas for Philosophy, Literature and Religion*, ed. Adriaan Peperzak (New York: Routledge, 1995), 194.

16. Veling, "In the Name," 283.

17. As quoted in Veling, "In the Name," from Gustavo Gutiérrez, "Liberation, Theology and Proclamation," in Claude Geffré and Gustavo Gutiérrez, eds., *Theology of Liberation, Concilium* 6, no. 10 (June 1974): 59.

18. Emmanuel Levinas, "Revelation in the Jewish Tradition," in *The Levinas Reader*, ed. Sean Hand (Oxford: Blackwell, 1989), 209.

19. Veling, "In the Name," 279.

20. Veling, "In the Name," 281.

21. This "O" in "Other" is deliberately ambiguous, denoting God as neighbor.

22. Veling, "In the Name," 292, quoting Levinas, *Difficult Freedom: Essays on Judaism* (Baltimore: The Johns Hopkins University Press, 1990), 18, 26.

23. David Power, "Communion within Pluralism in the Local Church: Maintaining Unity in the Process of Inculturation," in *The Multicultural Church: A New Landscape in U.S. Theologies*, ed. William Cenkner (Mahwah, NJ: Paulist Press, 1996), 79–101.

24. Ibid., 93–94.

25. Ibid., 94.

26. Ibid.

27. Ibid.

28. Ibid.

29. William B. Gudykunst and Young Yun Kim, *Communicating with Strangers: An Approach to Intercultural Communication*, 2nd ed. (New York: McGraw Hill, 1992), 255.

Appendix V (pages 215–21)

1. Some of this can be found in chapter 3 under "Politics."

2. Stephen Sykes, *Power and Christian Theology* (London: Continuum, 2006).

3. Geert Hofstede and M. Bond, "Hofstede's Cultural Dimensions," *Journal of Cross-Cultural Psychology* 15 (1984): 417–33. This quotation, 419.

4. Eric H. F. Law, *The Wolf Shall Dwell with the Lamb* (St. Louis: Chalice Press, 1993), 19–27. Eric Law, Episcopal (Anglican) priest, has spent more than twenty years working with multicultural communities in the United States and beyond. His objective is to help them really work together by providing information and developing skills in individuals and communities. Much of his work is highly relevant to this book's purpose, though he is dealing with parish or ad-hoc communities rather than explicitly with permanent and residential communities.

5. William B. Gudykunst and Young Yun Kim, *Communicating with Strangers: An Approach to Intercultural Communication*, 2nd ed. (New York: McGraw Hill, 1992), 47, in reference to Geert Hofstede, *Culture's Consequences* (Beverly Hills, CA: Sage Publications, 1980).

6. Eric H. F. Law, *The Wolf*, 57–69.

7. Ibid., 57–58.

8. Ibid., 58.

9. David Nygren and Miriam Ukeritis, *The Future of Religious Orders in the United States: Transformation and Commitment* (Westport, CT: Praeger, 1993). For the Research Executive Summary, *Origins* (September 24, 1992): 258–72.

10. Ibid., 266–71.

Bibliography

Adler, Peter S. "Beyond Cultural Identity: Reflections on Cultural and Multi-cultural Man." In *Intercultural Communication: A Reader*, edited by Larry Samovar and Richard Porter. Belmont, CA: Wadsworth, 1987.

Aixala, J., ed. *Other Apostolates Today: Selected Letters and Addresses of Pedro Arrupe, SJ*. Vol. 3. St. Louis: Institute of Jesuit Sources, 1981.

Arbuckle, Gerald A. *Culture, Inculturation, & Theologians: A Postmodern Critique*. Collegeville, MN: Liturgical Press, 2010.

Arnett, R. *Communication and Community*. Carbondale, IL: Southern Illinois University Press, 1986.

Arrupe, Pedro. "Letter to the Whole Society on Inculturation." In Aixala, *Other Apostolates Today*, 172–81.

Asuncion-Lande, Nobleza, ed. *Ethical Perspectives and Critical Issues in Intercultural Communication*. Falls Church, VA: Speech Communication Association, 1978.

Austin, J. L. *How to Do Things with Words*. Oxford, UK: Clarendon Press, 1962.

Barnlund, D. "The Cross-Cultural Arena: An Ethical Void." In Asuncion-Lande, *Ethical Perspectives and Critical Issues in Intercultural Communication*.

Barnsley, J. *The Social Reality of Ethics*. London: Routledge, Kegan, Paul, 1972.

Beattie, John. *Other Cultures: Aims, Methods, and Achievements in Anthropology*. New York: The Free Press, 1964.

Bell, Catherine. *Ritual Theory, Ritual Practice*. Oxford, UK: Oxford University Press, 1992.

Bellah, Robert, et al. *Habits of the Heart*. Berkeley: University of California Press, 1985.

Benedict, Ruth. *Patterns of Culture*. New York: Houghton Mifflin, 1934.

Bennett, Janet M., and Milton J. Bennett. "Developing Intercultural Sensitivity: An Integrative Approach to Global and Domestic Diversity." In *Handbook of Intercultural Training*, 3rd ed., edited by Dan Landis, Janet M. Bennett, and Milton J. Bennet, 147–65. Thousand Oaks, CA: Sage Publications, 2004.

Bennett, Milton J. "Becoming Interculturally Competent." In *Toward Multiculturalism: A Reader in Multicultural Education*, 2nd ed., edited by Jaime S. Wurtzel, 62–77. Newton, MA: Intercultural Resource Corporation, 2004.

———. "A Developmental Approach to Training for Intercultural Sensitivity." *International Journal of Intercultural Relations* 10 (1986): 179–96.

———. "Toward Ethnorelativism: A Developmental Model of Intercultural Sensitivity." In *Education for the Intercultural Experience*, 2nd ed., edited by M. Paige, 21–71. Yarmouth, ME: Intercultural Press, 1993.

———. "Transition Shock." In *International and Intercultural Communication Annual*, vol. 4, edited by N. Jain. Falls Church, VA: Speech Communication Association, 1977.

Berger, Peter, and Thomas Luckmann. *The Social Construction of Reality: A Treatise on the Sociology of Knowledge*. New York: Anchor Books, 1967.

Bernstein, Basil. "Elaborated and Restricted Codes." In *Communication and Culture*, edited by A. Smith. New York: Holt, Reinhart, and Winston, 1966.

Bernstein Basil. "Social Class, Language, and Socialization." In *Language and Social Context*, edited by P. P. Gigliolo. New York: Penguin Books, 1972.

Beteille, André. "Inequality and Equality." In *Companion Encyclopedia of Anthropology*, edited by Tim Ingold, 1010–39. London: Routledge, 2002.

Bhaba, Homi, *The Location of Culture*. London: Routledge, 1994.

Biernatzki, William E. *Roots of Acceptance: The Intercultural Communication of Religious Meanings*. Rome: Editrice Pontificia Universita Gregoriana, 1991.

Bochner, Stephen. "The Social Psychology of Cross-Cultural Relations." In *Cultures in Contact: Studies in Cross-Cultural Interaction*. International Series in Social Experimental Psychology, edited by Stephen Bochner, vol. 1, 5–44. Oxford, UK: Pergamon Press, 1982.

Bruteau, Beatrice. *The Holy Thursday Revolution*. Maryknoll, NY: Orbis Books, 2005.

Buber, Martin. *I and Thou*. New York: Scribner, 1958.

————. *Between Man and Man*. New York: Macmillan, 1965.

Cada, Lawrence, and Raymond Fitz. *Shaping the Coming Age of Religious Life*. New York: Seabury Press, 1977.

Cenkner, William, ed. *The Multicultural Church*. Mahwah, NJ: Paulist Press, 1996.

Chomsky, Noam. *Syntactic Structures*. The Hague, Holland: Mouton, 1957.

Coleman, John. "Pastoral Strategies for Multicultural Parishes." *Origins* (2000): 497–505.

Costas, Orlando. "Conversion as a Complex Experience." In *Down to Earth: Studies in Christianity and Culture*, edited by Robert Coote and John Stott. Grand Rapids, MI: Eerdmans. Also in *Occasional Essays* 1, no. 5 (1985): 21–44.

Couturier, David. "At Odds with Ourselves: Polarization and the Learning Cultures of Priesthood." *Seminary Journal* 9, no. 3 (Winter 2003): 64–71.

Dawkins, Richard. *The Selfish Gene*. Oxford, UK: Clarendon Press, 1976.

Deregowski, J. B., et al. *Expiscations in Cross-Cultural Psychology: Selected Papers from the Sixth International Congress of the International Association for Cross-Cultural Psychology Held at Aberdeen, July 20–23, 1982*. Lisse, NL: Swets and Zeitlinger, 1983.

Derrida, Jacques. "Cogito and the History of Madness." In *Writing and Difference*. London: Routledge, 1978.

Dietterich, Inagrace. *The Gospel in Our Culture* 8, no. 3 (September 1996): 1–6.

Dorr, Donal. *Spirituality and Justice*. Maryknoll, NY: Orbis Books, 1984.

Dunbar, Robin. "Culture, Honesty, and the Freerider Problem." In *The Evolution of Culture: A Historical and Scientific Overview*, edited by Robin Dunbar, Chris Knight, and Camilla Power, 194–213. Edinburgh, UK: Edinburgh University Press, 1999.

Dupré, Wilhelm. "Multiculturalism and Xenophobia: Reflections on a Common Dilemma." In Wijsen and Nissen, *Mission Is a Must*, 62–77.

Earley, Christopher P., and Ang Soon, eds. *Cultural Intelligence: Individual Interactions across Cultures*. Stanford, CA: Stanford University Press, 2003.

Eilers, Franz-Josef. *Communicating Between Cultures: An Introduction to Intercultural Communication*, 4th ed. Manila: Logos Publications, 2012.

Fernandez, Pedro. "Constructing Religious Community: A Spiritan Reading." *Spiritan Horizons* 8 (Fall 2013): 25–38.

Fox, Robin. *Kinship and Marriage: An Anthropological Perspective*. Cambridge Studies in Social Anthropology. Cambridge, UK: Cambridge University Press, 1967/1988.

Frankl, Viktor. *Man's Search for Meaning*. New York: Pocket Books/Simon and Schuster, 1959.

Friedli, Richard. "Interkulturelle Theologie." In *Lexikon Missionstheologischer Grundbegriffe*, edited by Karl Müller and Theo Sundermeier, 181–85. Berlin: Reimer Verlag, 1987.

Friedli, Richard, Jan A. B. Jongeneel, Klaus Koschorke, Theo Sundermeier, and Werner Usdorf, eds. *Intercultural Perceptions and Prospects of World Christianity*. Frankfurt: Peter Lang, 2010.

Friedman, M. *The Confirmation of Otherness*. New York: Dell, 1983.

———. Foreword to *Communication and Community*, by R. Arnett, vii–xix. Carbondale, IL: Southern Illinois University Press, 1986.

Gallagher, Michael Paul. *Clashing Symbols: An Introduction to Faith and Culture*. London: Darton, Longman & Todd, 1997.

Geertz, Clifford. *The Interpretation of Cultures*. New York: Basic Books, 1973.

———. "On the Nature of Anthropological Understanding." *American Scientist* 63, no. 1 (January–February 1975): 47–53.

Gittins, Anthony J. "Belief and Faith, Assent and Dissent." *New Theology Review* no. 3 (August 1989): 65–85.

———. "Beyond Hospitality? The Missionary Status and Role Revisited." *Currents in Theology and Mission* (1994): 164–82.

———. "Developing Mature Ministers for Diverse Cultural Contexts." *Reflective Practice: Formation and Supervision in Ministry* 29 (2009): 9–22.

———. Foreword to *Culture, Inculturation, and Theologians: A Post-Modern Critique*, by Gerald Arbuckle, xi–xvii. Collegeville, MN: Liturgical Press, 2010.

———. *Ministry at the Margins: Strategy and Spirituality for Mission*. Maryknoll, NY: Orbis Books, 2002.

———. *A Presence That Disturbs: A Call to Radical Discipleship*. Liguori, MO: Liguori Publications, 2002.

———. "Spirituality and Mission: Body, World, and Experience of God." *New Theology Review* 23, no. 4 (November 2010): 62–73.

Goffman, Erving. *Asylums: Essays on the Social Situation of Mental Patients and Other Inmates*. Garden City, NY: Anchor Books, 1961.

———. *The Presentation of Self in Everyday Life*. New York: Doubleday, 1959.

———. *Stigma: Notes on the Management of Spoiled Identity*. Englewood Cliffs, NJ: Prentice-Hall, 1963.

———. *Strategic Interaction*. Philadelphia: University of Pennsylvania Press, 1969.

Gorringe, T. J. *Furthering Humanity: A Theology of Culture*. Hants, UK: Ashgate Publishing, 2004.

Greeley, Andrew. *The Catholic Imagination*. Berkeley: University of California Press, 2000.

Green, Anna. *Cultural History: Theory and History*. New York: Palgrave Macmillian, 2008.

Grimes, Ronald. *Beginnings in Ritual Studies*. Waterloo, Canada: Ritual Studies International, 2013.

Gross, Rita M. "Excuse Me, But What's the Question? Isn't Religious Diversity Normal?" In *The Myth of Religious Superiority*, edited by Paul Knitter, 75–87. Maryknoll, NY: Orbis Books, 2005.

Guder, Darrell. *Missional Church*. Grand Rapids, MI: Eerdmans, 1998.

Gudykunst, William B. *Bridging Differences: Effective Intergroup Communication*. Newbury Park, CA: Sage Publications, 1991.

———, ed. *Cross-Cultural and Intercultural Communication*. Thousand Oaks, CA: Sage Publications, 2003.

Gudykunst, William B., and Stella Ting-Toomey. *Culture and Interpersonal Communication*. Newbury Park, CA: Sage Publications, 1988.

Gudykunst, William B., and Young Yun Kim. *Communicating with Strangers: An Approach to Intercultural Communication*. 2nd ed. New York: McGraw-Hill, 1992.

———. *Communicating with Strangers: An Approach to Intercultural Communication*. 4th ed. New York: McGraw-Hill, 2003.

Hall, Edward T. *Beyond Culture.* New York: Anchor Books, 1976.

———. *The Hidden Dimension.* New York: Anchor/Doubleday, 1966.

———. *The Silent Language.* Greenwich, CT: Fawcett Publications, 1959.

———. "A System for the Notation of Proxemic Behavior." *American Anthropologist* 65 (1963): 1003–26.

Hammer, Mitchell. *Intercultural Development Inventory,* http://idiinventory.com.

Hick, John, and Paul Knitter, eds. *The Myth of Christian Uniqueness.* Maryknoll, NY: Orbis Books, 1987.

Hofstede, Geert H. *Culture's Consequences.* Beverly Hills, CA: Sage Publications, 1980.

———. "Dimensions of National Cultures in Fifty Countries and Three Regions." In Deregowski, et al., *Expiscations in Cross-Cultural Psychology.*

Hollenweger, Walter. *Erfahrungen der Leibhaftigkeit. Interkulturelle Theologie.* 2nd ed. Munich, 1990.

Hunsberger, George, and Craig van Gelder, eds. *The Church Between the Gospel and Culture.* Grand Rapids, MI: Eerdmans, 1997.

Ingold, Tim, ed. *Companions Encyclopedia of Anthropology.* London: Routledge, 2002.

Jain, N., ed. *International and Intercultural Communication Annual.* Vol. 4. Falls Church, VA: Speech Communication Association, 1977.

Jampolsky, G. *Out of Darkness and Into the Light.* New York: Bantam, 1989.

Klopf, Donald W., and J. McCroskey. *Intercultural Communication Encounters.* Pearson, NY: 2007.

Koyama, Kosuke. "'Extend Hospitality to Strangers'—A Missiology of *Theologia Crucis.*" *International Bulletin of Missionary Research* 82 (1993): 283–95.

Kristeva, J. *Strangers to Ourselves.* New York: Columbia University Press, 1991.

Landis, Dan, ed. *Handbook of Intercultural Training.* 3rd ed. Thousand Oaks, CA: Sage Publications, 2004.

Lane, Harlan. *The Wild Boy of Aveyron.* Cambridge, MA: Harvard University Press, 1975.

Eric H. F. Law. *The Bush Was Blazing But Not Consumed: Developing a Multicultural Community Through Dialogue and Liturgy*. St. Louis: Chalice Press, 1996.

————. *Inclusion: Making Room for Grace*. St. Louis: Chalice Press, 2000.

————. *Sacred Acts, Holy Exchange: Faithful Diversity and Practical Transformation*. St. Louis: Chalice Press, 2002.

————. *The Wolf Shall Lie Down with the Lamb: A Spirituality for Leadership in a Multicultural Community*. St. Louis: Chalice Press, 1993.

Lee, Jung Young. *Marginality: The Key to Multicultural Theology*. Minneapolis: Fortress Press, 1995.

Lonergan, Bernard. *Method in Theology*. London: Darton, Longman & Todd, 1972.

Magesa, Laurenti. *What Is Not Sacred? African Spirituality*. Maryknoll, NY: Orbis Books, 2012.

Martin, Judith K., ed. "Theories and Methods in Cross-Cultural Orientation." *International Journal of Intercultural Relations* 10, no. 2 (1986).

Meier, John P. *A Marginal Jew: Rethinking the Historical Jesus*. 4 vols. New York: Doubleday, 1991–2009.

Messner, Wolfgang. *International Communication Competence: A Toolkit for Acquiring Effective and Appropriate Intercultural Communication*. Bangalore, India: Messner Consulting & Training Pvt, Ltd., 2013.

Messner, Wolfgang, and N. Schäfer, eds. *The ICCA™ Facilitator's Manual. Intercultural Communication and Collaboration Appraisal*. London: Createspace, 2012. www.globusresearch.com.

Michael, S. M. "Interculturality and the *Anthropos* Tradition." *Verbum, SVD* 54, no.1 (2013): 60–74.

Moloney, Francis Xavier. *A Hard Saying: The Gospel and Culture*. Collegeville, MN: Liturgical Press, 2001.

Moore, Nina. *Nonverbal Communication: Studies and Applications*. New York: Oxford, 2010.

Müller, Karl, and T. Sundermeier, eds. *Dictionary of Mission*. Maryknoll, NY: Orbis Books, 1997.

Murray, Pat. "Intercultural Leadership." UISG Assembly, Rome, Italy, May 7, 2013. Unpublished manuscript.

Nguyen, van Thanh. "Biblical Foundations for Interculturality." *Verbum, SVD* 54, no. 1 (2013): 35–47.

Nissiotis, Nikos. "Conversion and the Church." *The Ecumenical Review* 19, no. 3 (July 1967): 261–70.

Nowak, Martin A., and Sarah Coakley, eds. *Evolution, Games, and God: The Principle of Cooperation.* Cambridge, MA: Harvard University Press, 2013.

Ong, Walter. *Orality and Literacy: The Technologizing of the Word.* New York: Routledge, 1982/2002.

Peck, M. Scott. *The Different Drum: Community Making and Peace.* New York: Simon and Schuster, 1987.

Rambo, Lewis. "Conversion." In *Dictionary of Pastoral Care and Counselling,* edited by R. Hunter. Nashville, TN: Abingdon Press, 1990.

Rhoads, David. *The Challenge of Diversity: The Witness of Paul and the Gospels.* Minneapolis: Augsburg Fortress, 1996.

Roberts, Simon. *Order and Dispute.* Harmondsworth, UK: Penguin Books, 1979.

Sacks, Jonathan. *The Dignity of Difference: How to Avoid the Clash of Civilizations.* London: Continuum, 2003.

———. *The Home We Build Together: Recreating Society.* London: Continuum, 2007.

Samovar, Larry, and Richard Porter, eds. *Intercultural Communication: A Reader.* 3rd ed. Belmont, CA: Wadsworth, 1982.

———. *Intercultural Communication: A Reader.* 5th ed. Belmont, CA: Wadsworth, 1987.

Scheuerer, F-X. *Interculturality—A Challenge for the Mission of the Church.* Bangalore, India: Asian Trading Co., 2001.

Schreiter, Robert. *The New Catholicity: Between the Global and the Local.* Maryknoll, NY: Orbis Books, 1997.

Sen, Amartya. " 'Social Exclusion': Concept, Application, and Scrutiny." *Social Development Papers,* 1. Office of Environment and Social Development. Asian Development Bank. Manila, 2000.

Shorter, Aylward. *Toward a Theology of Inculturation.* London: Geoffrey Chapman, 1988.

Sillitoe, Paul. "Why Spheres of Exchange?" *Ethnology* 45, no. 1 (Winter, 2006): 1–26.

Simmel, Georg. "The Stranger." In *Georg Simmel: On Individuality and Social Forms*, edited by Donald N. Levine, 143–49. Chicago: University of Chicago Press, 1971.

Smith, A. *Communication and Culture*. New York: Holt, Rinehart, Winston, 1966.

Smith, Wilfred C. "Idolatry in Comparative Perspective." In *The Myth of Christian Uniqueness*, edited by John Hick and Paul Knitter, 53–68. Maryknoll, NY: Orbis Books, 1987.

Sobrino, Jon. *Witnesses to the Kingdom: The Martyrs of El Salvador and the Crucified Peoples*. Maryknoll, NY: Orbis Books, 2003.

Spadaro, Antonio. "A Big Heart Open to God: The Exclusive Interview with Pope Francis." *America* (September 30, 2013): 15–38, here 28.

Spellers, Stephanie. *Radical Welcome: Embracing God, the Other, and the Spirit of Transformation*. New York: Church Publishing, 2006.

Spitzberg, B. H. "A Model of Intercultural Communication Competence." In *Intercultural Communication: A Reader*, edited by L. A. Samovar and R. E. Porter, 375–87. Belmont, CA: Wadsworth Publishing, 2000.

Spivak, Gayatri Chakravorty. "Can the Subaltern Speak?" In *Marxism and the Interpretation of Culture*, edited by C. Nelson and L. Grossberg, 271–313. Basingstoke, UK: Macmillan Education, 1988.

Steindl-Rast, David. "Belonging to Community: Earth Household and God Household." In *Fugitive Faith*, 102–17. Maryknoll, NY: Orbis Books, 1999.

Stonequist, Everett. *The Marginal Man*. New York: Russell and Russell, 1961.

Sykes, Stephen. *Power and Christian Theology*. London: Continuum, 2006.

Tan, Jonathan. *Asian American Theologies*. Maryknoll, NY: Orbis Books, 2008.

Tracy, David. *The Analogical Imagination: Christian Theology and the Culture of Pluralism*. New York: Crossroad, 1981.

Turner, Victor. *The Forest of Symbols*. Ithaca, NY: Cornell University Press, 1967.

Usdorf, Werner. "The Cultural Origins of 'Intercultural' Theology." In *Intercultural Perceptions and Prospects of World Christianity*, edited by Richard Friedli, 81–105. Frankfurt, Peter Lang, 2010.

Van Gennep, Arnold. *The Rites of Passage*. London: Routledge and Kegan Paul, 1908/1977.

Venter, Dawid. "Mending the Multi-Coloured Coat of a Rainbow Nation." *Missionalia* (1995): 316–17.

Wallis, Jim. *The Call to Conversion*. San Francisco: HarperSanFrancisco, 1981.

Walls, Andrew. "The Ephesian Moment." In *The Cross-Cultural Process in Christian History*, 72–82. Maryknoll, NY: Orbis Books, 2002.

Wiebe, Rudy. *The Blue Mountains of China*. Toronto: McClelland and Stewart, 1970.

Wijsen, Frans, and P. Nissen, eds. *'Mission Is a Must': Intercultural Theology and the Mission of the Church*. Amsterdam/New York: Rodoni, 2002.

Williams, Raymond. *A Vocabulary of Culture and Society*. New York: Oxford University Press, 1985.

Wurtzel, Jaime S., ed. *Toward Multiculturalism: A Reader in Multicultural Education*. 2nd ed. Newton, MA: Intercultural Resource Corporation, 2004.

Young Yun, Kim, and William B. Gudykunst, eds. *Theories in Intercultural Communication*. Newbury Park, CA: Sage Publications, 1988.

Index

Made in the USA
Lexington, KY
28 June 2017